Short Bike Rides® Series

Short Bike Rides®

in and around

Los Angeles

Second Edition

Robert M. Winning

The Globe Pequot Press

Guilford, Connecticut

Help Us Keep This Guide Up to Date

Every effort has been made by the author and editors to make this guide as accurate and useful as possible. However, many things can change after a guide is published–establishments close, phone numbers change, facilities come under new management, etc.

We would love to hear from you concerning your experiences with this guide and how you feel it could be made better and be kept up to date. While we may not be able to respond to all comments and suggestions, we'll take them to heart and we'll also make certain to share them with the author. Please send your comments and suggestions to the following address:

The Globe Pequot Press
Reader Response/Editorial Department
P.O. Box 480
Guilford, CT 06437

Or you may e-mail us at:

editorial@globe-pequot.com

Thanks for your input, and happy travels!

Copyright © 1993, 1998 by Robert M. Winning

Short Bike Rides is a registered trademark of The Globe Pequot Press

Library of Congress Cataloging-in-Publication Data

Winning, Robert.
  Short bike rides in and around Los Angeles / Robert M. Winning — 2nd ed.
    p.   cm. — (Short bike ride series)
  Includes index.
  ISBN 0-7627-0209-5
  1. Bicycle touring—California—Los Angeles Metropolitan Area—Guidebooks. 2. Los Angeles Metropolitan Area (Calif.) —Guidebooks.
I. Title. II. Series
GV1045.5.C22L678 1998   98-2526
917.94'930453—dc21   CIP

✿ This text is printed on recycled paper
Manufactured in the United States of America
Second Edition/Third Printing

About the Author

After working for several years in the defense industry and as an executive at Capitol Records, Robert Winning spent sixteen years as vice president of International Administration at Warner Bros. Bob continues to hold a devout interest in bicycling and rides approximately 9,000 miles a year. He and a small team of cyclists rode from Los Angeles to Boston in 1986, and he wrote about his experiences during this trip in *Bicycling Across America* (Wilderness Press). He organizes an annual two-week-long van-supported bicycle tour somewhere in North America. He has appeared as an expert witness on bicycle safety for the California Department of Transportation and lives with his wife in West Hills, California, a Los Angeles suburb.

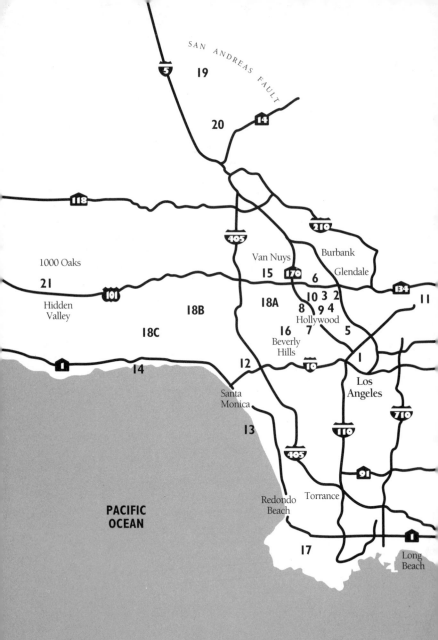

Contents

Introduction

This book is for people who are about to visit Los Angeles and are unfamiliar with the city, and it's for those who already live in L.A. but for one reason or another haven't yet really seen it. It's also for people who live in L.A. who want to do some bicycle riding just for the fun of it. It most certainly is *not* a book about bicycling. It's just that when it comes to seeing and appreciating Los Angeles and its environs, a bicycle has many advantages over a car.

Generally speaking, the rides are easy round trips that can be done in a few hours; the destinations are places of interest, not necessarily places of fame. For example, though rides pass by such famous places as the Chinese Theater and Olvera Street, there are many other rides past places like Marilyn Monroe's high school and Hansel and Gretel's House in Beverly Hills, places of interest that are fun to get to and see.

Some cities enjoy good press. The mere mention of names like Seattle or Portland brings forth images of carefree cyclists plying perfectly smooth streets devoid of traffic. Los Angeles enjoys no such idealized reputation. In fact L.A. bashing is very much in vogue at the moment; yet for me and thousands like me, greater Los Angeles is the best urban bicycle-riding area in the world.

The striking thing about Los Angeles, at least when viewed from a bicycle, is its size—not its 3,000,000-plus population, but its physical size. It covers 465 square miles! That's a lot of geography, especially when you consider that it excludes places like Beverly Hills, Santa Monica, Burbank, and other rather sizeable cities that are part of the megalopolis. The rides in this book include much more than L.A.'s basic 465 square miles. It just so happens, for instance, that some of the most fascinating territory is in the Santa Clarita Valley and Canyon Country, part of a bicycle rider's Los Angeles, but outside of its political definition.

I remember the first time I saw Los Angeles. It was 1957; I was a mere pup, and L.A. was a different place from what it is today, although as the French say, "The more things change, the more they stay the same."

The freeway system, which like Disneyland will never be complete, was embryonic back then. Traffic was horrendous—arguably worse than it is today. Hollywood was somewhat cleaner, but it was never what you'd call pristine. The movie studios were right where they are today—anywhere but in Hollywood itself. They were then owned by moguls, not Japanese megacorporations. The tallest building was city hall, and the main library stood out because of its unique Byzantine architecture. Of course, that was before it burned—twice. Olvera Street and the city's birthplace were undergoing their hundredth (give or take a few) restoration. English was the primary language downtown, and Angels' Flight, a 1-block-long cog railway on Bunker Hill, was still standing at its original location. (Now it's back, in a slightly different place, after a twenty-year hiatus.)

There used to be a trolley line called the Red Cars. The Red Cars are fondly remembered today, but no one seems to remember that they disappeared because no one rode them. Contrary to currently popular mythology, the air in L.A. was not pristine back then. In fact the Indians called the San Fernando Valley the "Valley of Smoke." But even now, even downtown, there are very few days when the smog is bad enough to put a crimp in your bike riding. And nothing today crimps bike riding as much as the old Red Car tracks used to.

The San Fernando Valley was indeed less crowded in the fifties than it is today. The Hollywood Freeway ended abruptly and ignominiously at Woodman Avenue. There was no Golden State Freeway, San Diego Freeway, Simi Valley Freeway, or Ventura Freeway. That's why traffic, in spite of the city's low population, was horrendous.

My father used to say, "The thing that really bothers me is that someday we're going to look back on now as the good-old days." Well, now is the time to see Los Angeles. These are the good-old days for bicyclists. Not too many years ago, the streets were potholed and narrow, with frequent constrictions like cholesterol-clogged arteries. It was, and is, city policy to put through basic, narrow roads where needed. These roads are widened by owners of adjacent land when they develop it. As a result, during the development of suburban areas, there were frequent narrowings, and the basic roads were potholed, awaiting a developer's improvements. With the development of

2

suburban areas, the much-maligned L.A. transportation system improved. Today the streets are well surfaced; they extend everywhere; and because of the elimination of the "clots" in the "arteries," bicycling is safer and easier than ever before.

Bicycles and bicycling accessories seem to have improved to match the riding conditions. The introduction of rearview mirrors, for example, makes riding around sprawling Los Angeles easier and safer.

And then there are the things that Los Angeles always had and always will have: a beautiful 20-mile-long, palm-fringed beach; a unique, picturesque, and historic center; three mountain ranges, snow-capped some of the year, guarding the flanks; an entertainment industry unrivaled anywhere; and, of course, a marvelous climate that is very nearly perfect. This is where the Beautiful People, and the Rich and Famous, and the Wannabes, and Ordinary Folks with and without bikes—but all with cars—live and play. This is where American taste and trends and style and fashion get their start. And as luck would have it, the best way to absorb all of this is on a series of short bike rides. Beyond all that, the object of this book is not only to see it all, but to have fun doing it.

In Los Angeles, when you ask someone, "How far is it from here to there?" the answer is nearly always a seeming non-sequitur: "What time of day will you be going?" You look puzzled but answer, "Ten in the morning." The person then estimates, "It'll take you so many minutes."

You see, to an Angeleno (as people from Los Angeles are called) the city isn't measured in miles; it's measured in minutes. Car-minutes. Distances, therefore, are longer during rush hours and when the Dodgers are playing. Beaches are farther away on sunny summer weekends. Places near freeways are closer. Bicycle distances, however, are indeed measured in miles, and although lots of Angelenos ride bikes, few can tell you how far it is in miles from here to there.

So, you'll need a good map of the city. Thomas Bros. makes some excellent ones, which include every point of interest, street, and large hole in the ground. But the Thomas maps are expensive, and because they're so detailed, you really have to know your way around before you can use them well. The Automobile Club of Southern California (a branch of AAA) also produces excellent city maps, which are free to AAA members nationwide. Perhaps best of all, AAA maps fit in a bike-jersey pocket.

Since this book was written by a bicyclist for bicyclists, all distances are in miles, even though the author is an Angeleno. In fact, most of the distances given are accurate, or at least precise, to the tenth of a mile. Frequently, a mileage will appear as *about;* this is an effort to prevent precision from exceeding accuracy.

Although estimated riding times are listed for each ride and all ride options in this book, as a rule I have assumed that for our purposes, speed is of no concern. "Approximate Pedaling Times" given for each ride are just that: *very* approximate times that you will actually *be* pedaling. Not included are the time-outs for *seeing* things (or eating, or stopping just for the heck of it). Furthermore, pedaling times are adjusted to the "slowest common denominator"; hence, while such things as big hills are taken into account, average riding times are generally geared (pun intended) to riders who have had little recent riding experience. These times will seem excruciatingly slow to experienced riders.

Los Angeles has been called "seventy-six suburbs in search of a city." I admit that there is some truth to this description. I don't know if there are exactly seventy-six suburbs, but the fact is that few Angelenos ever see downtown. I myself get there every couple of years, whenever I want to show a visitor around. The city of Los Angeles is divided willy-nilly into named districts—suburbs, if you will—places like Hollywood, Westwood, Palms, Glassell Park, and Bel-Air. The San Fernando Valley, itself a part of L.A., is divided into numerous communities, including West Hills, Woodland Hills, Mission Hills, Granada Hills, North Hills, and even some places without *Hills* in the name, including Reseda, Studio City, Canoga Park, Chatsworth, Northridge, and Van Nuys. It's easier to name the places that are *not* part of the city of Los Angeles: Glendale, Burbank, Pasadena, Beverly Hills, Santa Monica, the city of San Fernando, plus several others.

L.A. also is divided into large subareas—e.g., downtown, Westside, Eastside, San Fernando Valley, Canyon Country, and, of course, the now-infamous South-Central. Each area has its attractions and its

4

repulsions. In this book I've tried to avoid the latter, but some of the real attractions are surrounded by places that aren't so great to see by bike (or any other means of transportation). It's not practical to close your eyes, so just pedal on through places you don't like, and I guarantee that in minutes you'll be someplace you do like. That's one of the things that makes Los Angeles special.

I imagine that some folks picking up this book will wonder about the area affected by the 1992 riots. Well, as indicated above, there are places in every city where one simply does not deliberately go on a bicycle. The bulk of this book was written long before the riots; no rides went into the affected area then, and none go there in the present version. The main reason is that the riot area is not of interest to sightseeing cyclists; affluence, or lack of it, has nothing to do with it—we do tour Skid Row. There are *vast* areas of the city where there was no rioting that are also ignored in this book. With 465 square miles to choose from, this guidebook excludes a couple of hundred square miles that are of little interest to a two-wheeling tourist, of which the riot area occupies 8 square miles.

Likewise, some people may wonder about the 1994 earthquake. Well, it was indeed a big one, maybe not *the* big one, but big enough. It left large areas of the San Fernando Valley in ruins, and if not ruined, severely damaged. A few scars remain, but by and large the Valley has bounced back and is better than ever. Among the good things that arose from the earthquake's ill wind, to mix metaphors again, is that every major street has been resurfaced, and the Valley is now, more than ever, a great place to ride a bike.

The city is quite easy to get around in, and although it looks unbelievably vast and complex from the air (as well as from the ground for that matter) the layout is, for the most part, logical. For example, throughout the city, odd-numbered locations are on the north and west sides of the streets. Even numbers, therefore, will be found on the south and east. Numbers are lowest in the east and south, and progress higher toward the west and north. Streets—that is thoroughfares with *Street* in the name, run east/west. So, for example, Strathern Street runs nearly 20 miles from Burbank to West Hills. It begins, presumably, with 1 Strathern Street at its eastern end, and it ends with 25000 or so at its western terminus. Avenues run north/south, with 1 at the south end and 12000 or so at the north end. Most boulevards run north/south, but they *can* run east/west. They are almost always very busy thoroughfares. Ways, lanes, drives, and a host of other designations can run any which way.

Nearly all streets and avenues are interrupted in their progress here and there. (Boulevards are not: They go all the way through from beginning to end without interruption.)

The numbers on the streets, avenues, and boulevards continue upward, without regard to the interruptions. So, for example, a street that goes uninterrupted for several miles like Saticoy Street, which abruptly ends at Van Nuys Airport, will have numbers from 1 to about 15800, when it bumps into the airport; Saticoy Street then begins again on the west side of Van Nuys Airport with 17000 and continues until its next interruption. Many streets have a dozen or more interruptions between 1 and 25000, and many avenues are interrupted six times or more between 1 and 12000. But if you are in the 18000 block of a street, you may rest assured that *every* east/west street directly north and south of you also will be in the 18000 block. Likewise, if you are in the 8000 block of an avenue, every avenue directly east and west of you will be in its 8000 block.

Wilshire Boulevard, Sepulveda Boulevard, and Sunset Boulevard, to name just three major streets, are exceptions to the numbering rule, but they *are* uninterrupted from beginning to end. Also, all of the foregoing applies only to the city of Los Angeles. Other cities in Los Angeles *County*—e.g., Pasadena, Beverly Hills, Burbank, Glendale, and Santa Monica—may have different naming and numbering rules.

Equipment for L.A. Riding

Odometers

No matter what kind of bicycle you ride, you should have an odometer. When I was a kid, an odometer was a little counter with a starwheel at one end. The counter was fork-mounted. Every time the wheel rotated, a spoke-mounted striker would advance the star-wheel one-fifth of a turn with a rather loud click. The counter registered the wheel rotations, and voila—mileage!

In the 1970s belt-driven devices became common, and they are still in use today. A wheel-mounted pulley is connected to a counter-mounted pulley by a large O-ring belt. The counter registers mileage. This kind of odometer has two advantages over the star-wheel: First, it is mercifully quiet. Second, it computes cumulative mileage since the unit was installed, *and* it computes trip mileage; it can be reset at the beginning of every ride, or every turn, for that matter.

Most odometers are now computerized. They range in price from $20 to $80, or so. Even the cheapest ones measure cumulative distance, trip distance, and current speed. More expensive ones give you the time of day, current speed, average speed, maximum speed, cumulative distance, distance since midnight, elapsed time, and distance since the last turn. For riding in Los Angeles, you will need an odometer that gives trip distances to the nearest tenth of a mile. (Most electronic computers give it to the nearest hundredth.)

Locks and Chains

I once left my bike unlocked outside the public library in Canoga Park. It was gone when I came out ten minutes later. Annually thereafter for many years, I would go into a bike shop to buy a cable and lock. After years of buying cables and locks that would have easily towed the battleship *New Jersey,* I opted for a three-dollar set I found at the local auto-parts store. About ten years ago I realized that the kids who were looking to filch a bike were looking for ones that were unlocked. No security setup will thwart a real criminal, but a lightweight cable-and-lock set will keep L.A.'s band of klepto-kids at bay.

The cable I use is made of plastic-coated steel braid, maybe 3 millimeters in diameter. The lock is solid brass, a half-inch square and a quarter-inch thick. The whole business weighs 2 ounces. I've been using this arrangement for ten years, and I have evidence that kids have been attracted to my unattended bike but settled for easier pickings.

This is the setup I recommend for riding in Los Angeles. Mind you, I don't recommend leaving a bike secured as described above overnight or even for hours. But a light cable and lock will do the trick while you're walking around a point of interest or having a snack. A totally unsecured bike, though, is as good as gone.

The Bicycle

You should *enjoy* the rides in this book; you should not be conscious of any discomfort during them. Your bicycle is your tool for seeing Los Angeles, and the correct tool is a good road bike. If you were to tour the innumerable mountain trails in and around L.A., you'd need a mountain bike (and a different book). But, if you're going to ride in L.A., you're going to encounter hills. The really hilly rides in this book are so marked; should you encounter a nasty hill in the midst of an otherwise mildly rolling or flat ride, you get no extra points for trying to ride up it—show it who's boss, and walk up. I won't tell anyone.

If you are renting a bike, forget the above caveats; you won't have a choice, and the bike selected for you will probably be a mountain bike or a "hybrid." (A hybrid bike is neither fish nor fowl. It isn't a really good mountain bike and it isn't a really good road bike. It *will* get you from Point A to Point B, though, and perhaps that's sufficient, but if you are going to buy a bicycle, buy the best *road bike* you can afford.)

Helmets

Let's get the helmet thing out of the way right away: *Never* ride a bike without one. Not for a mile; not for a yard; not in the driveway; not even for a Short Bike Ride.

Contrary to common belief, most bicycle injuries, including head injuries, are unrelated to cars and traffic. Most injuries occur when you fall, and most falls are caused by road hazards, attention lapses, and collisions with other bikes. The speed you are going on the crashing bike has less to do with the extent of injuries than you'd think. Many racers swear that they'd rather crash at 20 mph than 5— not that you're given the choice. When you crash at 20 mph, you slide and roll and generally spread yourself, literally, all over the road;

no one point on your body takes all of the crash forces. At 5 mph, you just fall over, and whatever hits the ground first absorbs nearly all of the force of the fall.

If you're an average-size person on an average-size bike, you'll fall on your shoulder and hip, and you'll be *really* sore for an average of a couple of weeks. If you're unlucky, as well as average, you'll fall in whole or in part on your head. It's a fall from considerable height—5 feet or more—with a good deal of weight behind it. Just picture getting dropped on your head from a height of 5 feet. Ouch!

Helmets are designed to absorb and redistribute the force of such a fall, and while such a fall can, if all things go wrong, actually *kill* you, a helmeted head usually escapes totally unscathed.

Clothing

Bike clothing has come into fashion. When currently fashionable bicycle clothing first came out, I thought it was a conspiracy to demonstrate just how ugly and unflattering an article of clothing could get. Bicycle garb, chiefly shorts and jerseys, is designed to show every bulge and flaw. Even Calvin Klein's models would show an unwanted bump here and there. It appears, however, that the human eye/mind connection can get used to anything. After you've seen something often enough and long enough, you cease to see it at all. After two or three years of seeing bike shorts and jerseys on everyone, I stopped noticing physiological anomalies that are hidden by normal clothing. This occurred not only with me but with the public at large, and somewhere along the line, bike clothing became *fashionable*. I still have a hard time believing it, especially when I see people wearing unpadded bike shorts with wild designs on the legs.

Regardless, bicycle clothing is another case of using the correct tool for the job to be done. Your bike won't reject you if you insist on riding it wearing jeans and a T-shirt. It's like using a dime instead of a screwdriver, though, and you really should ride a bike with bicycle clothing. We'll start with shorts.

Bicycle shorts are tight-fitting in the legs, so that they don't ride up the thighs. They're longish, ending just above the knees, so that the up-and-down motion against the saddle doesn't chafe. They have a pad in the seat to distribute the pressure of the saddle onto the "sit-bones" and away from sensitive soft tissues. You don't wear underwear with bike shorts, because underwear has seams that come between you and the saddle, giving rise to one of the most uncomfortable sensations experienced by humans since the rack. Most cycling shorts don't have pockets (although some do), which brings me to jerseys.

Bicycling in a T-shirt is fine. A lot of really experienced cyclists do it all the time. But T-shirts, like shorts, generally don't have pockets. And, T-shirts tend to ride up in back. Jerseys are cut long in back, so that when you lean forward over the handlebars there's no exposed skin on your back. This is not a matter of modesty; it's a matter of sunburn, and it's even more important than you'd think, since bicycle shorts are cut extra low in back. A jersey gives the comfort of a T-shirt and has three generous pockets in back, in which some folks carry snacks, a windbreaker, maps, route slips, car keys, and repair items.

There are really only two other special items of bike clothing worthy of mention here: gloves and shoes. Bicycle gloves, like shorts, are padded in such a way as to spread pressure away from sensitive areas. In the case of the hand, the sensitive area is the carpal tunnel in the heel of the hand. Without gloves, with flat bars, it will take ten minutes for your hands and fingers to start to tingle, and not too much longer to become painful and/or numb. For $12 or so you can get a good pair of gloves that will delay the onset of these problems. For $25 the delay is longer. With flat bars, though, the problem is probably inevitable, even on a short ride. This is because flat handlebars, those that don't curve down like ram's horns, afford only one position for the hands. Dropped bars, the downward-curved ones, afford five positions, and by moving your gloved hands around the various positions, you can delay the onset of tingling, numbness, and/or pain indefinitely.

Shoes are a whole subject in themselves. Again, it's a case of choosing the right tool for the job at hand, or in this case, at foot. If your bike has toe clips, you should invest in touring shoes. These have stiff rubber soles that transmit more of your leg power to the pedals. Toe clips position your foot on the pedals correctly—i.e., so that the ball of each foot is directly over the pedal's spindle. You may use tennis or running shoes for bicycling, but you may find that the pedal "cage" cuts into the sole, which will cause you to feel pressure on your foot. If you are visiting Los Angeles and all you have are a pair of running shoes, don't let that stop you from taking a Short Bike Ride.

Cleats and cleated shoes are not covered here, because if you know about them, you're already sufficiently informed, and if you don't know about them, you wouldn't be using them on these Short Bike Rides, anyway.

A final word about bicycle clothing as it relates to Los Angeles: Any place you encounter on these rides will accept you in bicycling attire. Los Angeles is a very informal city, and it has become even more so in recent years. Furthermore, there's a kind of Angeleno admiration for physically active people, so I know of no stores, restaurants, or museums that will turn away cyclists for reasons of dress. Well, darn few anyway, and exceptions are so noted.

Repairs and Repair Equipment

Flat tires are the bane of a bicyclist's existence. This is one area in which mountain (fat-tire) bikes are superior to road bicycles: They rarely get flat tires. Mind you, a flat tire is an entirely survivable occurrence; it needn't ruin your day or your ride. All you need are the proper tools: two tire levers, one or two spare tubes, a pump, and know-how.

The pump is usually mounted somewhere on the bike's frame and is simple to operate.

The two tire levers are also simple to use. After removing the wheel from the bike (it's usually secured by a flip-lever quick release), slip one of the levers under the edge of the tire and pry up, using the lip of the rim as a fulcrum. Do the same with the second lever about 4 inches away from the first, and slide it around the rim, until the tire is off the rim all the way around on one side.

Pull out the punctured tube. Feel around the inside of the tire to determine what caused the puncture. Whatever it was—glass, thorn, nail—remove it. If you can't find the cause, keep looking until you lose patience.

With the pump, put a couple of puffs of air into the spare tube and insert the valve stem in the valve hole. Install the rest of the tube. Let the puffs of air out—they were put in only to give the tube shape.

Beginning *opposite* the valve stem, push the tire back onto the rim. When you get to the valve stem, the job will become more difficult. Keep pushing, *hard,* and eventually the darned thing will pop onto the rim.

Inflate the tire as hard as you can get it or until you feel that enough is enough. Then reinstall the wheel.

When you remount the wheel, make sure that it is evenly placed between the brake pads. If it's a rear wheel (four out of five flats are in the rear), the wheel should be centered between the chain stays, too. The quick-release mechanism should be tight, but not too tight. (You should be able to release it without resorting to a crowbar, jack handle, pneumatic hammer, or similar device.)

And that's all there is to it. For a first-timer, it should take about ten minutes. Someone like me, who gets three or four flats a month, sometimes all on the same ride, can fix a flat in five minutes or less—until he or she runs out of spare tubes. Then the real fun begins!

In the event that a tire goes flat, and you have neither the know-how nor the spare tube that are required, in Los Angeles there's normally a bike shop within a twenty-minute walk. Just ask any passerby.

One item of optional equipment I strongly recommend is a rear-view mirror. These come in a variety of types, but I believe the best to be the Third Eye helmet-mounted mirror. It provides a wide-angle view of the road behind you. If you are riding with someone else and, as is frequently the case, you are riding single file, a rearview mirror literally permits you to keep an eye on your companion. If he or she gets stopped at a traffic light (and you don't), or gets a flat tire, or has to stop for any reason, the rearview mirror is the way you'll find out. If you're riding alone, and you want to change lanes or turn left, the rearview mirror is the only way for you to determine that it is safe to do so without taking your eyes off the road ahead or turning your head to look over your left shoulder. While your head is turned, your front wheel can get into all manner of difficulties, and you may be using your helmet before you know it.

One final item of equipment you will probably want to carry: a water bottle. On most of the rides in this book, you will be within five minutes of a drink, and generally speaking, your pace will not be such that you'll become dehydrated. Nevertheless, water bottles are cheap (a few bike shops *give* them away), your bike probably has a water-bottle cage on the downtube, and you may as well carry some liquid with you. On a Short Bike Ride you will definitely not need any of the fancy performance-enhancing drinks or electrolyte replacements.

Safety

Los Angeles is different from any other city I've ridden in—and that's a *lot* of cities! First off, the traffic in L.A. is heavy. There are things you can do about that. If you're going to be around town for an extended period, do the rides in outlying areas during the week, and do the rides downtown on weekends, preferably Sundays. In other words, use common sense and stay out of the busiest places at the busiest times. But if you're new to L.A., you may stumble into very busy places simply because you didn't know they were there.

Take heart. Escape is minutes away. If you're riding on Sunset Boulevard in Bel-Air, for example, and you find the 50,000-car-per-day volume to be a bit much, any side street will take you into a quiet (and unbelievably wealthy) neighborhood with *no* traffic at all. You may have to zigzag considerably to make east/west progress without traffic, but it can be done, and it will be interesting at that, although it will raise minor havoc with your route "Directions at a Glance" mileages. Likewise, in the San Fernando Valley, Ventura Boulevard and other east/west streets are very congested during normal business hours. A 1-block detour to the north or south will get rid of the traffic. (Drivers don't seem to realize this, so let's just keep it between us.)

Always ride on the right side of the street, just as you would if you were driving a motor vehicle. In fact, motor-vehicle rules apply equally to bicycles in California, except that on a bike, you must ride as far to the right "as practical." This means that you should not ride in the gutter (the concrete strip adjacent to the curb), and you can ride farther out into the traffic lane than you normally would, if there are potholes or other obstacles along your normal course of travel. Most Angeleno motorists are aware of the rule, and most will give you no problem. There are a few who may blow horns at you, yell at you, or shake their fists and other appendages at you, but the *vast* majority will give you all of the road that you need.

On the other hand, be careful, and don't do unexpected things. All sudden things are unexpected. Always check behind you to make sure that your next maneuver will be acceptable to motorists lurking back there.

Los Angeles traffic is uncommonly well organized. On most busy streets there is a "left-turn storage lane," sometimes two. Get into the storage lane in such a way that after completing the left turn you are as close as practical to the right curb. If you are instructed (by a sign) to turn only with a green arrow, then wait for the arrow. Sometimes it's a long wait, especially if there are no cars to trip the sensors. Wait, anyway.

Where there is no left-turn storage lane, turn left from a point as far to the right as possible, and complete your turn so that you are as close as practical to the right curb.

On super busy streets, you can always do a "chicken left." This is a left turn accomplished by using the pedestrian walk buttons and signals. If you do use this perfectly valid system for turning left against otherwise impossible odds, be sure to act as a pedestrian: Do not ride your bike; walk with it, as though you were really a pedestrian. Get on and ride away *after* you've completed the left turn. The reason for this is that pedestrian crosswalks are recessed from the corners, and if you mount your bike in the crosswalk, a car turning right can hit you (not to mention the danger you present to other pedestrians).

Cars are permitted to park at the curb almost everywhere in Los Angeles and its surrounding communities. Many streets, particularly in the San Fernando Valley, have 12-foot-wide bike lanes that accommodate parked cars. People are permitted to sit in their cars. Why people sit in their cars is something of a mystery, as is the reason why eventually they abruptly decide not to continue sitting there. The result is that after observing a long line of parked cars as you ride alongside them, a car door will suddenly pop open. Some of the most serious bike accidents involve this occurrence. The only consolation is that it usually causes very extensive damage to the car, but breaking a couple of large bones and losing half your teeth can ruin your entire day.

The only defense against the car-door syndrome is constant vigilance. Look for *motion* in parked cars. Before anyone opens a car door, he or she *moves*. If you're lucky you will see this motion and be able to get out of the way before the door flies open. A secondary defense is to ride as close to the left edge of a bike-lane-with-parking as possible. And in general, ride as far to the left of parked cars as you can without obstructing motorized traffic.

Many, if not most, streets in Los Angeles have alleys running between them. Alleys are tempting alternate routes for bicyclists wishing to avoid heavy traffic. In suburban areas the alleys provide access to residents' garages, municipal utilities, and trash collectors on appropriate days. Alleys are not visibly maintained by the city. Therefore, they are frequently littered with broken glass. Furthermore, they are often blocked by service vehicles and are dead-ended. If these factors aren't enough to keep you out of alleys, people leaving their aforementioned garages enter the alley blind; they cannot see into the alley until the hood of the vehicle clears the boundary fence. (Unlike Eastern neighborhoods, *all* property in L.A. is fenced.) A person on a bicycle in an alley is a sitting duck for even well-intentioned motorists leaving their garages, which they usually do at 55 mph.

We've talked about streets, avenues, and boulevards, and we've given more space to L.A.'s rather unique alleys than they deserve, so it's time we mentioned bike paths. These are different from bike routes or bike lanes. A *bike route* is a route that meanders through various neighborhoods designated by some local politician who thinks that having a bike route in his district lends it an air of suburbia. Some of the rides in this book follow bike routes for part of their distance; it is pure coincidence.

A *bike lane* is defined by a white line some distance out from the curb; the space between the line and the curb is dedicated to bicycle use (although cars may park in some of them). In another uncanny coincidence, parts of some of the rides in this book follow bike lanes. (Caution: most bike-lane lines are now made of plastic bonded to the pavement; these lines are very slippery when wet. Do not ride on them.)

A *bike path*, sometimes called a *bikeway*, is a hard-paved surface, separated from roadways intended primarily for motorized traffic. Most bike paths are "multiuse" pavements, from which motor vehicles are excluded. There are two kinds of multiuse bike paths. One kind is a real multiuse path on which you'll find, among others, skateboarders, rollerskaters, runners, race-walkers, and carriage-pushing nannies. All such activities are legal and encouraged, the taxpayer theoretically getting more bang for the buck than for a dedicated bike path, which in theory is for bicycle use exclusively. Casual observation of the multiuse path and the dedicated bike path in Los Angeles reveals little or no difference. That is why I will recommend only one bike path among the Short Bike Rides.

Statistically, in Los Angeles and everywhere else in the world, bike paths are less safe than city streets. This is so for dedicated bike paths, and it is even more so for multiuse bike paths. I have mentioned above that the vast majority of bicycle accidents do not involve cars; many involve other bikes. On a dedicated bike path, there are numerous collisions with other bikes, in large part because most of the bike path's users are inexperienced, and to a lesser extent because bicycles are inherently somewhat unstable; that leads to minor disasters when a whole bunch of bikes are thrown together on the narrow roadway. Further, stir into the pot unauthorized users, like runners, and you have an inordinate number of runner/bicyclist collisions, and bicycle/bicycle collisions, which occur when a bike rider swerves into opposing traffic to avoid a runner (or skateboarder, jet-skier, or what have you). Dedicated bike paths have signs threatening dire legal consequences to unauthorized users, but no one I know has ever been cited for such use, even though such a violation is much more likely to cause injury than a cyclist rolling through a four-way stop.

When a bike path is not dedicated (i.e., multiuse), and few of L.A.'s are, it is an accident that's found a place to happen. This is further exacerbated by Angelenos' penchant for dreaming up strange, new, and usually risky pastimes. If someone invents a way to travel by means of a caster attached to the nose, you can be certain that that someone will be from Los Angeles, and that he or she will try it out on the bike path that passes by Venice. Nevertheless, that very bike path, the one that passes by Venice, is the only one I recommend as a Short Bike Ride. Some things are simply worth the risk.

Climate

Los Angeles has four distinct climate zones: coastal, basin, valley, and mountain. The coastal zone is very moderate, 10°F cooler than the other zones in summer, 10°F warmer in winter; it is frequently cloudy or chilly in the mornings. The Los Angeles Basin is a little warmer than the coast in the summer and cooler in winter; statistics for the Basin are the ones that appear in your newspaper. The valleys, specifically the San Fernando Valley and the San Gabriel Valley, are at least 10° warmer than the Basin in the summer and at least 10°F cooler in winter: temperatures over 100°F in the summer are not unusual, and temperatures around freezing are common in winter. Although one hears many transplanted Easterners complaining that there are no seasons in Los Angeles, only people permanently confined indoors can fail to notice the difference between summer and winter. There is no swimming in Los Angeles in winter, even though L.A.'s swimming pools make it look like the Land of Ten Thousand Lakes from the air.

Regardless of climate zone, Los Angeles has a weather pattern called "persistence," meaning that the odds are very great that tomorrow will be the same as today. Don't worry about the rain—it happens only twenty days per year at most, rarely affects all 465 square miles of city, and hardly ever lasts more than a few hours. Smog, incidentally, is over publicized and rarely affects bicycle riding, although it can obscure otherwise spectacular views. In short, bicycling in Los Angeles is a 12-month, 345-days (or more) per-year activity.

This Is the City!

Location:	Civic Center
Mileage:	4.5 miles (a little more if one takes side trips to numerous interesting places)
Approximate pedaling time:	½ hour
Terrain:	Good surface throughout, with a few modest hills
Traffic:	Can be unnerving on weekdays and at times on Saturdays
Things to see:	Avila Adobe, Bunker Hill, Children's Museum, Chinatown, City Hall, Courthouse, Federal Building, Little Joe's Restaurant, Little Tokyo, Historic Theater District, Million Dollar Theater, Music Center, Olvera Street, Parker Center, Philippe's, Plaza, Skid Row, Triforium, Union Station, and more

This is a tour of the heart of Los Angeles, warts and all, to mix metaphors. Although it has been said that L.A. is seventy-six suburbs in search of a city, this is unarguably the city's center—the place the seventy-six suburbs are supposedly looking for. The fact that the rest of the city would continue to exist, even thrive, if this heart were cut out, doesn't detract from the power and uniqueness of the city's civic center.

Downtown Los Angeles is unlike any other city. It is a peculiar mixture of several cultures, of old and new, and of twenty-first-century high tech and 1920s grubby. The four-level freeway inter-

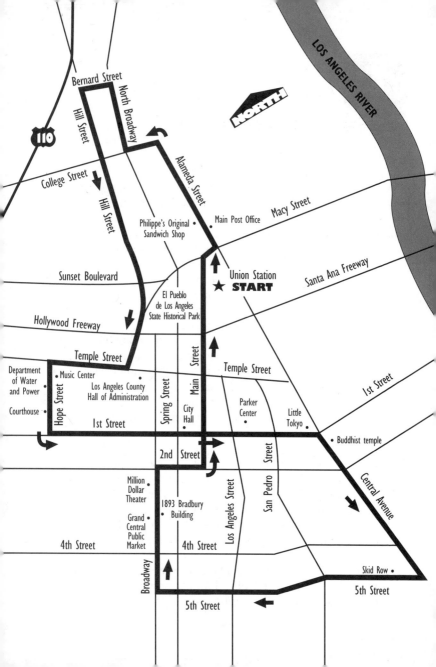

DIREC-TIONS at a glance

0.0 Right out of the Union Station parking lot.
     Head north on Alameda Street
0.3 Left onto College Street
0.3 Right onto North Broadway
0.4 Left onto Bernard Street
0.4 Left onto Hill Street
0.7 Right onto Temple Street
0.9 Left onto Hope Street
1.2 Left onto 1st Street; cross Spring Street; cross Los Angeles Street
2.0 Right onto Central Avenue
2.5 Right onto 5th Street
3.3 Right onto Broadway
3.7 Right onto 2nd Street
3.8 Left onto Main Street; pass over Hollywood Freeway
4.5 Back to Union Station

change and new sky-scraping glass tubes are in stark contrast with Skid Row and Broadway. Further, the boundaries of each district within the downtown area are quite sharp; one moment you're in Chinatown, the next in L.A.'s historic Mexican quarter, and the next in Little Tokyo. The Thomas Bros. map of downtown Los Angeles lists eighty-three points of interest. This ride obviously falls short in the point-of-interest count, but it does pass within eyeshot of virtually every point listed by Thomas Bros. So, if you see something not discussed in the following paragraphs, by all means detour to what caught your eye, and enjoy!

As in any big city, there's a parking problem in the downtown area, so take advantage of being on two wheels, and park your car outside of the congested area, preferably in as safe a place as possible. I recommend the parking lot at Union Station. It is fairly inexpensive, safe, and within walking distance of most of the things you'll want to return to for a closer look.

Union Station itself is a point of interest. It was among the last, if not *the* last, of the great train stations built in this country. It was built by a coalition of the Union Pacific, Southern Pacific, and Atchison, Topeka, and Santa Fe railroads. It has been featured in innumerable movies and television shows, and a walking tour through the cavernous waiting rooms will bring back memories of a bygone era. If you're too young to remember the bygone era, this is an opportunity to savor a bit of Americana that will never return. Union Station is also the terminus for L.A.'s budding subway system, Metrolink, Amtrak, and bus system. After returning from your bike ride, a thorough exploration of the terminal and a round trip on the Red Line subway is strongly recommended. The terminal renovation and MTA (Metropolitan Transit Authority) building are reported to have cost $300 million. Some of this money was spent in a spectacular manner, and you really should see it.

Across the street from Union Station is **El Pueblo de Los Angeles State Historical Park.** It's the re-creation of Los Angeles' earliest days as a Spanish pueblo and unlike any other state park you'll ever see. Within its boundaries are several points of interest best seen on foot. Olvera Street, all of a short block long, is Los Angeles' first (i.e., oldest) street and first (i.e., premier) tourist trap. The street, a brick-paved alley, really, was named for pioneer Augustin Olvera. It was reconstructed in 1930 as a Mexican shopping street, lined with restaurants and shops, with a center divider of street-vendor stalls. The street has been renovated and rejuvenated several times in the past decade or two, and it retains a certain charm and attractiveness, even though most of the goods for sale are, well, shoddy. But on Olvera Street you can forget that you're in the heart of L.A. and pretend for a short while that you're south of the border a couple of hundred years ago. Since Olvera Street is a public way, albeit closed to vehicular traffic, admission is free.

At the east end of the street, incidentally, is an open air stand–cum–restaurant that has probably the best *taquitos* in town. Confections on the street run toward the *very* sweet; you can just about feel your teeth rot as you chew, but you probably should give the cactus candy a try anyway. There are better Mexican restaurants just about anywhere in Los Angeles, but for atmosphere there are a couple along the alley that can't be beat.

In the middle of Olvera Street, at number 10 on the south side, is the **Avila Adobe**, built by Don Francisco Avila in 1818. It is Los Angeles' oldest adobe and probably its oldest building. Avila was mayor of Los Angeles and its richest citizen. None of my history books says whether he was wealthy before becoming mayor or as a result of becoming mayor, but the fact is that this adobe was quite something in its day. It has been restored, and the furnishings give a sense of what it was like to be rich in Los Angeles in the early to mid-nineteenth century. For the record, it wasn't so good. Better to be middle class now. Admission is free.

Almost directly across the street from the Avila Adobe, at 17 West Olvera Street, is **Pelanconi House**, one of the first brick buildings in the city, built in 1855. It is named for its second owner, Antonio Pelanconi. What happened to its first owner and why it wasn't named for him, I don't know. Today the structure is a private residence, and I imagine its tenants would not appreciate your knocking on the door to ask this burning question.

At the south end of Olvera Street is the **Plaza**, on which stand **Pico House** and the **Old Plaza Firehouse**. The Plaza was the heart and soul of Los Angeles in the 1830s and 1840s, and these days it comes alive on Cinco de Mayo (May 5th), a major, festive Mexican holiday. Cinco de Mayo commemorates the 1867 Mexican overthrow of the French emperor Maximillian. Approximately one third of L.A. residents are of Mexican origin, and the holiday is celebrated with gusto in that country. The festivals have followed the emigrants to their new homes in Los Angeles. The Old Plaza Firehouse, which was built in 1884, is now a museum displaying early Firefighting equipment. Admission is free, and if you enjoy looking at old stuff in a refurbished genuine firehouse, you'll *love* this place.

Across Main Street, at number 535 North, is the **Plaza Church**, whose official name is Church of Our Lady of the Queen of the Angels (which is an exact translation of the original Spanish name for Los Angeles). The original adobe structure was built in 1818 by local Indians; it is the oldest church in Los Angeles. The building has been restored and enlarged over the years, but it retains typical mission-style lines.

If you turned right out of the Union Station parking lot or if you pass through the north end of Olvera Street, you will be on Alameda Street. One block along Alameda on the right is L.A.'s **Main Post Office**. It is notable for its enormity and its WPA murals by Boris Deutsch. Its address, for the record, is 900 Alameda Street.

Diagonally across the street from the Post Office (at 1001 North Alameda Street) is **Philippe's Original Sandwich Shop**. It was here that the French-dip sandwich was invented in 1908. (The people at Philippe's say it was named for a policeman nicknamed Frenchy who dipped his roast beef sandwiches in gravy.) At this writing the price of a cup of coffee was still 10 cents; the floors were still covered with sawdust and the tables with linoleum. Circus people meet there on Mondays, and the everyday crowds are a cross section of Los Angeles society. And yes, the French-dip sandwiches are good.

Continue past Philippe's on Alameda to College Street and turn left. You will soon know for sure that you ain't in Kansas anymore. In fact, you'll think you're in Hong Kong or Taipei. After 1 block, turn right on Broadway. On your right is **Little Joe's Restaurant**, an Italian eatery in the heart of New Chinatown. Little Joe's has been in this location since the forties. The original Chinatown came later—in the fifties to be precise. Little Joe's is an excellent restaurant with moderate prices. Chinatown's main drag is Broadway (from about 700 to 1000 North), though there's lots of activity on side streets. The street signs are bilingual (English/Chinese), and it is amazing how many locals speak only Chinese. There are a couple of shopping districts on either side of Broadway at around 800 North, where one can find Oriental treasures ranging from real junk to not-too-awful.

Take your first left on Bernard Street; in a few yards turn left on Hill Street, then turn right on Temple Street. Immediately on your left is the **Los Angeles County Hall of Administration**. After 2 blocks turn left on Hope Street. You'll see the **Music Center** on your left and the **Department of Water and Power** on your right. Both are striking buildings. The Department of Water and Power was designed by A. C. Martin in 1964; the ponds in front of the building serve not only the aesthetic purpose of reflecting the glass structure but also dissipate heat from the air-conditioning system.

The Music Center was completed in 1969. It is to Los Angeles what Lincoln Center is to New York. It consists of the **Dorothy Chandler Pavilion**, the **Mark Taper Forum**, and the **Ahmanson Theater**. For many years the Oscars were awarded in the Dorothy Chandler Pavilion. It is still the home of the Los Angeles Philharmonic Orchestra and the site of other major musical performances, including many Broadway shows before, during, or after their runs on the Great White Way. The Mark Taper and Ahmanson theaters are just that: theaters. While there is a core group of theater- and concertgoers in Los Angeles, and while the quality of this particular collection of brick and mortar is arguably unmatched in this country, the Music Center has horrendous parking and traffic problems, the tickets are expensive, and it is located far away from where people live. Nevertheless, attending a performance at one of the Music Center entities is a memorable and rewarding experience.

The Music Center occupies a full city block. At the end of the block, turn left on 1st Street. Before completing the turn, you will see straight ahead the Bunker Hill Towers, fine and *expensive* residential skyscrapers built in 1968 on the site of one of the city's least desirable neighborhoods. Bunker Hill's structures were razed in the early sixties for all of the redevelopment that you see from the Music Center to the Towers. The construction on your right as you complete the turn onto 1st Street is going to be the **Disney Auditorium**, built with contributions—massive ones—from Walt Disney's heirs and corporations at their philanthropic best. The cost of this building will eventually reach into the hundreds of millions of dollars. The history of its construction is, fittingly, like that of an overbudget movie, like *Titanic* or *Heaven's Gate*. Although construction has been plagued by political, architectural, design, and money problems, its final form will rival the Sydney (Australia) Opera House for audacity of design. Ultimately, beyond the year 2000, it will replace the Dorothy Chandler Pavilion as the home of L.A.'s cultural highlights.

On your left on the block just past the back of the Dorothy Chandler Pavilion is the **Courthouse**. You saw the front of this building weekly if you watched *L.A. Law*. To your left, 2 blocks farther along, as you cross Spring Street, you'll see **City Hall**, star of *Dragnet* and other shows, as well as being, well, city hall. Built in 1928, it was the tallest building in the city until 1957. It was (and is) twenty-seven stories high, and, until 1956, there was an ordinance limiting building heights to thirteen stories. The city fathers passed the ordinance for the express purpose of keeping City Hall the most exalted edifice in town. There are forty-five-minute guided tours (by appointment only) that include a terrific view from the observation deck on the twenty-seventh floor. Ironically the city jail used to be on the twenty-sixth floor; it had great views—by appointment only, too. City Hall may be closed to visitors while earthquake repairs and earthquake-proofing are under way. Completion is expected in late 1998.

Ride 1 block farther and you'll cross Los Angeles Street. Look left and you'll see **Parker Center**, headquarters for the Los Angeles Police Department and star of additional innumerable television dramas, not to mention news broadcasts. It's always a good idea to obey traffic laws, but in this neighborhood, it becomes imperative.

Continue on 1st Street and you'll soon arrive in **Little Tokyo**. I have visited Big Tokyo, the one in Japan, and there is absolutely no question in my mind that Los Angeles' version is more authentic. It is nothing like Chinatown, so don't skip it, thinking that once you've seen one Orientaltown you've seen 'em all. Little Tokyo is what Big Tokyo should be. You can save thousands of dollars by riding these streets instead of flying to Japan. The New Otani Hotel at the corner of 1st and Los Angeles Streets, which opened in 1977, is nothing short of fantastic, offering everything you'd find in a top-flight Tokyo hotel.

Turn right on Central Avenue, and you'll soon pass a spectacular **Buddhist temple** that starred in an episode of *Remington Steele,* among other shows. Turn right on **5th Street**, and you'll find yourself in another world—**Skid Row**. This is not exactly the kind of place you'll want to linger, but hardly anyone goes to Skid Row (on a temporary basis), and it's an eye-opener. A right on Broadway takes you away from that world and into another, where in quick succession you'll pass the **Grand Central Public Market**, the **Bradbury Building**, and the **Million Dollar Theater**.

The Grand Central Public Market at 317 South Broadway was built in 1920, and 200,000 shoppers come every week to buy everything considered edible by somebody. There are hundreds of independent businesses within the market's walls, and some of them have utterly fantastic takeout food. The famous Farmers Market in the Fairfax district is featured on a different ride. Take this opportunity to savor the exotic and exciting atmosphere of this unique market.

Across the street, at 304 South Broadway, is the 1893 Bradbury Building, plain of exterior but fantastic inside. Here and there I've mentioned television shows and movies that various landmarks have appeared in, but if I were to do that with the Bradbury Building there wouldn't be space left in the book for any other points of interest. It is open to the public and is free.

Right next to the Grand Central Public Market is the Million Dollar Theater. Built in the 1920s, the theater is currently a bit rundown and features Spanish-language films. But it cost a million semolians to build back in the days when a buck was a buck, and you can see from the façade that it was once a grand place indeed.

In fact, up and down South Broadway, between 3rd and 9th Streets, there are movie palaces of the past that have been lovingly restored. Bear in mind that these places reflect a time when the movie was the king of entertainment, vaudeville was queen, and Los Angeles was the undisputed capital of the motion picture business. L.A. still is, but these theaters reflect a grander time, a time when all 15,000 seats were occupied day and night, every day and every night. It was a time when the stages held court to by every famous vaudevillian and the screens were filled with the faces and figures whose every sniffle and peccadillo was breathlessly reported in the world press. If you're riding a bicycle, you're probably too young to recognize the names; even I don't recognize many of them, and I'm older than you, so I'll skip the roster of has-beens and let your imagination run wild. The entire theater district is listed in the National Register of Historic Places; elsewhere, such as New York, the register lists only individual theaters.

The **Los Angeles Theater** at 615 South Broadway—although it's the first theater mentioned here because of its low address number—was the last movie palace built on Broadway. It is probably the most luxurious of them all; its new owners poured more than $2 million into refurbishments in the 1980s, making the Los Angeles the best-preserved theater of the lot. Bear in mind that the place was built in 1931 at a cost of $1 million. Charlie Chaplin's *City Lights* premiered here, with Albert Einstein reportedly the evening's guest of honor. All Twentieth Century Fox films premiered at the Los Angeles for many years. If you have a chance, return to the Los Angeles, and tour the building; a movie is included in the ticket price.

The **Palace Theater** at 630 South Broadway opened in 1911; it's the oldest continuously operating theater in downtown Los Angeles. It was originally part of the Orpheum Circuit vaudeville theater chain. It's five stories high, four of which are occupied by the auditorium, with the top floor used as rehearsal space. The second balcony is reputed to be haunted.

The **State Theater** at 703 South Broadway (at 7th Street) was built in 1921 and was L.A.'s most successful downtown theater. Its builder, Marcus Loew, formed Metro-Goldwyn-Mayer three years later, and for many years MGM pictures premiered at the State Theater. It is reputed to be the largest brick veneer building in Los Angeles.

The **Orpheum Theater** at 842 South Broadway opened in 1926 as a second Orpheum Circuit outlet. The theater is now known mainly for its Wurlitzer organ, maintained by the Los Angeles Theater Organ Society. A demonstration/recital is well worth the side trip.

Turn right on 2nd Street and left on Main Street. You're now in the heart of Old and Modern L.A. Here are the **Triforium** (also known as the **Municipal Juke Box**)—City Hall has been referred to as the Municipal Joke Box—Fletcher Bowron Square and Mall; and the **Children's Museum**. The Triforium is a sixties-looking collection of multicolored anodized aluminum junk, er, modern sculpture, on the corner of Main and Temple at 310 North Main Street. It is hooked up to a now-dysfunctional and obsolete computer that once coordinated a light and musical chime show. No modern Los Angeles guidebook mentions it, but when it was built in the mid-sixties, it was supposed to be L.A.'s symbol. Fortunately, Los Angeles has other candidates for that honor.

The Triforium is located on Fletcher Bowron Square. Bowron served as mayor in the twenties, thirties, and forties. Sharing this site is the **Children's Museum**. It's full of things that kids can touch, as well as exhibits of what goes on beneath the streets, old-time crafts, and a kids' TV station that they can help run. Hey, this is L.A.!

Directly across the street is the **Federal Building**. This is not the Federal Building that hosts demonstrations; *that* one is in Westwood, convenient to UCLA and the demonstrators. This Federal Building is just a big office building crammed full, one supposes, with federal employees doing whatever they do. On the ground floor, however, is a bookstore that has every single book published by the U.S. Government Printing Office. It is fabulous! (On the Alameda Street side is an interesting three-story-tall sculpture of four sheet-metal guys walking toward one another on a collision course; they are full of random holes, as though shot innumerable times by huge shotguns.)

Continue on Main Street, crossing over the Hollywood Freeway; the **murals** on the walls of the sunken freeway were painted to dress the town up for the 1984 Olympics and are now beginning to show signs of distress. Nevertheless, they're worth a quick stop, especially since a look over your shoulder will reward you not only with a view of a mural but of City Hall as well. Keep going for a block or so, and you'll be back at Union Station, where, with any luck, you'll find your car as you left it, hubcaps and all.

For Further Information

Bradbury Building tour (213) 626–1893
Children's Museum (213) 687–8800
City Hall tour (213) 485–2121
Last Remaining Seats (for information on restored theaters and events) (213) 896–9114
Music Center (213) 972–7211
U.S. Government Printing Office Store (213) 239–9844

Getting There

All freeways in southern California go to downtown L.A., one way or another. Find out from a friendly local where you are in relation to downtown (north, south, east, or west) and which freeway goes there. Whatever freeway it is, get on it headed for Los Angeles or downtown. Do not ask locals for details about exits, freeway changes, or street directions. You'll get unnecessarily confused.

Union Station is at the Alameda exit of the Hollywood (US–101) Freeway. All freeways eventually cross or merge with the Hollywood Freeway. Warnings of freeway changes are given beginning 3 miles from the point where you have to change and every $\frac{1}{4}$ mile thereafter, until it's too late and you've missed your turn. So, no matter which freeway you use initially, keep following the signs to downtown (or Los Angeles) and then get on US–101/Hollywood Freeway. Sooner or later you'll come to the Alameda exit, and Union Station, which is well posted, is right there.

Griffith Park Overview

As mentioned in the Introduction, Los Angeles is a big basin ringed by mountains. Downtown and the oldest sections of town are separated from the northern area by a range of relatively low mountains, called the Santa Monicas on the west and the Hollywood Hills to the east. At the eastern end of the Hollywood Hills is Griffith Park. The park is separated from the rest of the Hollywood Hills by Cahuenga (pronounced cah-wen´-gah) Pass, which links the community of Hollywood and the rest of L.A. to the San Fernando Valley. The US–101 (Hollywood) Freeway passes through Cahuenga Pass, and modern four-banger engines have a hard time holding speed, much less accelerating, through it from the Hollywood side, which is somewhat lower in elevation than the Studio City/San Fernando Valley side. I mention this as forewarning and for information, because one of the rides goes through Cahuenga Pass, alongside the freeway.

Bikes, incidentally, *are* allowed on freeways, when there is no viable alternative route. Since there is a perfectly good street (Cahuenga Boulevard) alongside the Hollywood Freeway, bikes are strictly *verboten* on this particular freeway. Why you'd want to ride on the Hollywood Freeway, anyway, is a matter for you to discuss with your psychiatrist. And while we are digressing, the term *freeway* does not refer to the cost of riding on such a road; it means that the road is free of cross traffic. A toll road, of which California has only one—a short one in Orange County—can be a freeway—and vice versa, I suppose.

Griffith Park is bounded on the west by the Hollywood Freeway, on the east by the I–5 (Golden State) Freeway, on the north by the SR–134 (Ventura) Freeway, and on the south by Los Feliz Boulevard. I have no idea why Los Feliz Boulevard wasn't replaced by a freeway. As you will see in an upcoming ride, there is sufficient traffic to warrant a freeway there. When you come to Los Feliz Boulevard, be extra cautious because of the heavy traffic you're almost certain to find there.

Griffith Park is a mountain, or four mountains, depending on how you count. Actually, it's a big mountain with at least four named peaks: Mount Bell (elev. 1,587 feet), Mount Chapel (elev. 1,622 feet), Mount Hollywood (elev. 1,625 feet), and Mount Lee (elev. 1,640 feet). The peaks are connected by saddles, and there is a nice network of lightly traveled two-lane roads linking the mountains. The famous Hollywood sign is on Mount Lee's southwest flank (see Rides 4 and 9).

The park is named for Col. Griffith J. Griffith. (With such unimaginative parents, it's a wonder he wasn't named Griffith G. Griffith.) In 1896 he gave the city of Los Angeles a Christmas gift: 3,015 acres of beautiful, mountainous land. It was, even then, the largest city park in the world. It was so big and so remote that it lay outside the city limits until 1910. The park has annexed additional land since then, and its present size, my guidebook says, is 4,063.87 acres, give or take a square foot or two. The city of Beverly Hills, to give you an idea of relative size, occupies 3,647 acres.

In 1912 Griffith gave the city $100,000 to build an observatory. We will visit the completely refurbished observatory on the third ride in the Griffith Park series. In addition to the observatory, which you'll immediately recognize from its starring role in innumerable movies and television programs, the park boasts three major golf courses, the Greek Theater (alfresco light opera), Travel Town (antique trains and free parking), the L.A. Zoo, the Fern Dell Nature Museum, and the Autry Western Heritage Museum, among numerous other attractions. Hollywoodland Girls Camp and Griffith Park Boys Camp are both located in the park, separated by a couple of miles of impassable hills, forest, and other obstacles that make mingling unlikely. (None of the three rides visits either camp.)

Incidentally, a glance at a map of the Griffith Park area will immediately reveal that there are two famous cemeteries within what one would expect to be park boundaries—Forest Lawn Memorial Park and Mt. Sinai Memorial Park. They are the resting place for hundreds of the formerly rich and famous as well as thousands of ordinary, and permanent, Angelenos. There are quite a few exceptions, of course, but nearly all famous folk who have died in Los Angeles in the past fifty years are interred there. Griffith made the establishment of the two cemeteries in this location a quid pro quo for giving the park to the city.

You will note that several rides in this book use Travel Town as a starting point. That's because Travel Town is centrally located, is something of an attraction in itself, and has ample free parking. As luck would have it, Travel Town is near the lowest elevation in all of Griffith Park. The first ride in the Griffith Park series is pleasant and undemanding. It remains more or less at the same elevation as Travel Town while passing some truly interesting and pretty sites.

The second Griffith Park ride, The Mineral Wells Loop, is a little less easy, as it includes a significant climb past Mineral Wells on a hill dubbed by local cyclists "Trash Truck Hill." (There's a landfill near Mineral Wells, and during the week there is frequently a parade of trash trucks wending their way to the dump. Eventually, the landfill will be a golf course or woodland or some other public-use ground bearing no resemblance to its current use.)

The third ride, the Griffith Observatory Loop, is less moderate than the others, as it climbs up to the observatory. The ancient Greeks, or Chinese, or somebody, noticed that celestial observations are best done from high up, and even in offbeat L.A. that tradition is followed. The observatory, therefore, being an honest-to-goodness astronomical observatory (and planetarium), is located on high ground. This is not a killer ride, but neither is it a ride for those whose day will be ruined by hills.

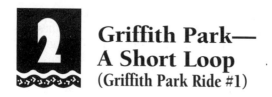

Griffith Park—
A Short Loop
(Griffith Park Ride #1)

Location:	Griffith Park
Mileage:	9 with a 4-mile option
Approximate pedaling time:	¾ hour, plus ½ hour for the 4-mile option
Terrain:	Excellent; two-lane roads, quite flat, tree-shaded
Traffic:	Light
Things to see:	Travel Town, Los Angeles Zoo, Griffith Park Carousel, golf courses, pony rides, Autry Western Heritage Museum, Pioneer Aviators' Airport (*Casablanca* Airport), Los Angeles Live Steamers' Miniature Railroad, and more; the 4-mile option includes the Los Angeles River, Forest Lawn Memorial Park, Mt. Sinai Memorial Park, and the Warner Bros. back lot

This ride will give you a good overview of the park, and it passes several of the park's major attractions. On your way back to Travel Town, as you pass the Visitor Center and Ranger Headquarters, there's an intersection on the left. If you turn there, you can complete the last part of the Mineral Wells Loop (Griffith Park Ride #2), which includes a hill—a pretty big hill. If you don't take that option, you may continue to the zoo and the Autry Western Heritage Museum. From there you can backtrack on Crystal Springs Drive to Griffith Park Drive and turn right to complete the second ride, or you can continue on Crystal Springs Drive to Travel Town. If you're in doubt, read the ride de-

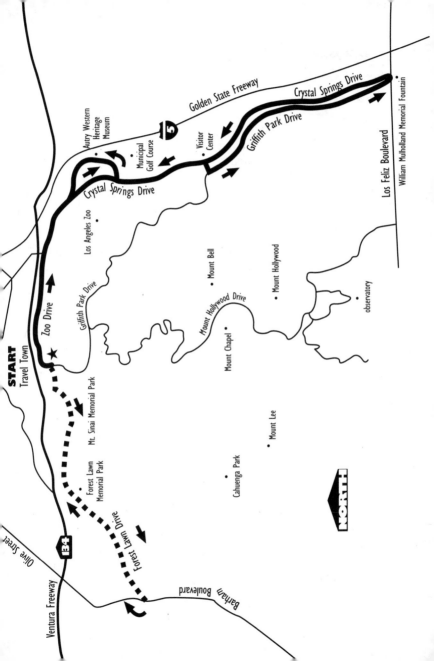

0.0	Right from Travel Town parking lot onto Zoo Drive
1.6	Zoo Drive becomes Crystal Springs Drive
2.6	Right at stop sign (after golf course)
2.8	Left at stop sign; go past carousel
3.4	Right onto Griffith Park Drive at T (may not be marked)
4.7	U-turn; Griffith Park Drive becomes Crystal Springs Drive
6.9	Right, continuing on Crystal Springs Drive (may not be marked); turns left after 0.1 mile and passes Autry Western Heritage Museum
7.2	Left onto Zoo Drive (no choice)
8.7	Left into Travel Town parking lot

Four-mile Extension

8.7	Left onto unmarked road (instead of going into Travel Town parking lot)
8.9	Left onto Forest Lawn Drive
10.9	U-turn at Barham Boulevard
12.9	Right onto unmarked road
13.1	Straight into Travel Town parking lot

scription for the second ride, and decide then. In any event, this ride is on gently rolling ground. Crystal Springs Drive and Griffith Park Drive are two-lane asphalt roads. Although both roads have generous bike lanes marked on the right side, they are frequently cluttered with eucalyptus leaves, bark, seeds, and twigs. The traffic, even on weekends, is bearable. If you want to make this a less-than-gentle ride, you can race through the loop as fast as you can; indeed, hundreds of bicycle racers use this loop every week for training.

Before you even roll away from the starting point, here are a few words about **Travel Town**. This place is an unabashed paean to railroading. It is, in fact, a museum with the largest collection of steam locomotives in the western United States. It also houses a vast array of railroad equipment dating from the 1880s through the 1940s—everything from parlor cars to sleepers and diners, from freight cars to urban trolleys, short-line and experimental, all in a shaded, almost wooded, setting. Travel Town was dedicated in 1952, following the aggressive promotion of Charley Atkins, a steam-powered-railroad enthusiast. The Los Angeles Live Steamers Club offers rides on a scale-model train around the perimeter of Travel Town. Birthday parties for kids and adults can be held aboard two cars that are available days and evenings. Try it! It's the next best thing to actually going on a train ride.

Turn right out of the Travel Town parking lot onto Zoo Drive. Almost immediately, the road turns right. Bear right when Zoo Drive turns after 1.2 miles or so. You will soon pass the entrance to the **Los Angeles Zoo** on the right.

The zoo covers about 113 acres, not including the 28-acre parking lot. It is one of the better zoos in the United States, although, to be candid, it isn't as good as the San Diego Zoo. On the other hand, it's 150 miles closer than the San Diego Zoo, and that counts for a lot. Adventure Island is a section of the zoo set aside for kids. It has a sea lion exhibit, mountain lions, and small city-dwelling animals like skunks, opossums, spiders, and the like. There's a fascinating interactive computer display that provides various smells with the touch of a button and the ability to examine insects under a microscope. In 1990 and early 1991 the rest of the zoo underwent renovation, and further renovation and modernization is planned for 1998–2000. The koala exhibit is unique, in that koalas, being nocturnal animals, normally are asleep and hidden during zoo visiting hours. As far as I know, the L.A. Zoo is the only one in the world where the koalas are housed in an enclosed building, where, through the magic of electric lights, the habitat resembles Australia in moonlight. After the zoo closes, the lights come on and the koalas, thinking it's daytime, go to sleep. At least that's what I'm told. The zoo is segmented into continental areas, with all animals indigenous to a particular continent exhibited together.

On the site of what is now the zoo parking lot and the Autry Western Heritage Museum was the first **airfield** in the area. During

World War I it was a key airport and served as such until after World War II. There is some disagreement on this, but it is rumored that it was this airfield that appears in *Casablanca*. William Boeing learned to fly here, and Glen Martin used it as his home base until World War II. Amelia Earhart flew from this airfield regularly, and it was from here that she left on her final flight, during which she disappeared. After World War II, Quonset huts were erected here to house returning veterans and their families. The community was called Roger Young Village, after the war hero. Alas, not even a plaque can be found to commemorate any of these claims to fame. As you look over the sea of asphalt and automobiles, though, take note that you are looking at one of the premier parking lots in the world.

Zoo Drive appropriately changes its name after you pass the zoo, 1.5 miles from Travel Town, to become Crystal Springs Drive. Continue on Crystal Springs Drive for 1.3 miles to the stop sign at the intersection with Griffith Park Drive. Turn right here and follow the road around to the left. You will be on Griffith Park Drive for 1.6 miles.

If you're feeling peppy, you can pick up the Mineral Wells Loop (Griffith Park Ride #2) here, or you can wait for a second chance on the way back, or a third chance at a later date. If you don't follow the road around to the left past the carousel, but instead follow Griffith Park Drive around to the right, you'll find yourself on the last, and hardest, part of the Mineral Wells Loop. If you pass the entrance to the Harding Park Golf Course, Club House, and Driving Range, you'll know that you missed the left turn for the first ride and are on the second ride. If you like a tough hill, you'll like the Mineral Wells Loop. If you belong on the first ride, the Griffith Park Short Loop, turn around and bear right at the bottom of the hill.

Almost immediately after bearing left, you will come upon the carousel, which is officially called the **Griffith Park Merry-Go-Round**. I don't know what the difference between a carousel and a merry-go-round is, but I do know that this one is of moderate size, authentic, old, completely refurbished, and a lot of fun!

After passing (or even visiting) the carousel, bear right at the bottom of the grade, and you'll be on Griffith Park Drive. (Griffith Park

Drive and Crystal Springs Drive are one-way roads, separated by a few feet and some oleander shrubbery, but are generally not visible to one another.) When you come to a busy intersection, you have reached Los Feliz Boulevard. Across the street on the right is the **William Mulholland Memorial Fountain**, which sits dormant or shoots water high into the air in innumerable varying patterns. If it's in the shooting mode when you arrive at the intersection, it's worth a foot-trip across Los Feliz to watch a really nice and free show. If it's in the dormant mode, which it seems to be nearly all the time, don't bother risking life, limb, and bike. (To learn more about William Mulholland, chief architect of Los Angeles' vital and sophisticated water system, see Ride 19.) Make a U-turn instead. The roadway going back into the park is Crystal Springs Drive.

Almost immediately after you turn around onto Crystal Springs Drive, you'll see model train rides, pony rides, and stage coach rides on the right, as well as a drinking fountain or two and rest rooms.

About 2.2 miles from the U-turn from Griffith Park Drive onto Crystal Springs Drive, the road turns sharply to the right, skirts the southern edge of the zoo parking lot, and after 0.2 mile, turns left (north). In about 0.1 mile you will come to the entrance of the **Autry Western Heritage Museum**. When I first heard of this place—it opened in 1990—I assumed that Gene Autry had donated his saddle, his stuffed horse, Champion, and his fake six-shooters to the city, and erected a magnificent structure to house these memorabilia. Well, it turns out that it's Roy Rogers whose stuffed horse, Trigger, is housed in a museum (in Apple Valley, 100 miles northeast). While this museum pays ample tribute to movie Westerns—in fact, you can actually take part in one—its focus is on our Western heritage. Urban and urbane though we may now be, it's really just a few years ago since this was the Wild West. Orcutt Park, to give you a sense of historical perspective, is a historical/botanical garden where the discoverer of oil in this area lived; he died about thirty-five years ago.

The Autry Western Heritage Museum is a must-see. There are seven permanent exhibits, dubbed "Spirits": the Spirits of Discovery, Opportunity, Conquest, Community, Cowboy, Romance, and Imagination. In the Heritage Theater there's an ongoing show illustrating each of the Spirits; the show, which features unique special effects, was designed by Walt Disney Imagineering. The museum, incidentally, sports one of the great museum gift shops. There's no charge to enter the gift shop, which features unique Angeleno and Western memorabilia.

After passing the museum, bear left and continue for about 1.75 miles back to Travel Town. Just before turning left into the parking lot, there is a sharp left bend in the road; this is the beginning of Griffith Park Drive. If you continue straight ahead and pass the entrance to the parking lot, you will soon find yourself confronted by a substantial hill, Trash Truck Hill. The Mineral Wells Ride comes down this hill; the Griffith Observatory Ride (Griffith Park Ride #3) goes up it on its way to Griffith Observatory.

Four-mile Extension

If you'd like to extend the ride a bit on flat ground, turn left instead of returning to Travel Town. This will take you past Mt. Sinai and Forest Lawn memorial parks. On your right is the Los Angeles River. The Disney Studio and Warner Bros. are clearly visible on the opposite bank of the river. The distance from Travel Town to Barham Boulevard is 1.5 miles, so by going to Barham and back, you can add 4 gentle and quite interesting miles to the ride.

Griffith Park—
Mineral Wells Loop
(Griffith Park Ride #2)

Location:	Griffith Park
Mileage:	4 (8 with the 4-mile flat extension)
Approximate pedaling time:	½ hour
Terrain:	Excellent—two-lane, well-paved; flat, except for one challenging hill
Traffic:	Light
Things to see:	In addition to most of the highlights of Griffith Park Ride #1, some of the more beautiful scenery in the park in the area of Mineral Wells

This is not *really* a separate ride from the Short Loop (Griffith Park Ride #1), but the only way to include it in the book, as it deserves to be, was to give it a number. Probably the best way to do this ride is to do the Short Loop (Griffith Park Ride #1) and immediately do the Mineral Wells Loop (Griffith Park Ride #2), assuming that you don't kill too much time at the zoo and Western Heritage Museum. The hill that goes past the Harding Golf Course and Mineral Wells Picnic Area is really a nice one. An underlying purpose of all the rides in this book is to let you get acquainted with various parts of Los Angeles, places you'll want to come back to by car and/or share with others. This ride accomplishes these things, and it includes a great downhill that lets you coast into the parking lot at the end. What more can one ask for?

The Short Loop and the Mineral Wells Loop share the first 2.8 miles. During these miles you'll pass the **Los Angeles Zoo**, two golf courses, and the **Autry Western Heritage Museum.** You'll also pass the Los Angeles Zoo parking lot, arguably the most historic parking lot anywhere. For more details on these and other attractions, see the introduction and description for Ride 2.

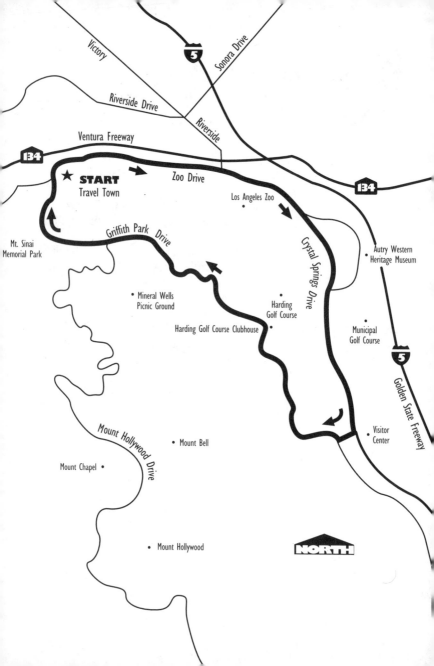

DIREC-TIONS at a glance

0.0	Right from Travel Town parking lot onto Zoo Drive
1.6	Zoo Drive becomes Crystal Springs Drive
2.6	Right at stop sign (after golf course)
2.8	Right at stop sign; go toward golf course. Crystal Springs Drive eventually becomes Griffith Park Drive.

4.2 Right into Travel Town parking lot. (For a flat 4-mile extension, turn left instead of right, and follow the directions at the end of Ride 2.)

When you get to the stop sign at Griffith Park Drive, turn right. You may detour briefly to look at, or even ride on, the **carousel**. If so, instead of going up the hill to the right, follow Griffith Park Drive 0.1 mile to the left, or follow your ears to the distinctive merry-go-round music. After you're done with the carousel, backtrack and climb the hill. You've procrastinated long enough.

As you climb the hill, **Mineral Wells Picnic Ground** will be on your left, 1.2 miles from the turn onto Griffith Park Drive, about 0.4 mile beyond the **Harding Golf Course Clubhouse**.

About 1.7 miles from the turn onto Griffith Park Drive is a narrow paved road on the left. This road leads to the **Griffith Park Observatory**, the main feature of the third Griffith Park ride. Keep going straight to complete the Mineral Wells Loop Ride.

Once you start down the north side of **Trash Truck Hill**, you can pick up considerable speed. The road surface is very good, except after the rare rainstorm, and traffic is usually light. A certain amount of caution should be exercised, though, as trash trucks and other vehicles of the gas-guzzling variety have been known to stop just around a blind curve. The scenery on both sides of the hill is just great. You'd never know you were in the heart of a city with a population in excess of seven million. At the bottom of the hill, 2.4 miles from the turn onto Griffith Park Drive, on the right-hand side, is the Travel Town parking lot. (If you wish to add a very flat 4-mile extension to your ride, turn left instead of going into the parking lot and follow the directions for the extension at the end of the Ride 2.)

Griffith Observatory Loop
(Griffith Park Ride #3)

Location:	Griffith Park
Mileage:	14
Approximate pedaling time:	1½ hours
Terrain:	Excellent two-lane rural roads, but hilly and difficult
Traffic:	Light, except at the Griffith Observatory and on Los Feliz Boulevard
Things to see:	The most beautiful parts of Griffith Park, Griffith Observatory, museum, and planetarium, and the most spectacular vistas of any city in the world

This ride does not have any *killer* hills; but it does include a long climb up the side of a mountain (Mount Hollywood) to the Observatory.

No one has died doing this ride; in fact, it is done daily by cyclists of the road-racing persuasion. "Yes," I hear you say, "but I'm not a road racer or any other kind of racer, so let's forget it." Not so fast; you bought this book to take nice rides to worthwhile places, and this is one of them. You really shouldn't miss the Griffith Observatory because of a little hill. Okay, okay, a big hill. But it's a relatively gentle climb. It's just a little long. You bought and paid for those low gears, so get into your lowest, take your time, watch the scenery, and before you know it, you can be gulping a big soda at the Observatory Snack Bar. Ponder such things as why the eucalyptus trees lining the road shed their bark and not their leaves, and you'll forget that you're gaining a thousand feet or so.

Start this ride by turning left out of the Travel Town parking lot.

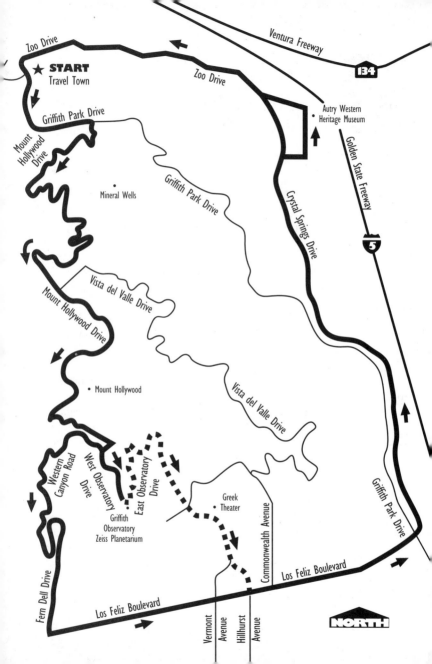

DIREC-TIONS at a glance

0.0	Left from Travel Town parking lot onto Griffith Park Drive
0.7	Right onto Mount Hollywood Drive (go around gate, if closed)
5.0	Right onto West Observatory Drive
5.4	Enter observatory parking lot
5.6	Right onto West Observatory Drive
6.0	Left onto Western Canyon Road (first left)
7.2	Western Canyon Road becomes Fern Dell Drive
8.0	Left onto Los Feliz Boulevard
10.2	Left onto Crystal Springs Drive—entrance to Griffith Park (walk your bike)
12.4	Right, continuing on Crystal Springs Drive (may not be marked); turns sharply left after 0.1 mile and passes Autry Western Heritage Museum
12.7	Left onto Zoo Drive (no choice)
14.2	Left into Travel Town parking lot

This puts you on Griffith Park Drive. About 0.7 mile up the hill is an intersection with a road from the right, Mount Hollywood Drive. This turn occurs at the top of Trash Truck Hill. At the time of writing, it is not a well-marked turn, but it's hard to miss. There is a real temptation to keep going straight, since that's downhill, but try to overcome the urge to take the easy way out.

At the time of this writing, there is also a ROAD CLOSED sign and a steel-tube gate across the road. The reason originally given by the Powers That Be for this situation is L.A.'s seemingly interminable drought. What that has to do with it is anyone's guess. The drought is over—has been for several years—but the gate is still closed. Anyhow, Mount Hollywood Drive is in excellent condition; it is now totally free of traffic; using it on a bike is completely legal, so look at it as a bicyclist's million-dollar scenic bikeway.

The right turn onto Mount Hollywood Drive marks the beginning of a long and winding climb up to the observatory. You'll be on

Mount Hollywood Drive for 4.2 miles. (I *told* you this was a big park!) The scenery is spectacular and unique to Los Angeles. This is a gentle ride, if you sit back and enjoy it; if you push yourself, the climb can really get to you. For some reason, when the road is open to motorized traffic, people park here and there along the way to polish their cars. If you want to blend in, park your bike for a few minutes, whip out a can of Meguire's wax, and polish your steed.

After 4.2 miles turn right on West Observatory Drive. This is a fairly steep climb, but it lasts less than 0.4 mile, and when you reach the top, you're *there!* And what a there there is! The **Griffith Observatory** is at the back of the parking lot. You'll recognize it immediately.

There's an overpriced snack bar at the northwest end of the parking lot, but it's the only game in town, and if the ride up the mountain bestowed an insatiable craving for park food, it's there for you.

Griffith Observatory was built with a $100,000 gift from Col. Griffith J. Griffith in 1912. The first thing you'll notice after dismounting your bike and approaching the building is the spectacular view of Hollywood and downtown L.A. In fact, it's safe to say that it's a view rivaled by only a few in the world; even the views from the top of the Eiffel Tower and the Empire State Building can't compare with this!

The observatory's twin refracting telescopes, with 12- and 9½-inch lenses, are available for public use from dusk to 10:00 P.M. The staff usually aim the telescopes at an interesting object—e.g., Saturn—and visitors line up for a few seconds' peek at the wonder. (The lines are short, but since the telescopes don't function during daylight hours, don't attempt this ride for telescopic viewing.) The observatory also houses a very good museum, with a focus (pun intended) on matters astronomical, that is worth seeing during daylight hours, and during the week the odds are in your favor that there will be a movie or television show being shot on the grounds. The building was completely renovated in 1990, and the grounds are kept immaculate.

The 650-seat **Zeiss Planetarium**, dedicated in 1935 and completely renovated in 1990, presents spectacular shows every hour or so. The new projector is one of the biggest and best anywhere, and the lecturers seem to have a nice easy delivery and a great sense of humor.

The **Laserium** is a laser-light show that has been operating since the late 1970s. The shows are presented by Laser Images, Inc. and consist of abstract laser-light images projected on the planetarium ceiling, moving in time with well-selected musical accompaniment.

No description of the observatory would be complete without mentioning the bust of James Dean at the edge of the canyon separating the observatory from the Hollywood sign. (In fact, one of the best views of the Hollywood sign is from the observatory.) Why James Dean's bust is located here is a mystery to me. But if you're a James Dean fan, you have another reason to go to the observatory.

When you've had your fill of the views, the snacks, the museum, James Dean, the Hollywood sign, and everything else the observatory has to offer, leave the parking lot by the road (*West* Observatory Drive) to the left of the parking lot (with the observatory behind you). You can make a mistake here and unwittingly go down *East* Observatory Drive. Not to worry—if that happens, when you reach the first intersection (after 0.4 mile), turn left and go through the tunnel. The tunnel, incidentally, has been featured in numerous movies, TV shows, and commercials. If you have followed the directions correctly, the tunnel will be on your left when you reach the first intersection out of the parking lot. (Riding through tunnels, however short, makes me nervous, and that's why I routed you down *West* Observatory Drive.)

Take your first left onto Western Canyon Road; after 0.8 mile this becomes Fern Dell Drive. Fern Dell was once one of the most beautiful sections of Griffith Park. It is a narrow strip of land following a rustic creek completely engulfed by ferns of all kinds. In recent years the area's rising population has had a major (adverse) impact; the stream has become trash-laden, and traffic through the Dell has become very heavy on weekends. After 0.8 mile on Fern Dell Drive, turn left onto Los Feliz Boulevard. After 2.1 miles of heavy traffic, you'll come to Crystal Springs Drive at the Mulholland Fountain entrance to Griffith Park.

For a different, but almost equally scenic, route to Los Feliz, leave the observatory parking lot via West Observatory Drive; turn right onto Vermont Canyon Road, which becomes Vermont Avenue, and stay on these roads for 2.0 miles. You will wind your way down the mountain past the **Greek Theater.** This is a 6,000-seat outdoor theater leased by the city to an operator to put on stage shows, light opera, and ballet. These events are never held during daylight hours, but after seeing this idyllic setting, you may be tempted to attend a show.

It's a beautiful (downhill) ride through the canyon and the high-rent district all the way to Los Feliz Boulevard, where you turn left. Once on Los Feliz, continue for 1.8 miles to Crystal Springs Drive, where you'll once again be out of city traffic.

Whichever route you use to descend from the observatory, Crystal Springs Drive and the (re)entry into Griffith Park are at the bottom of the rather steep hill, with the Mulholland Fountain on the right. Be careful turning left onto Crystal Springs Drive; moving over into the left lane can be very hazardous, and the green light that permits the turn gives a new meaning to the term split second. A "chicken left," where you stay to the right and cross as a pedestrian, is recommended.

Upon turning onto Crystal Springs Drive, you are 4.0 flat-to-slightly-rolling miles from Travel Town. See Ride #2 for landmarks and points of interest along Crystal Springs Drive, between Los Feliz and Travel Town. Upon arrival back in Travel Town, you will have gone about 15 miles, and what unforgettable miles they were!

For Further Information
(Griffith Park Rides)

Autry Western Heritage Museum (213) 667–200
Greek Theater (213) 410–1062
Griffith Observatory & Planetarium (213) 664–1191
Laserium (818) 997–3624
Los Angeles Zoo (213) 666–4090
Travel Town Party Reservations (213) 662–5874
Travel Town Railroad (213) 662–9678

Getting There

Travel Town is at the northeast corner of Griffith Park. From points east and west of Griffith Park, take the SR–134 (Ventura) Freeway to the Victory Boulevard exit. Within 50 feet of the exit there is a T intersection with Zoo Drive. Travel Town is on the right. Follow the signs.

From the north or south, take the I–5 (Golden State) Freeway to the Griffith Park/Los Angeles Zoo/Western Heritage Museum exit. Follow the ZOO DRIVE signs north and then west, past the museum to Travel Town.

This Is the City, Too!

Location:	South of Griffith Park almost to downtown
Mileage:	23 miles without the Tommy's Famous hamburger detour; 26 miles with the detour
Approximate pedaling time:	2¾ hours without detour; 3¼ hours with detour
Terrain:	Good pavement all the way; quite easy, essentially flat, although there are a couple of very short but steep hills
Traffic:	Mostly moderate, with a few bad intersections
Things to see:	Griffith Park, Fargo Street and the steepest streets in the city, Aimee Semple McPherson's Angelus Temple, Tommy's Famous hamburger joint, L.A.'s first oil wells, Echo Park, Elysian Park, Dodger Stadium, Police Academy, L.A.'s Victorian district, Silver Lake, and much more

This is a ride through some of the early-to-modern history of the city. Bear in mind that Angelenos consider anything occurring in a previous year to be History. Any event occurring more than ten years ago is Really History. So, Aimee Semple McPherson, who died in 1944, is treated in much the same manner as pioneer, early settler, and local hero Jose Vicente Feliz, who died more than a 150 years earlier. Corporal Feliz was granted **Rancho Los Feliz**; Colonel Griffith J. Griffith

DIREC-TIONS at a glance

0.0	Right out of Travel Town parking lot onto Zoo Drive
1.75	Zoo Drive becomes Crystal Springs Drive—follow past zoo, golf course, and carousel
4.6	Cross Los Feliz Boulevard—becomes Riverside Drive
6.3	Right onto Allesandro Street
7.1	Left onto Glendale Boulevard
8.7	Left onto Colton Street
8.8	Left onto Douglas Street
9.0	Right onto Cortez Street
9.1	Left onto Edgeware Road
9.3	Left onto Carroll Avenue
9.5	Right onto Edgeware Road
9.7	Left onto Douglas Street
10.0	Left onto Allison Avenue, immediately followed by a right onto Sunset Boulevard and a left onto Elysian Park Avenue
10.4	Right onto Dodger Stadium Ring Road
11.4	Right on unmarked road opposite left field stands to Academy Road (follow signs to Academy)
11.7	Right onto Academy Road
12.1	Left onto Elysian Park Drive
13.6	Left onto Stadium Way at T intersection
14.0	Right onto Academy Road
14.2	Leave park; name changes to Morton Avenue
14.5	Right onto Scott Avenue
14.8	Stop at Glendale Boulevard, scratch head, and decide whether you want a Tommy's Famous hamburger, chili, and fries or would rather continue the tour

To Go to Tommy's Famous

14.8	Cross Glendale Boulevard
14.9	Left onto Alvarado Street
16.3	Right onto Beverly Boulevard
16.6	Right into Tommy's Famous parking lot; after pigging out:

16.6	Right onto Rampart Boulevard
16.9	Right onto Temple Street
17.2	Left onto Alvarado Street
18.1	Right onto Scott Avenue
18.2	Left onto Glendale Avenue; this is the corner where the detour to Tommy's Famous began

To Skip Tommy's Famous (or to continue after the side trip)
(Mileages on left assume you've "done" Tommy's; mileages on right assume you skipped Tommy's)

18.2 (14.5)	If you skip Tommy's, turn right onto Glendale Boulevard; if you go to Tommy's, turn left onto Glendale Boulevard. Whatever you decide to do, head north on Glendale
19.0 (15.3)	Left onto Earl Street
19.1 (15.4)	Right onto Silver Lake Boulevard
19.3 (15.6)	Left onto Armstrong Avenue
19.7 (16.0)	Right onto West Silver Lake Drive
19.8 (16.1)	Left onto Rowena Boulevard
20.3 (16.6)	Right onto Griffith Park Boulevard
20.5 (16.8)	Right onto Los Feliz Boulevard
21.2 (17.5)	Left onto Crystal Springs Drive
24.4 (20.7)	Crystal Springs turns left and becomes Zoo Drive
26.0 (22.3)	Left into Travel Town parking lot

acquired the *rancho* (which means "farm" in Spanish) from Feliz's heirs, and it was a piece of Rancho Los Feliz that Griffith gave the city as its park. Los Feliz Boulevard, which cuts through the rancho, and a small adobe next to the ranger station in Griffith Park, are all that remains of the corporal. Not to denigrate Griffith's generosity, but Rancho Los Feliz was so big that there was *plenty* left over for him after his gift to the city. Griffith Park was, in fact, only about 5 percent of Rancho Los Feliz.

It's interesting to note that a mere corporal in the service of Spain was given such a magnificent spread, and that it took a full colonel in the U.S. Army to acquire it from him. There appears to have been severe rank inflation in the military since those days. If this were going on now, Feliz and Griffith would be four-star generals. Parenthetically, Corporal Feliz was a commandant and judge during Los Angeles' first nineteen years of existence.

The starting point for this ride is Travel Town (see Ride 2 for more details on Travel Town). After going on other Short Bike Rides that start at Travel Town, you may have spotted parking lots closer to Los Feliz Boulevard. I picked Travel Town because this ride calls for the peace of mind that goes with a park setting for a beginning and end. The ride is very urban, and the parks make for a nice contrast.

Turn right out of the Travel Town parking lot. Almost immediately the road turns right again, and you have little choice but to follow it. This is Zoo Drive. It, too, bears right after you pass Victory Boulevard, and 1.75 miles from the starting point, it changes its name to Crystal Springs Drive. Continue on Crystal Springs Drive, past the zoo entrance and the golf courses to the stop sign at Griffith Park Drive. You can go straight ahead here, but for scenic purposes I recommend a right turn; go up the slight incline and bear left past the carousel. The road goes down a rather steep grade, turns right, and then straightens out for the rest of the ride through the park. You'll come to Los Feliz Boulevard 4.6 miles from the Travel Town entrance.

Eventually, you'll get a green light. You can use the time to determine if the **William Mulholland Memorial Fountain** across the street is functioning and to see if you can discern a pattern to the volleys of water being shot skyward. When you finally do get a green light, cross the street quickly, because the duration of that green light gives a new meaning to the term *split second*. Crystal Springs Drive ends at Los Feliz and becomes Riverside Drive. The Los Angeles River is indeed less than a block away on the left. Parenthetically, the much-heralded Los Angeles River Bikeway, a $17 million-plus project funded in the main by federal money, is located along the river; at this writing, a 3-mile leg has been completed. This leg extends north from Los Feliz Boulevard, and you might enjoy traveling on it. The entire bikeway is scheduled to be completed around 2007, although other estimates run between 2003 and never. You'll be on Riverside for 1.7 miles.

The first overpass you ride under is the **Red Car Overpass.** It is now Hyperion Street, but it was originally built as a railroad bridge for L.A.'s famed Red Cars. Los Angeles had horse-drawn street cars from 1888 to 1902. In 1901 Henry Huntington, about whom you'll read more when we visit San Marino and the Huntington Library (see Ride 11), established the Pacific Electric Railroad, commonly known as the Red Cars. The lines ran everywhere. I mean *everywhere.* There were hundreds of miles of track, and wherever they ran, housing tracts soon followed. Wherever in the present-day megalopolis you may be, if you see a group of old homes, you can be sure that a Red Car line once ran nearby. The last trolleys ran in Los Angeles in 1960; those very machines can still be seen, however, in Tijuana, Mexico, Guatemala, and other locales where they don't look especially inviting.

Immediately after passing under the SR–2 (Glendale) Freeway, turn right on Allesandro Street. Right away you'll be faced with a hill. It's a very noticeable hill, but anyone can climb it, given the will and patience. Also, it's mercifully short. As you're climbing, you'll notice the SR–110 (Pasadena) Freeway humming along slightly below you on the right. Look left and you'll see some amazing sights. The streets on the left are unbelievably steep; in fact, a couple are so steep that they are paved with stairs. Cove Street has one of these staircases.

Just when you think you've seen it all, you'll come to Baxter Street, and, a short block farther along, **Fargo Street,** 0.6 mile from the turn onto Allesandro Street. You *must* stop to look at Fargo Street, the steepest paved street in Los Angeles. Before the city will accept delivery of a new fire truck, it is road tested on Fargo Street—presumably going *up* it. Whether the truck is any good after wrenching its guts out climbing the hill is another matter. The concrete street was paved in the twenties, and it's nothing short of a miracle that the wet concrete didn't just slide down the hill. For the statistically minded, it has a 33 percent grade, rising 300 feet in 300 yards.

History was made here in 1968 when Darryl Levesque of Upland, then a member of the Los Angeles Wheelmen, was challenged by a fellow member to climb Fargo Street on a tandem with his wife. The Levesques made it to the top. Every year since then, the L.A. Wheelmen have sponsored a January attack on the hill. In recent years there have been about 125 riders trying and 50 or 60 succeeding in the attempt to climb to the top. The number of attempts and the percentage of successes are increasing annually. (At this writing, though, only five women have accomplished the feat.)

A woman living on Fargo Street told the *L.A. Times* in 1982 that the most annoying thing about living there was the Saturday-night screams of teenage girls. Apparently it's a great place to scare the daylights out of a date by driving over the lip of the hill at full throttle. Bad as screams in the night are, the residents say that the street's celebrity status is even tougher to deal with.

This ride does not even attempt the climb, but you really must push your bike at least partway up the hill. You'll see why UPS and bill collectors avoid calling on Fargo Street residents. From the lofty perch at the top there's a magnificent view of Griffith Park and a good deal of the rest of town. The view is spectacular even partway up.

You'll be on Allesandro Street for a total of 0.8 mile, after which you'll turn left on Glendale Boulevard. After 0.75 mile you'll come to **Angelus Temple** on the left. It is said that in 1920 Aimee Semple McPherson arrived in Los Angeles with $100, a tambourine, and a rare brand of charisma. A fiery, puritanical evangelist, she built a huge following on pulpit theatrics. Angelus Temple, a magnificent structure costing somewhat more than $100, was built by McPherson in 1923. She also established the first religious radio station, KFSG, at about that time. In 1926, at the height of her popularity, she disappeared. It was national, 2-inch-headline stuff. A couple of weeks later she reappeared, not looking too devastated, with a story that she'd been kidnapped.

Various theories about what *really* happened have been batted about for years, but the one that is supported by a great deal of circumstantial evidence and seems to be accepted by modern cynics, myself included, is that McPherson was vacationing in Hermosillo, Mexico, with her lover. No one will ever know for sure, but the general consensus is that kidnapping, while pretty exciting, is less glamorous than a Puritan's tryst on the seamy side of the Border.

A mere 0.1 mile beyond Angelus Temple is **Echo Park** and its famous lake. The lake was built by the city as a reservoir in 1885. Mr. and Ms. John Q. Public, who have a modest suburban ranch-style place in the Valley, generally think that Los Angeles pipes all of its water from the soggy North. Not so. In fact, most of L.A.'s water comes from the Colorado River and local wells. Regardless of where the water comes from, it is stored in numerous reservoirs all over town. Several of them, like Echo Park Lake, are located in city parks. The lake in Lincoln Park (originally called Eastlake) was once a reservoir; MacArthur Park (originally called Westlake) has a large lake, and Lafayette Park has an unnamed lake/reservoir. Echo Park Lake, incidentally, was drained and dredged in 1988. Fifty years of gunk (muck, old shoes, shopping carts, and generally unsavory detritus) was removed and the lake was refilled. Its famous lotus beds were reestablished, and if you're visiting when they're in bloom, they're a memorable sight.

Continue on Glendale Boulevard for 1.1 miles and turn left on Colton Street. As you make the turn, Rockwood Street will be behind you. At the top of the short, very steep hill is the site of one of the first **oil wells** in Los Angeles, which stood on property owned by Emma Summers, a music teacher. (There's really nothing to see there, and it's certainly not worth the steep climb, only to have to make a U-turn to get back to where you are now.) Now that you've turned onto Colton, look to your immediate left on Patton Street, as you climb a little on Colton; you'll come upon another old oil well.

Oil was discovered in Los Angeles County in the town of Newhall (see Ride 20) in 1876. An oil boom really got going in 1892, when Edward L. Doheny, whose name graces a number of L.A.'s highlights, struck black gold at the corner of Colton and Patton. That well has disappeared, but the ones at Colton and Douglas are almost exactly the same age and, like the first well, were originally hand-dug. The holes measured 4 by 6 feet and were 155 feet-deep. By 1900 there were 1,100 oil wells in this area.

After 0.1 mile on Colton Street, turn left on Douglas Street. After 0.2 mile turn right on Cortez Street. After 0.1 mile on Cortez, turn left on Edgeware Road. This is **Angeleno Heights**, which was an elegant neighborhood in the late nineteenth century. Settled in 1886, it was L.A.'s first suburb. It has been undergoing more or less constant restoration for the past ten or more years, and today it sports some of the best examples of authentic Victorian architecture to be found in California. Stay on Edgeware for 0.2 mile and turn left on Carroll Avenue. After 0.2 mile turn right on Edgeware Road.

No, you are not going crazy; you *were* at this turn not so long ago, but Edgeware Road curves around 180 degrees, and when you turned left on Carroll Avenue, it took you back to Edgeware. Now, turn right on Edgeware and continue 0.2 mile to Douglas Street.

Turn left on Douglas. Continue 0.3 mile to Allison Avenue, where you'll jog right on Sunset Boulevard and left on Elysian Park Avenue. Stay on Elysian Park Avenue for 0.3 mile. Then turn right on Dodger Stadium Ring Road. You'll soon come to **Dodger Stadium.**

This is the place where the Brooklyn Dodgers of Ebbets Field became the Los Angeles Dodgers in 1956. The stadium seats 56,000 around its natural grass field. The ring road is more than a mile around, and you get the feeling that this is not just a stadium, it's Big Business! The Dodgers were sold by the O'Malley family to Rupert Murdoch's News Corp. in 1997, and what was always big business will become even bigger business. It was also Big Politics before and for some time after its 1956 construction in Chavez Ravine, a very run-down neighborhood whose inhabitants were displaced by the city. Needless to say, it's best to visit the stadium when the Dodgers aren't playing.

After a little less than a mile on Dodger Stadium Ring Road, turn right on an unmarked road opposite the left field stands. (You pass the right field stands first, so this right turn comes about 0.2 mile after you begin to pass the stands.)

After 0.3 mile turn right on Academy Road; follow Academy Road to the right. On your left is the real honest-to-goodness **Los Angeles Police Academy**, the one that stars in *Police Academy*, and its many sequels. The place is usually a beehive of activity, hopefully more efficient than depicted in the movies.

Stay on Academy Road for 0.4 mile, turn left onto Elysian Park

Drive. You are now in **Elysian Park**. Follow Elysian Park Drive through a winding tour of Elysian Park, which will undergo several name changes. At this writing the roads in and around the park are in somewhat poor repair, so beware of potholes. After about 1.5 miles you'll come to a T intersection with Stadium Way. Turn left and ride 0.4 mile to Academy Road, where you turn right. After about 0.25 mile, when you leave the park, the name changes to Morton Avenue. Ride for 0.3 mile on Morton, turn right on Scott Avenue. After 0.3 mile you'll come to Glendale Avenue.

If you've developed a craving for something really Angeleno (and after all these turns who wouldn't?), go straight across Glendale Boulevard on Scott Avenue to Alvarado Street. Turn left on Alvarado; stay on Alvarado for 1.4 rather grubby urban miles. Turn right on Beverly Boulevard. On the right, after about 0.3 mile, at 4575 Beverly at the corner of Rampart Boulevard, is **Tommy's Famous** hamburger joint. Open 24 hours per day, 365 days a year, Tommy's Famous makes *the* L.A. burgers. And Tommy's fries are fantastic, too. And as long as you're there, try the chili. No, you wouldn't bring the Queen of England (or any other royalty) to Tommy's Famous; you wouldn't even bring her to this neighborhood, but this is the ultimate in stand-up dining.

Turn right on Rampart Boulevard, go up the slight incline for 0.25 mile, and turn right on Temple Street. Turn left on Alvarado Street, and in short order you'll be back to Scott Avenue. Turn right on Scott; after 1 block, turn left on Glendale Avenue. (If you skipped Tommy's, turn right on Glendale Avenue.) Ride on Glendale for 0.8 mile, and take a left onto Earl Street, where you ride for a block to a right turn on Silver Lake Boulevard.

The lake is in evidence here. It is a working reservoir, and its surroundings reflect the poshness of the old neighborhood. **The Silver Lake District** is making a comeback. Any puddle with a shoreline attracts the Angeleno well-to-do, and this neighborhood may someday rise again. In the meantime, enjoy the place as a real landmark.

Now it's time to head back to the barn. After 0.2 mile on Silver Lake Boulevard, turn left on Armstrong Avenue. After 0.4 mile on Armstrong, turn right on Silver Lake Drive followed by, after 0.1 mile, a left on Rowena Boulevard. Stay on Rowena for 0.5 mile; turn right on Griffith Park Boulevard. The name of this street is deceiving; it is *not* the best way to get back to Griffith Park. After 0.2 mile turn right onto Los Feliz Boulevard, where you'll stay for 0.7 mile—and an exciting 0.7 mile it is! It's downhill with heavy traffic, and you will want to turn left at the bottom of the hill. It's best to do a "chicken left" (i.e., walk your bike) at Crystal Springs Drive. You'll recognize the intersection, with the Mulholland Fountain on the right and Griffith Park's entrance on the left.

Once you've made the turn into the park, stay on Crystal Springs Drive for 3.2 miles. It's rolling terrain with light to moderate traffic (light during the week and frequently moderate on weekends). After about 2.8 miles without a turn, something of a record for this ride, Crystal Springs Drive turns right and then left, skirting the zoo parking lot and passing the **Autry Western Heritage Museum**. For more information about this fabulous museum, see Griffith Park Ride #1. About 3.2 miles from Los Feliz, the road turns left and becomes Zoo Drive. Stay on it for 1.6 miles, and after a left turn you'll find yourself at the entrance to the Travel Town parking lot. Whew!

For Further Information

Autry Western Heritage Museum (213) 667–2000
Griffith Park Headquarters (213) 665–5188
Los Angeles Zoo (213) 666–4090
Travel Town (213) 662–5874

Getting There

Travel Town is at the northeast corner of Griffith Park. From points east and west of Griffith Park, take the SR–134 (Ventura) Freeway to the Victory Boulevard exit. Within 50 feet of the exit there is a T intersection with Zoo Drive. Travel Town is on the right. Follow the signs.

From the north or south, take the I–5 (Golden State) Freeway to the Griffith Park/Los Angeles Zoo/Western Heritage Museum exit. Follow the ZOO DRIVE signs north and then west, past the museum to Travel Town.

Hollywood(s) Overview

There is a Hollywood. It's a part of the Los Angeles megalopolis, a few miles from downtown. It's another of L.A.'s seventy-six communities in search of a center. While it is famous primarily for being the Movie Capital of the World, it isn't, and maybe it never was, except for a relatively brief period in the twenties. The real motion-picture capital is arguably Burbank, though the cluster of Burbank, Studio City, and Universal City is a strong contender for the title. If you throw in television, the cluster almost certainly is more important than the next-biggest competitor, Culver City. The point is that way down the list, you'll find Hollywood, the geographical place 7 miles from downtown Los Angeles.

Not that Hollywood doesn't have its share of glamour. It is still the home of a studio or two, and it boasts the Hollywood Walk of Fame, Frederick's of Hollywood, Max Factor, the Egyptian Theater, the Chinese Theater, and a couple dozen record companies, Capitol Records being housed in the most conspicuous building. The Hollywood of yesteryear had many small studios that contributed greatly to today's entertainment industry, but all of the real old-timers, except Paramount Pictures, are gone.

For this reason, I've included two Hollywood rides (and a short side trip to the Hollywood Bowl). They will cover the real Hollywood, the Hollywood that you'll find on L.A.'s maps, and the Hollywood of Burbank and Studio City. Bear in mind that whole books, very large books, have been written about Hollywood, so these rides and the descriptions that accompany them are no more than a quick overview of the highlights. So if, in the course of one of the rides, you come across something that you find fascinating that isn't mentioned here, I hope you'll understand.

The Hollywood in Burbank, Toluca Lake, Universal City, and Studio City

Location:	Start in southeastern San Fernando Valley
Mileage:	17
Approximate pedaling time:	1½ hours
Terrain:	Well-paved streets and roads; flat
Traffic:	Some heavy traffic at certain locations on weekdays; weekend traffic is usually light throughout
Things to see:	Walt Disney studio, Warner Bros. studio, Universal studio, Universal CityWalk, NBC and CBS studios, Campo de Cahuenga, Forest Lawn and Mt. Sinai cemeteries

The best place to start this ride is Travel Town in Griffith Park. Turn right out of Travel Town's parking lot onto Zoo Drive, which almost immediately turns right. After 0.9 mile you'll come to the point where Riverside Drive/Victory Boulevard intersects on the left. (It's the first left after leaving Travel Town.)

Turn left; go over the SR–134 (Ventura) Freeway and down through the park to the next intersection, about 0.3 mile. Turn left; this will put you on Riverside Drive. Almost immediately you'll find yourself in a nice residential area. After 0.7 mile you'll pass the **Los Angeles Equestrian Center** on your left. This was the site of the 1984 Olympics' equestrian events. It is reputed to be among the best equestrian centers in the world. Another 0.4 mile will put you abreast of the **General Motors Training Center** on the right, the surprisingly small facility where Mr. Goodwrench is trained. About 0.5 mile beyond that you'll come to the **Disney studio**.

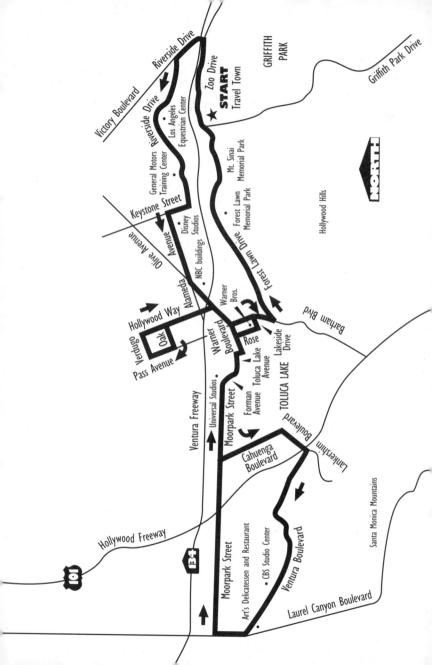

DIREC-TIONS at a glance

0.0	Right from Travel Town parking lot onto Zoo Drive
0.9	Left onto Riverside Drive (possibly renamed Victory Boulevard); go over SR–134 (Ventura) Freeway
1.2	Left onto Riverside Drive
2.9	Right onto Keystone Street
3.2	Left onto Alameda Avenue
4.2	Right onto Hollywood Way
4.3	Left onto Oak Street
4.5	Right onto Pass Avenue
4.8	Right onto Verdugo Avenue
5.0	Right onto Hollywood Way
5.7	Right onto Olive Avenue
6.2	Right onto Lakeside Drive to end
6.3	Right onto Rose Street
6.5	Left onto Warner Boulevard
6.6	Left onto Clybourn Avenue
6.7	Right onto Toluca Lake Avenue
7.1	Right onto Forman Avenue
7.2	Left onto Moorpark Street
7.7	Left onto Cahuenga Boulevard
8.2	Left onto Lankershim Boulevard
8.7	Right onto Ventura Boulevard
10.7	Right onto Laurel Canyon Boulevard
11.1	Right onto Moorpark Street
14.0	Right onto Clybourn Avenue
14.2	Left onto Warner Boulevard
14.5	Right onto Pass Avenue
14.9	Left onto Forest Lawn Drive
16.7	Right onto Griffith Park Drive (probably not marked) with sign to Travel Town and L.A. Zoo
16.9	Enter Travel Town parking lot

Disney, which had its beginnings on Hyperion Avenue in Glendale, moved to its present fifty-one-acre location in August 1939. *Pinocchio* was the first picture produced here. There are three landmarks of note from your vantage point at the intersection of Riverside Drive and Keystone Street. The first is a giant satellite dish used by the Disney Channel. The second is the Disney water tower. Most studios have a water tower, proclaiming, I suppose, that they are small towns, islands of fantasy in a surrounding sea of the real world. These towers tend to be colorful and to display well-known logos. In this case, the logo is Mickey Mouse and Uncle Walt's well-known signature. The third landmark is the Animation Building, completed in 1997. It has a four-story-tall wizard's hat above the main entrance and film sprocket–shaped windows winding around the irregular shape of the upper story. As wild as this architecture is, wait'll you see the Disney Administration Building.

Turn right on Keystone Street and you'll get a better view of the water tower. (If you continue straight on Riverside Drive, you'll be disappointed: there's nothing visible from the street except big beige buildings.) On the left on Keystone Street is the Disney back lot. You can catch a glimpse of the back lot's innards through breaks in the ivy-covered chain-link fence.

After passing 0.25 mile of frustratingly hidden studio property, turn left on Alameda Avenue. The Disney studio continues on the left, and after 0.2 mile, on the left, at the corner of Buena Vista Street, is the **Disney Administration Building**. You can't miss it; it'll knock you off your bike! It's a hulking, multistory, red sandstone structure with an enormous portico. In the triangular space supporting the roof is a row of six of the Seven Dwarfs, each 10 feet tall, arms upraised, supporting a small platform. On the platform, just underneath the peak of the roof and occupying the most important position of all, is Dopey. He holds up the roof's peak. Before the building was completed in 1990, there was speculation that Mickey Mouse would hold up the peak. The significance of Dopey being at the top is debated by nearly everyone who sees this truly magnificent paean to Disney's characters.

About 0.3 mile past the Disney studio, on the left, you'll come to the first of several **NBC buildings**, and just beyond that, at 3000 West

Alameda Avenue, the main NBC studio, office center, and production facility. Tours of the NBC facilities are available, and they're quite worthwhile. Tickets to various NBC television shows are readily available at no cost. (See "For Further Information" for the phone number.)

At the NBC studio, Olive Street cuts across Alameda at a sharp angle, creating an oddly shaped and busy intersection. Be careful crossing it. On your left you'll see more of NBC. The basic studio dates back to the 1950s, but there has been a great deal of expansion and renovation, and nearly all of the visible structures are from the late 1980s and 1990s.

The **Warner Bros. water tower** soon will be visible on your left. (The *Brothers* of Warner Bros., incidentally, is always abbreviated, and you will reveal your unfamiliarity with show biz if you spell it out.) When you get to Hollywood Way, turn right, away from the Warner Bros.' water tower; we'll get back to it in due course. At the corner of Hollywood Way and Olive Street is the **WEA** (Warner/Elektra/Atlantic) **Building**. WEA is the distribution arm of the record company and videotape division.

Turning right on Hollywood Way takes you to the former **Columbia Ranch**, the official name of the old Columbia Pictures Burbank studio. The present-day ranch, now part of Warner Bros., is a mere shadow of its old self. When originally occupied by Columbia in 1930, the ranch covered more than 100 acres. Today it occupies forty-one, with a dozen sound stages and lots of outdoor sets. Go around the block, turning left on Oak, right on Pass, right on Verdugo, and right again upon your return to Hollywood Way. You'll be seeing some outdoor sets very close up, and peering through the gate at Oak and Hollywood Way provides a very good view of a typical studio's exterior interior—exterior referring to the outsides of the buildings; the interior referring to the usually hidden area inside the perimeter walls and fences. Turn right at Olive (the end of the street).

One block farther along on Olive, on the right (north) is the **Glass Building** (at 3950 Olive Street). It is the only building in Los Angeles with actual curved glass panels; other round buildings, such as the Capitol Records Building and the Bonaventure Hotel, actually have flat panes arranged in a circle.

Directly across the street is Warner Bros.' **Main Administration Building.** It's a Mediterranean- style building with lush tropical foliage in front. The official address is 4000 Warner Boulevard, but it's really on Olive Street. Take a side trip up the driveway, past the front doors, and back onto Olive Street. The Warner water tower is much in evidence, as is the guard gate, through which no one passes unless employed by Warner or one of the more than one hundred independent producers that call the studio home. The Warner Bros. water tower, you may know, is the home of the Animaniacs, who are some of Warner's zanier cartoon characters. The Animaniacs are not drawn on the water tower; they *live* in it, as anyone under the age of eight can tell you. If you are visiting Los Angeles with anyone around eight years of age, they will want you to take them to see this water tower.

There is even less to see at Warner Bros. than at Disney. The studio was built in 1929 after a move from the geographic Hollywood. During dark financial days for Warner and Columbia Pictures, Columbia joined Warner at this site and formed the Burbank Studios. By 1990 Warner's health was restored and further invigorated by a merger with *Time* magazine (actually Time, Inc.), and Columbia was booted out. Columbia, meanwhile, was bought by Sony, renamed Sony Pictures, and the Japanese company has relocated to Culver City.

Follow Olive Avenue left around the western boundary of the studio. This takes you southward, with the studio on the left. The gigantic, blocks-long wall is covered with billboards touting the latest Warner Bros. movies and television shows. The innards of the Warner studio are not very enticing. The streets are unnamed, and the buildings, of which there are dozens, have such fanciful names as *Building 19,* or *Stage 8.* There are some thirty sound stages, and while they are uninteresting barnlike structures on the outside and airplane hangar–like caverns on the inside, a lot of very interesting things do go on in them. Alas, sets are closed to the public (and nearly all employees). Outdoor sets, while open to employees, are diminishing in size, number, and importance with the advent of location shooting. (One advantage of location shooting to a bicyclist, though, is that at any given moment, somewhere in Los Angeles there are thirty or

71

more movies and TV shows being filmed, and the odds of your stumbling onto one of the "shoots" is quite high.) Warner does run tours of the studio on a rather limited and pricey basis. If you are interested in the *real* workings of a *working* studio, you will love the Warner tour and it will be worth the money.

After 0.25 mile on Pass Avenue, turn right at the **Smoke House**. This was once a major watering hole for studio personnel who wanted to "take a lunch" outside of the commissary. It is no longer what it once was, but the food is still good and reasonably priced, and there's a fair chance you'll see someone famous. (Be forewarned, however, that bicycle clothing at the Smoke House is not appropriate.)

If you were to go straight ahead, instead of turning at the Smoke House, you'd come to Forest Lawn Drive on the left, a good way to get back to Travel Town; on the right, behind the Smoke House and across the river, is the back of the Universal studio, and at the top of the hill straight ahead is the passage to **Lake Hollywood** (see Ride 10). Forest Lawn Drive, incidentally, is the route by which we'll return to Travel Town.

Follow Lakeside Drive around to the right. The offices of **Shamrock Productions** and other independent movie producers are on the left and right, and at the point where the street turns right to become Rose Street, you'll pass the entrance to the Lakeside Country Club. There is a lake in there—**Toluca Lake**. It's privately owned by the truly rich and famous. You can see the lake from the country club's driveway, along with ducks, geese, and swans. It is said that W. C. Fields, angered by the quacking noise, once tried to cream some geese with an oar while sailing Toluca Lake's otherwise untroubled waters.

After 0.2 mile turn left on Warner Boulevard. Stay on Warner to the T intersection with Clybourn Avenue, turn left. The left (east) side of Clybourn is Burbank and the right side is Toluca Lake. Toluca Lake is a part of the city of Los Angeles, and you will soon see that it's one of the nicer parts. It was, and to some extent still is, home to many show-biz celebrities. In the days of the "star system," when players were under contract to a particular studio, a home in Toluca Lake meant that you could walk to Warner Bros. and Universal. We will zigzag through the picturesque streets on the way to the next stop, the **Universal studio.**

A right on Forman Avenue and a left on Moorpark Street will take you past Bob Hope's house, which begins at the corner of Arcola (the entrance is at 10346 Moorpark Street) and ends at Ledge Avenue. It's totally hidden behind a high, ivy-covered wall. Jonathan Winters's house is at 4301 Arcola Avenue, so double back and turn left (north) at Arcola. Winters has actually been seen by cyclists, and he doesn't seem to mind being recognized. On the off chance that you do see him, you can talk to him, but don't ask for an autograph. Return to Moorpark Street and turn right. If you go farther north to Riverside Drive, you'll come to beautiful downtown Toluca Lake. Depending on the day of the week and the time of day, there are celebrities to be seen here, with the odds running about nine to one against. In any case, there's a good breakfast or lunch to be had at Paty's—at the corner of Riverside Drive and Clybourn Avenue. Bicyclists are welcome there—there's even a bike rack—and the food is excellent, though somewhat expensive. If you wish, you can eat at the sidewalk tables in view of your bike and the passing scene. There's a Bob's Big Boy coffee shop for the more price conscious, and a Marie Callender's restaurant for those who don't mind waiting for a table. Directly across Clybourn Avenue from Bob's is a restaurant that used to be owned by Robert Redford, but is no longer. This structure's other claim to fame is that it was the very first International House of Pancakes (IHOP).

Take Moorpark Street about 0.5 mile to Cahuenga Boulevard. About a 0.5 mile after the turn, the street joins Lankershim Boulevard; bear left onto Lankershim. Almost immediately after the turn onto Cahuenga, you'll pass the **Technicolor labs** on the left, and soon thereafter you'll begin to pass the Universal studio, officially known as Universal City Studios Inc. Universal is unlike Disney and Warner Bros. For one thing, the facilities give the impression of being newer; they're sixties/seventies-style smoked-glass towers. Also, Universal welcomes visitors. Sort of. The *real* studios—the sound stages where TV shows and movies are *really* being shot—are just as much off-limits to the public and just as dreary as in the other studios. But, sensing that there was a buck to be made, Universal created a pseudostudio that makes a small effort to show visitors what a studio is like. The original Universal tour did a pretty good job of that, but today's tour is more amusement park than genuine studio tour. Nevertheless, it's worth the time and (considerable) money if you've never been to Los Angeles and you want to see everything. The address—100 Universal Plaza—doesn't help very much. The studios are on the east side of Lankershim Boulevard, 1 block north of the intersection with Ventura Boulevard. Universal, incidentally, was bought lock, stock, and Western gun-barrel, by Japanese industrial giant Matsushita in 1990.

There is an extraordinarily steep climb up to where the action is on the left side of the street. A big sign directing traffic to the various attractions gives a new meaning to the term, "You can't miss it!" The "attractions" include, but are not limited to, the Tour, two big hotels, a multi-multi-screen movie theater complex, and at least two big, overpriced restaurants. Also at the top of the hill and reachable by car from another entrance altogether is Universal CityWalk. This is an idealized Los Angeles city street, sanitized, as it were, with a selection of movie theaters, restaurants, novelty and gift shops, buskers, and neon galore. Everything is of the highest quality, admission is free, and a good time is guaranteed. In short, don't miss CityWalk. It is to Los Angeles what Disneyland's Main Street is to old time middle-America. These attractions are definitely something you would not want to ride a bike to—the hill is something for bikes with very low gears and riders with very big thighs!

Directly across the street, though, is something of historical interest that you might want to look at: **Campo de Cahuenga**, State Registered Landmark (SRL) 151. It was here, on January 13, 1847, that the treaty between Mexico and the United States was signed, ending the Mexican American War. The signatories (mentioned here because of the number of places in California named after them) were Lt. Col. John C. Fremont and Gen. Andreas Pico. Near this site there was a skirmish between a band of rebel Californians led by Juan Alvarado (for whom a L.A. major street is named) and Governor Manuel Micheltorena's mini-army. Micheltorena, who retreated into Rancho Los Feliz, lost badly—you can tell, because nothing is named after

74

him—and Pio Pico was made governor in his place. The treaty became known as the Treaty of Cahuenga, after the adobe building in which it was signed. The building was erected by Thomas Feliz in 1845. Be forewarned, however, that the present building is a 1923 replica. The address is 3919 Lankershim Boulevard.

Having absorbed your quota of history, continue on Lankershim under the freeway, to the T intersection with Ventura Boulevard. This is the point where Ventura, fresh from a 20-mile journey from the suburbs, meets up with Cahuenga Boulevard, which proceeds to the left to the Hollywood Bowl, the John Anson Ford Theater, and the *real* (i.e., geographical) Hollywood. For the purpose of this ride, however, turn right onto Ventura Boulevard.

After 1.5 miles on Ventura, you'll come to the **CBS Studio Center** (on the right at Colfax Avenue). This is the site of the old Republic Pictures studios; virtually every Western movie ever made was made by Republic. Now, many CBS television shows are produced here.

Ventura Boulevard is a street with a personality problem. It is extraordinarily long, the west end petering out in Woodland Hills, more than 20 miles away. It ends, fittingly, I suppose, at the Motion Picture Country Home and Hospital, where show-biz folks frequently end their days. At the east end, which you just passed through, Ventura is a hodgepodge of one- and two-story commercial and retail buildings of undistinguished (to say the very least) architecture.

At Laurel Canyon Boulevard, 0.5 mile from the beginning of CBS at Colfax Avenue, begins Ventura Boulevard's first major, cohesive shopping district, downtown **Studio City**. At this writing, Studio City is going distinctly upscale. On the left (south) side of the street, at 12224 Ventura Boulevard, is **Art's Delicatessen and Restaurant**. Art's is the Caterer to the Stars, and many a meeting I attended while I was in show biz was fueled by cholesterol from Art's. A sign across the front of the building proudly proclaims, EVERY SANDWICH IS A WORK OF ART.

Backtrack to Laurel Canyon Boulevard, and turn left (north). Laurel Canyon, to the south, crosses the Hollywood Hills section of the Santa Monica Mountains. It's a tough climb on a narrow, winding road, which ends in the western part of Hollywood. It pops up in the news occasionally, because of the rather offbeat lifestyles of some of its inhabitants and an occasional spectacular and devastating brush fire. Laurel Canyon Boulevard to the north (the direction you are heading) passes the oldest, and at one time largest, shopping mall in Los Angeles, and along most of its route is a pretty dull street. (It was at that mall that the Great Shoot-out of 1997 occurred. The shoot-out, which involved dozens of police and a handful of extremely well-armed bank robbers, was televised worldwide, but a visit to the site will reveal only a tired old mall whose best days are behind it. "Move along folks, there's nothing to see.")

Approximately 0.4 mile from the turn onto Laurel Canyon Boulevard, turn right on Moorpark Street. This is a very pleasant thoroughfare that goes back through Studio City to Toluca Lake. The street bears left after 3.0 miles, just after you cross Cahuenga Boulevard, but you should keep going straight. You will recognize this as the same Moorpark Street you were on in Toluca Lake. One mile from Cahuenga Boulevard, you'll come to a T intersection with Clybourn Avenue. Turn right and take a left on Warner Boulevard. After 0.3 mile on Warner, turn right on Pass Avenue. (Be aware that the intersections of all east/west streets with Pass Avenue are blocked off with concrete barriers and threatening signs to prevent commuting motorists from using the residential streets as shortcuts to the studios. Bicyclists can—and should—walk their bikes around these barriers.) A little farther along, after you turn right, you'll again be directly across the street from the Warner Bros. studio. When you get to the Smoke House, *carefully* get into the left turn lane, and turn left on Forest Lawn Drive. You will have been on Pass Avenue for 0.4 mile.

After turning left on Forest Lawn, on your immediate left you'll see the concrete-lined Los Angeles River, and perched on the river's north bank, the Warner Bros. studio. You are looking at Wall Street, so named not because of any connection with stocks and bonds, but because this is the place where set walls (and doors, staircases, and associated indoor set accoutrements) are stored.

Forest Lawn Drive passes **Forest Lawn** and **Mt. Sinai cemeteries**. These are spectacular in their own way. They're certainly unique to California. Forest Lawn Memorial Park—Hollywood Hills, as it is formally known—has several rather eclectic tourist attractions, such as a full-scale replica of Boston's Old North Church, a replica of the Aztec temple at Tula, Mexico, and a copy of *The Last Supper*. It isn't to everyone's taste, and you may feel a little out of place going into Forest Lawn on a bicycle, so I'd recommend that if you're to "do" Forest Lawn at all, you visit by car. It's only a mile or so from Travel Town.

All along the first part of the ride on Forest Lawn Drive are good views on the left (north) of Warner's back lot. The Drive is on the south bank of the Los Angeles River, and the studio is on the north bank. The river is a relative trickle most of the year, but there is enough water to support some interesting waterfowl, and if you keep an eye peeled, you may spot an egret or some other showy bird. About 1.8 miles from the turn onto Forest Lawn Drive, bear right; Travel Town and your motorized vehicle are 0.2 mile farther along.

For Further Information

Art's Delicatessen and Restaurant (818) 762–1221
Campo de Cahuenga (818) 763–7651
NBC television show tickets (818) 840–3537
NBC tour information (818) 840–3572
Universal CityWalk (818) 622–4455
Universal Studio tour (818) 508–9600
Warner Bros. VIP Studio Tour (818) 954–6000

Getting There

Travel Town is at the northeast corner of Griffith Park. From points east and west of Griffith Park, take the SR–134 (Ventura) Freeway to the Victory Boulevard exit. Within 50 feet of the exit is a T intersection with Zoo Drive. Travel Town is to the right. Follow the signs.

From the north or south, take the I–5 (Golden State) Freeway to the Griffith Park/Los Angeles Zoo/Autry Western Heritage Museum exit, and follow the ZOO DRIVE signs north and then west past the museum to Travel Town.

The *Real* (Geographical) Hollywood

Location:	7 miles north of downtown Angeles, off the Hollywood Freeway (US–101)
Mileage:	11
Approximate pedaling time:	1½ hours
Terrain:	Good pavement throughout; one or two noticeable, but manageable, hills
Traffic:	Occasionally hairy
Things to see:	A&M Records/Charlie Chaplin Studio, Capitol Records, CBS Television City, Chinese Theater, Cinerama Dome, Fairfax District, Frederick's of Hollywood, George C. Page Museum, Hollywood Bowl, Hollywood Jazz Mural, Hollywood Memorial Cemetery, La Brea Tar Pits, Los Angeles County Museum of Art, Max Factor Beauty Museum, Miracle Mile, Pantages Theater, Paramount Pictures Studio, Petersen Automotive Museum, RCA Records, Walk of Fame, Wilshire Boulevard, and more

This ride starts at the Capitol Records Building at 1750 North Vine Street in Hollywood.

The thirteen-story building was designed "on spec" in 1940 by Charles Luckman. The design lay unloved, undisturbed, and unsold until 1954, when Capitol Records dusted it off and built the present structure. It was just a coincidence that it looks like a stack of

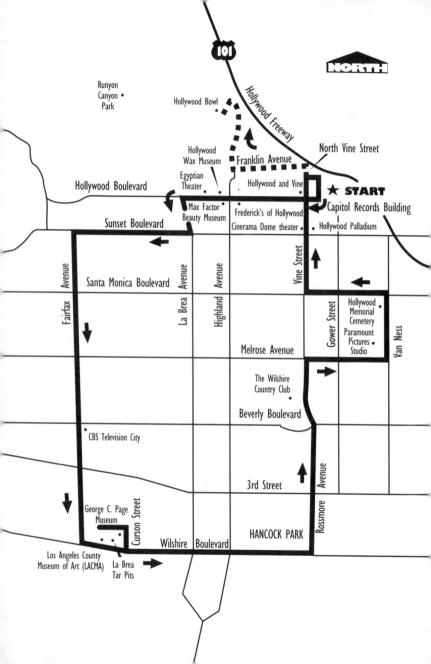

The REAL (Geographical) Hollywood

0.0 Start at parking lot next to Capitol Records Building, 1750 North Vine Street
0.1 Right onto Franklin Avenue
0.2 Right onto Argyle Avenue
0.4 Right onto Hollywood Boulevard
1.6 Left onto La Brea Avenue
1.8 Right onto Sunset Boulevard
2.8 Left onto Fairfax Avenue
5.3 Left onto Wilshire Boulevard
5.7 Left onto Curson Street; walk through park on left, and return to Wilshire Boulevard
5.7 Left onto Wilshire Boulevard
7.3 Left onto Rossmore Avenue
8.3 Right onto Beverly Boulevard
8.3 Left onto Rossmore Avenue
8.8 Right onto Melrose Avenue
9.4 Left onto Van Ness Avenue
9.9 Left onto Santa Monica Boulevard
10.5 Right onto Vine Street
11.3 Right into Capitol Records Building parking lot

Hollywood Bowl Bonus Side Trip

0.0 Start at parking lot next to Capitol Records Building, 1750 North Vine Street
0.1 Left onto Franklin Avenue
0.7 Right onto Highland Avenue
1.1 Left into Hollywood Bowl entrance. Walk your bike to make the left turn or use pedestrian tunnel. After touring the Bowl, return to Highland Avenue
1.2 Right onto Highland Avenue
1.8 Left onto Franklin Avenue
2.4 Right onto Vine Street
2.5 Left into Capitol Records Building parking lot

records. The pointed thing at the very top that most people think is supposed to look like a stylus is actually an ornament intended to give the building more height than the former thirteen-story height-limiting ordinance permitted. Tours of the building and its recording studios are conducted regularly. The floors, incidentally, are numbered 1 through 12 and E. E stands for Executive, the executives apparently being unable to cope with being on the thirteenth floor.

There is an enormous **mural** on the building's south wall, commemorating Hollywood Jazz: 1945–1972. The mural, by Los Angeles artist Richard Wyatt, was completed in 1991 and appears destined to be the latest, and one of the more spectacular, Hollywood tourist attractions.

Turn right (uphill) out of the parking lot and right again on Franklin Avenue. Radio Station **KFWB's studios** are just ahead. Take the first right (Argyle Avenue); turn right at the end of the block on Hollywood Boulevard. The building on your right at the corner of Hollywood and Argyle (at 6233 Hollywood Boulevard) is the **Pantages Theater**. It was built in 1929, seats about 2,900, and was the site of the Academy Award ceremonies throughout the fifties. It was a classic movie palace for many years, but it is now given over to live theater, mostly Broadway musicals.

The next corner is Hollywood and Vine. It escapes me why this is such a famous intersection. It will strike you as being rather grubby, and you will undoubtedly think that it was once a magnificent "Crossroads of the World," now fallen on hard times. I hate to disillusion you, but this intersection has been grubby for at least thirty years. In fact, I know folks who remember it from the thirties and forties, and they all attest to its grubbiness that far back. Nevertheless, a snapshot of the street sign is *de rigueur*.

You will note that the sidewalk has brass stars imbedded in chewing gum, red terrazzo, and concrete. Since 1958 the Walk of Fame has featured the names of stars, placed seemingly at random along Hollywood Boulevard. Each star, in addition to the featured brass name, has a brass bas relief symbolizing the source of the honoree's fame—e.g., a movie camera for a movie star, a microphone for a radio personality, a phonograph record for a recording artist. (Please don't ask what a phonograph record is. As far as I know, the organization that places the stars in the Walk of Fame has no bas relief symbol for a CD—yet.) There are now more than 3,000 stars on the Walk of Fame, and it's kind of fun to cover a block or two of them on foot. If you recognize more than half of the names, and you recognize the phonograph record for what it is, you're even older than I am.

Frederick's of Hollywood, famed for its racy lingerie, is on the left side of the street in a rather garish purple building at 6808 Hollywood Boulevard. Frederick's has gone somewhat respectable these days. Or maybe it's just that things that used to be unmentionable no longer are. Frederick's houses a world-famous, one-of-a-kind lingerie museum featuring undergarments of past and current stars.

A block or so farther along, on the left at Highland Avenue, is the **Max Factor Beauty Museum.** Max Factor, makeup artist to the studios for decades, now reoccupies the building it vacated when it was bought out in the corporate takeover wave of the eighties. The building itself, erected in 1931, is worth looking at. The museum has a display depicting how movie stars are made up and coiffed. Admission to the museum is free.

The **Hollywood Wax Museum** at 6767 Hollywood Boulevard is a kind of gloomy place, reminiscent of a failed Madame Toussaud's, which itself is a gloomy place.

The **Egyptian Theater** is a must-see. Fortunately it's hard to miss. Located at 6708 Hollywood Boulevard, it was built by Sid Grauman, a flamboyant impressario of the early days of the movies, in 1922. It is a showman's conception of an artist's dream of an architect's nightmare of what an Egyptian moving picture palace would have looked like in 2000 BC. Most of the original gewgaws are now gone, but you'll get the idea. Bear in mind that King Tut's tomb had been recently discovered in 1922. (Note: The Egyptian Theater closed its doors in 1992 after a long period of decline. At this writing its owners are planning to restore the site to its former glory.)

On the right side of the street is **Booksellers Row.** There's an awful lot of good browsing on this stretch of the boulevard. The biggest of the bookstores is B. Dalton Booksellers, a three-story structure at 6743 Hollywood Boulevard, rivaling, but not quite matching, Foyle's of London.

Musso and Frank, at 6667 Hollywood Boulevard, is Hollywood's oldest restaurant. It is expensive and crowded, but the food is good, and record-company executives like to "do" lunch there.

Across the street, at 7000 Hollywood Boulevard, is the **Hollywood Roosevelt Hotel.** It has been remodeled, renovated, and redecorated to a $35,000,000 fare-thee-well. It was built in 1927 and was the site of the first Academy Awards (in 1929). It is said that Errol Flynn concocted his recipe for gin in a tub behind the hotel's barber shop. In 1989 David Hockney painted the plaster bottom of the hotel's swimming pool with swirls. City officials ordered the pool closed and emptied on the grounds that swirls might be confusing to lifeguards. The state legislature stepped in and passed a law to the effect that the swirls were *not* confusing. (This sort of thing happens in Los Angeles all the time.) Ghosts of innumerable movie folk probably still stalk the hotel's renovated hallways. Indeed, it is said that the ghost of Montgomery Clift can be heard practicing the trumpet for *From Here to Eternity*—interesting, given that in real life, he didn't know one end of a trumpet from the other. The lobby of the hotel sports a large, late-twenties painting entitled *Hollywood Comes to Napoleon's Aid,* by Charles de Ravenne. The soldiers' faces are those of Charlie Chaplin, Douglas Fairbanks, William Powell, and others. Well, this *is* Hollywood!

The **Chinese Theater** at 6925 Hollywood Boulevard is another of Sid Grauman's grandiose confections, this one dating from 1927. It is his conception of a Chinese temple. One of many legends has it that actress Norma Talmadge accidentally stepped into a patch of wet cement in the forecourt. When Grauman saw this serendipitous accident, he rounded up Mary Pickford and Douglas Fairbanks and had them ruin their shoes, too. The rest is history. A few snapshots of the foot- and handprints in the cement are a must. You'll probably encounter a couple of dozen tourists wandering aimlessly, noses to the floor. You can probably walk around with your bike, but if you see a movie there, you'll most certainly have to leave it outside among the literal impressions of the celluloid famous. (There are *always* sleazy-looking guys milling about trying to sell maps to the movie stars' homes. Save yourself a few dollars, and don't buy one.) Seeing a movie at the Chinese, incidentally, is the *ultimate* film-going experience. Do it.

Turn left on La Brea Avenue. You have now traveled 1.25 miles on Hollywood Boulevard. About 0.25 mile down La Brea is Sunset Boulevard; 1 short block to the left, at the corner of Sunset and Highland, is Hollywood High School. This is a rather nice school, the subject of more than a few movies and the alma mater of a number of famous people. It was built in 1935, and it has classic streamlined modern lines.

Turn right on Sunset, stop, and look over your left shoulder at La Brea Avenue. Just downhill from your position is **A&M Records.** Its English Tudor–style buildings housed the Charlie Chaplin Studios in the twenties. It was here that "We Are the World" was recorded in 1985 by forty-five pop stars who, as A&M tells it, "checked their egos at the door." After 1.0 mile you'll come to Fairfax Avenue. Turn left and 0.8 mile downhill on the left, at the corner of Melrose Avenue, is **Fairfax High School.** Like Hollywood High, Fairfax High is alma mater to one heck of a lot of celebrities.

You'll now enter Los Angeles' answer to New York's Lower East Side, the Jewish Quarter. **Canter's Fairfax Restaurant Delicatessen and Bakery,** at 419 North Fairfax Avenue, is the quintessential Jewish-food emporium and the best representative of Fairfax Avenue's *ambience.* The food is very good, the service rude and crude, and the prices moderate—in other words, just what you'd expect.

After 1.4 miles from the turn onto Fairfax Avenue, at the corner of Beverly Boulevard, you'll see **CBS Television City.** This complex was built in 1952 and 1976 and was designed by Pereira and Luckman. There is a ticket window where free tickets for various television shows can be had for the asking. The actual address of CBS Television City is 7800 Beverly Boulevard.

Adjacent to CBS Television City, at the corner of Fairfax Avenue and 3rd Street, is the **Farmers Market.** The market was established in 1934, and in its heyday it hosted about 50,000 people daily. Like the Grand Central Public Market in downtown Los Angeles (see Ride 1), it was a collection of shops, food stalls, and restaurants under one big roof. During the forties and fifties, it was one of the top two or three tourist attractions in L.A. Today it's a bustling place, full of local and tourist alike. You can grab a bite to eat at one of the many shops.

This is a geologically active area; the nearby La Brea Tar Pits are still bubbling, and you'll probably get occasional whiffs of the crude oil that seeps up through the surface here and there. The area around 3rd and Fairfax burst into flame in 1989, when natural-gas accumulations exploded. Several businesses and homes were destroyed in an inferno that burned for several days. Geologists assure us that the natural gas is still seeping to the surface in the area, possibly right under your tires, but collectors and vents have been installed, and the chances of another explosion are remote.

Keep going down Fairfax Avenue to Wilshire Boulevard (1 city block from the Farmers Market). On the left is a part of an enormous (even by today's standards) housing complex, **Park La Brea Housing and Towers.** Covering 176 acres, it was built in the forties by Prudential Insurance, although it is now owned by other interests.

Turn left on Wilshire Boulevard. The former **May Company store** on the corner of Fairfax and Wilshire is a 1940 art deco structure, a true landmark. May Company has merged with Robinson's, and Robinson's-May is now part of Federated Department Stores, which closed the landmark store at Fairfax and Wilshire. Across the street is the **Petersen Automotive Museum**, an affiliate of the Natural History Museum of Los Angeles County. The official address is 6060 Wilshire Boulevard. The theme of the museum, which opened in 1997, is "From Memory Lane to the Fast Lane." If you have any affinity at all for automobiles, I mean other than dodging them on your bike, the Petersen Automotive Museum is a *must!*

Just ahead is the **Miracle Mile**. In 1920 A. W. Ross bought twenty acres between La Brea and Fairfax Avenues. The land was developed in the twenties and thirties as a prestigious shopping and office center. It is now a bit run-down, but it remains a prime concentration of art deco buildings.

After 0.1 mile from the turn onto Wilshire Boulevard, you'll come to the **Los Angeles County Museum of Art (LACMA)** on the left. Although it was founded in 1965, the largest and most conspicuous buildings were completed in 1986 and 1988. The address is 5905 Wilshire Boulevard. I can't begin to do LACMA justice in these pages—the Pavilion for Japanese Art alone has more than 32,000 square feet of display space. But now that you know where it is, you can explore it for yourself. There is a fee for nonmembers.

A bit farther along on the same block, at 5801 Wilshire Boulevard, is the **George C. Page Museum of La Brea Discoveries**. The museum was established in 1977 to display and interpret discoveries from the **La Brea Tar Pits**. It is nothing short of fabulous, particularly if the Tar Pits fascinate you, as they do me. Admission is free.

While we're on the subject of the La Brea Tar Pits, they are clearly visible from Wilshire Boulevard, but for an up-close-and-personal examination, turn left on Curson Street, and immediately turn left again; get off your bike and walk through the park. Here and there you'll come across tar seeping up through the grass. (Be careful, that stuff doesn't come off.) It was in the water-filled tar pits dotted here and there in the park that saber-tooth tigers and other prehistoric animals fell and were preserved for present-day scientists to study. The Tar Pits are a must-see for fossil lovers!

Return to Wilshire Boulevard and ride for 1.6 miles to Rossmore Avenue, where you turn left. You will cross 3rd Street after 0.5 mile. After another 0.5 mile, you'll come to Beverly Boulevard. The posh **Wilshire Country Club** is on the left. Jog right on Beverly and immediately jog left on Rossmore. This is definitely a high-rent district, where old money resides. A side trip around the neighborhood is rather nice. After another 0.5 mile you'll come to Melrose Avenue.

Turn right on Melrose; 0.25 mile on the left, at Gower Street, is the southwest corner of the **Paramount Pictures studio**, the last remaining studio in geographic Hollywood. Perched atop the corner of the building is the old RKO Studios sign (a globe rotating at the top of a radio broadcasting tower). RKO occupied the soundstages along Gower Street for many years, before a series of financial reversals led to Paramount's takeover of the property. The industry's affectionate name for the studio, reflecting the Westerns shot there, is "Gower Gulch." The main entrance to the studio used to be on Bronson Avenue; indeed, the Bronson entrance became famous from its use in

Sunset Boulevard. Continue a short distance on Melrose, and you'll come to the new double gate, which should be a familiar sight, owing to its use in numerous movies and TV promotional stunts.

A left turn on Van Ness, 0.3 mile from the corner of Gower, takes you along the eastern side of the Paramount Pictures studio. Halfway up the block on Van Ness is the end of the studio and the beginning of the **Hollywood Memorial Cemetery**, where Rudolph Valentino, Douglas Fairbanks, Jayne Mansfield, Jesse Lasky, Cecil B. De Mille, Mel Blanc, and Tyrone Power, among others, are interred. It is interesting to note that Cecil B. De Mille was one of the founders of Paramount Studios, which shares a wall with the cemetery. Douglas Fairbanks has the most impressive, or at least the most ornate, of the memorials in this sixty-five-acre refuge from Hollywood's hustle and bustle. Turn left onto Santa Monica Boulevard (0.5 mile from the turn onto Van Ness); the Hollywood Memorial Cemetery will be on your left, across the street.

Another 0.6 mile will put you at Vine Street, where you turn right. About 0.4 mile farther along is Sunset Boulevard. To the right on Sunset, at 6215, visible from Vine Street, is the **Hollywood Palladium**. Built in 1940, it was home to the Big Bands—all of them. Big Bands, you may have noticed, aren't the attraction they used to be, and it wouldn't surprise me at all if the Palladium became Something Else, too. But for the moment, suffice it to say that this is one Famous Place!

On the left, at 6360 Sunset, is the **Cinerama Dome theater**. This theater was originally built to house the then-new Cinerama widescreen special-format motion pictures. Now, ordinary first-run movies are shown in a really nice auditorium on a very large screen with excellent sound. It's another theater where moviegoing is a memorable experience.

On the corner of the next block is the **RCA Records building**. Just before you reach the famous crossroads of Hollywood and Vine, on the right side of Vine Street is the site of the old Brown Derby restaurant. It was the hangout for multitudes of movie stars and during the day for recording industry executives and artists. The restaurant, after many years of quiet decline, burned to the ground in 1988.

(It reopened in Pasadena, but it's not the same.)

You now have another view of Hollywood and Vine, and after 100 yards or so, you'll come to the parking lot at the Capitol Records Building and the Hollywood Jazz mural on the right.

Hollywood Bowl
Bonus Side Trip

Location:	North of Hollywood
Mileage:	2.5
Approximate pedaling time:	20 minutes
Terrain:	Good surface; one or two noticeable, but manageable, hills
Traffic:	Very urban; traffic on Highland Avenue may turn your hair gray
Things to see:	Hollywood Bowl

When you're finished with Ride 7, The *Real* Hollywood, you are ready for a short bonus ride to the Hollywood Bowl. It's only a short distance, and the traffic is memorable—if not downright intimidating—but it's worth it.

Turn right out of the Capitol Records parking lot and ride (or walk) uphill to the first corner (Franklin Street). Turn left on Franklin and go 0.6 mile to Highland Avenue. Turn right on Highland and go up the grade for 0.4 mile to the entrance to the Hollywood Bowl.

The Hollywood Bowl is an amphitheater, seating about 18,000. To say that it's famous is like saying that Los Angeles is large. The Bowl is the summer home of the Los Angeles Philharmonic Orchestra. To hear (and see) the 1812 Overture performed with live fireworks and thirty-six real cannons blasting away over the audience is a truly memorable experience! Cannons aside, the acoustics leave a great deal to be desired, but an evening at the Bowl should be experienced nonetheless. Early-comers can have a picnic at one of dozens of tables or at their seats. It gets chilly at night, so if you come for an evening performance, bring warm clothing. A seat cushion is also a must for all but those with a great deal of natural padding. Seat cushions and opera glasses can be rented at every performance. During the summer, Philharmonic rehearsals, *sans* gunnery, are free to the public (a very well kept secret—until now). The free rehearsals are on Tuesdays, Thursdays, and Fridays, beginning around 10:30 A.M. and running until 3:30 P.M. or so. For Patio Restaurant and/or Picnic Basket reservations, call a day ahead.

Bicyclists are permitted onto the Bowl grounds, and you may want to look around—it's really an overwhelming sight—and visit the museum adjacent to the Patio Restaurant. The museum features original Frank Lloyd Wright drawings of amphitheater shells and sound booths where you can hear recordings made at the Bowl by Stravinsky and others. This is a worthwhile side trip! Return to the Capitol Records parking lot by the same route. *Caution:* For variety, it is tempting to try a different route back to the parking lot, but turning onto any of the numerous side streets east of the Bowl will soon put you into mountainous terrain that you will live to remember with regret.

For Further Information

Canter's Fairfax Restaurant Deli and Bakery (213) 651–2030
Capitol-EMI Music (tours of Capitol Building) (213) 462–6251
CBS Television City (tickets and information) (213) 852–2624
Cinerama Dome Theater (213) 466–3401
G.C. Page Museum of La Brea Discoveries (213) 936–2230
Hollywood Bowl (213) 876–8742
Hollywood Bowl Museum (213) 850–2058
Hollywood Bowl Patio Restaurant and Picnic Baskets
    (213) 851–3588
Hollywood Roosevelt Hotel (213) 466–7000
Hollywood Wax Museum (213) 462–8860
Los Angeles County Museum of Art (213) 857–6111
Los Angeles Philharmonic Rehearsals (Hollywood Bowl)
    (213) 856–5400

Mann's Chinese Theater (213) 464–8111
Max Factor Beauty Museum (213) 463–6668
Musso and Frank Grill (213) 467–7788
Pantages Theater (213) 216–6666
Petersen Automotive Museum (213) 930–2277

Getting There

If you are coming by car, get off the US–101 (Hollywood) Freeway at the Vine Street exit, and the Capitol Records Building, a prominent L.A. landmark, will be very much in evidence. There is a parking lot abutting its southern wall. Metered parking is semi-available everywhere, but the time limit will not permit completion of this ride. Parking tickets at this writing are $30, so the parking lot—any parking lot—is cheaper.

The Hollywood Sign

Location:	Atop Mount Lee on the south side of Griffith Park, facing Hollywood
Mileage:	19
Approximate pedaling time:	2½ hours
Terrain:	Very difficult; there's a good deal of hill climbing
Traffic:	Light on side streets and hills; light to heavy on major streets, depending on time of day and day of week
Things to see:	One of the world's most famous and inaccessible landmarks, up close and personal; unmatched views of the world's most extensive and impressive city without having to rent a plane

This ride heads for a famous landmark that everyone sees but few visit. (If this sounds like some kind of riddle from someone who has taken one too many unhelmeted falls, so be it.) You're headed for the **Hollywood Sign,** the unofficial symbol of Los Angeles, along with the Capitol Tower, Disneyland, Grauman's (now Mann's) Chinese Theater, and a couple of dozen other contenders. The sign has appeared in countless pictures and advertisements and was recently restored to its original splendor (well, almost) with contributions from Gene Autry, Alice Cooper, Hugh Heffner, and thousands of concerned citizens (including me), some of whom may ride bikes.

The sign is much like the moon. It seems close enough at times to reach out and touch, and many try to bike or drive up there, but it always seems to be out of reach. In fact, it was not designed to be reached, only seen. When it was constructed in 1923, it read HOLLY-

DIREC-TIONS at a glance

0.0	Right from Travel Town parking lot onto Zoo Drive
1.7	Zoo Drive becomes Crystal Springs Drive
2.6	Right at stop sign
2.8	Left at stop sign—go past carousel
3.4	Right onto Griffith Park Drive at T (may not be marked)
4.7	Right onto Los Feliz Boulevard
5.0	Left onto Griffith Park Boulevard
5.6	Right onto Hyperion Boulevard
6.3	Hyperion becomes Fountain Avenue
7.6	Right onto Normandie Avenue
8.4	Left onto Franklin Avenue
9.5	Right onto Beachwood Drive
10.8	Left onto Ledgewood Drive
11.0	Right at Y onto Deronda Drive; ignore NOT A THRU STREET sign; Deronda becomes Mount Lee Drive
12.3	Arrive at Hollywood sign; after catching breath, return to Y intersection at Deronda.
13.6	Right at Y onto Rockcliff Drive
13.7	Right onto Ledgewood Drive
13.9	Left onto Mulholland Highway; bear right at Y—stay on Mulholland
14.3	Right onto Canyon Lake Drive
14.5	Left onto Tahoe Drive
15.0	Tahoe becomes Lake Hollywood Drive
16.0	Hollywood becomes La Suvida Drive
16.1	Left onto Primera Avenue
16.2	Right (first right) onto Lake Hollywood Drive
16.3	Right onto Barham Boulevard
17.0	Right onto Forest Lawn Drive
19.0	Right onto Griffith Park Drive (probably not marked) with sign to Travel Town and zoo
19.2	Enter Travel Town parking lot

WOODLAND. It was an advertisement for a then-opulent subdivision owned in part by movie-making mogul Mack Sennett. At 50 feet high and a city block long, it was the largest sign in the world. It was lit by 4,000 twenty-watt light bulbs spaced 8 inches apart, and it is said that in those presmog days, it could be seen for more than 50 miles. There was a full-time maintenance man whose primary job was to replace burned-out light bulbs—they didn't make 'em like they do now. In any event, the sign did its job: it sold real estate. It also served as a navigation aid to pilots in the less sophisticated days of flying, and it appeared as a prop in dozens of silent films.

Although the sign has always been difficult to reach, determined people have always managed to find a way. In the thirties, for example, Hollywood was mecca for movie hopefuls, and in 1932 a disillusioned would-be actress named Peg Entwhistle jumped to her death from the original letter *H*. Numerous other unsuccessful starlets also used various letters as "signing-off places," and in a macabre sort of way, this made the sign became even more famous and exotic. For many years practical jokers of all sorts have somehow found their way up the slopes of Mount Lee and done their thing. One group changed the sign to read HOLLYWEED, to protest California's new marijuana law decriminalizing possession of small amounts of the drug for personal use. And in 1992 a movie company obtained permission from the city—for a fat fee—to modify the *D* to accommodate a luscious cartoon character named Holli Would. Holli perched on the *D* for a couple of weeks; the fee paid for sign maintenance, though the movie (*Cool World*) flopped.

Sometime in the late thirties, the land on which the sign stands was donated to the city of Los Angeles as an addendum to Griffith Park. In 1949 the letters *L-A-N-D* were removed and a new letter *H* was put up. The sign immediately became the new symbol of the movie industry, then at its all-time peak (in terms of numbers of tickets purchased per capita). From then until 1978 the sign degenerated, along with much of Hollywood—the town, the industry, and the ambience. In 1973 the sign was declared Historical Landmark No. 111 by the Cultural Heritage Board, but this failed to halt its slide into disrepair and general seediness. Finally, in 1978, the gentlemen mentioned above and smaller contributors refurbished the sign at a cost of about $30,000 per letter.

But you really can't appreciate the grandeur of this symbol until you stand next to it, and it can be done by bike. Here's how:

Start in Griffith Park's Travel Town. Turn right out of the parking lot onto Zoo Drive, which becomes Crystal Springs Drive. Turn right at the stop sign after the golf course and take the first left. Go past the carousel, and bear right at the bottom of the hill. At Los Feliz Boulevard, turn right. After a 0.3 mile turn left on Griffith Park Boulevard. After 0.6 mile turn right on Hyperion Boulevard, which becomes Fountain Avenue after 0.75 mile. After 1.25 miles on Fountain, turn right on Normandie, and 0.7 mile later, turn left on Franklin. Turn right on Beachwood after 1.1 miles, and left on Ledgewood, where you'll stay for 0.2 mile. From Beachwood on, you'll be climbing in the old and still picturesque section of Hollywood that started the whole "glamour thing" to begin with. The streets will soon become narrow and steep, but keep going. Turn right on Deronda Drive at the Y, past the NOT A THRU STREET sign. There's a chain-link fence on the right; go around it, and 1.3 miles later, you'll be at your destination. Don't worry—you're not on private property, and although there are undoubtedly some weeds here found nowhere else on Earth, environmentalists gave up on Mount Lee long ago. Be careful of the rocks, sand, and debris and the steep hill. By the time you sidle up to the sign, you'll agree that anyone who wants to jump off it must *really* want to jump, as it's one heck of a trip getting there!

One of my riding buddies cautions against leaning your bike up against the protective fence. An ethereal voice from a hidden public address system will be heard saying something like, "Please do not lean your bikes against the fence. It sets off the alarm systems." The voice is deep enough, and until that moment, unexpected enough, to get immediate results. Soon after removing the offending bikes from the fence, the *basso profundo* voice will say "Thank you!"

To return, ride back to the NOT A THRU STREET sign. Turn right on Rockcliff Drive, right on Ledgewood Drive, and left on Mulholland at the Y. (*Note:* Keep right on the upper roadway; Mulholland bears right at the next Y; stay on Mulholland.) Turn right on Canyon Lake Drive, left on Tahoe Drive, which becomes Lake Hollywood Drive; you're now riding along the shore of Lake Hollywood. This becomes La Suvida Drive. Turn left at the top of the hill; you'll be on Lake Hollywood Drive again. You'll roll downhill to the intersection with Primera Avenue where you turn left; take your first right, which again is Lake Hollywood Drive, and in no time you'll be at a T intersection with Barham Boulevard, where you turn right. Stay on Barham for a fast, smooth 0.7 mile downhill. At the bottom of the hill, turn right on Forest Lawn Drive. (If you go straight, you'll get a very close view of Warner Bros. studios.) After a right onto Forest Lawn Drive and a right onto Griffith Park Drive, you'll soon (2.1 miles) be in Travel Town. The view on Forest Lawn Drive is primarily of well-kept cemeteries on the right and movie studio back lots on the left—neither very satisfying—but otherwise the road is great for cyclists, especially those who may be a bit pooped from climbing Mount Lee to the Hollywood Sign.

Getting There

Travel Town is at the northeast corner of Griffith Park. From points east and west of Griffith Park, take the SR–134 (Ventura) Freeway to the Victory Boulevard exit. Within 50 feet of the exit there is a T intersection with Zoo Drive. Travel Town is on the right. Follow the signs.

From the north or south, take the I–5 (Golden State) Freeway to the Griffith Park/Los Angeles Zoo/Autry Western Heritage Museum exit. Follow the ZOO DRIVE signs north and then west, past the museum to Travel Town.

Lake Hollywood

Location:	In the Hollywood Hills between Hollywood and Studio City
Mileage:	3.25 if you park your car at the lakeshore; 10.5 if you start at Travel Town
Approximate pedaling time:	45 minutes if you park your car at the lakeshore; 1¼ hours if you start at Travel Town
Terrain:	3.25-mile option: flat; 10.5-mile option: one killer hill in each direction
Traffic:	3.25-mile option: optimum, except that it is a popular runners' route, so you'll have to keep an eye out for foot traffic; there are two automobile barriers that will require you to dismount; 10.5-mile option: the route from Travel Town can involve heavy traffic, particularly at the corner of Forest Lawn Drive and Barham Boulevard, but it's quite manageable, and the time spent on busy Barham is very short
Things to see:	Gorgeous views of the Hollywood sign and Lake Hollywood in a unique and beautiful setting

Note: Lake Hollywood is a bona fide Los Angeles reservoir, and as such, it falls under the auspices of the Department of Water and Power. In its wisdom, the DWP closes the lake to visitors from time to time—e.g., after heavy rains. So, before embarking on this ride, you might want to call the DWP at (818) 909–3000 for the latest status report.

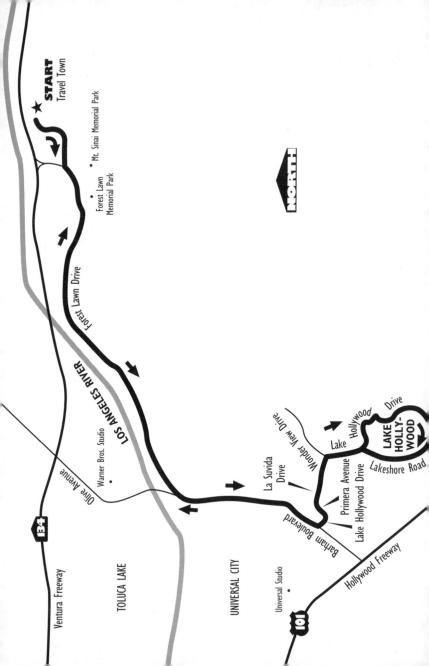

DIREC-TIONS at a glance

From Lakeshore

0.0 Left or right from Lake Hollywood Drive onto Lakeshore Road
3.3 Right or left onto Lakeshore Road

From Travel Town

- 0.0 Straight out of Travel Town parking lot onto unmarked road
- 0.2 Left onto Forest Lawn Drive
- 2.2 Left onto Barham Boulevard
- 2.9 Left onto Lake Hollywood Drive
- 3.0 Left onto Primera Avenue
- 3.1 Right onto La Suvida Drive
- 3.2 La Suvida becomes Lake Hollywood Drive
- 3.6 Left onto Lakeshore Road—circumnavigate Lake Hollywood
- 6.9 Left onto Lake Hollywood Drive (up steep hill)
- 7.3 Lake Hollywood becomes La Suvida Drive
- 7.4 Left onto Primera Avenue
- 7.5 Right onto Lake Hollywood Drive
- 7.6 Right onto Barham Boulevard
- 8.3 Right onto Forest Lawn Drive
- 10.3 Right onto Griffith Park Drive (probably unmarked)
- 10.5 Straight into Travel Town parking lot

Here's another of Los Angeles' best-kept secrets. Smack-dab in the middle of the megalopolis is a beautiful lake surrounded by lush semitropical vegetation and a perfect bicycling/running road. For more than half of its 3.25-mile length, the road is closed to motor traffic, and because so few people are aware of this gem, the nonmotorized traffic is pretty light, too. All of this gushing is about **Lake Hollywood**, otherwise known as the **Hollywood Reservoir**, a leaf-shaped body of water so clear that you can see the bottom in most places. At its deepest it's 183 feet deep, and according to the obligatory bronze plaque, it holds 2.5 billion gallons of water.

The reservoir is contained by a dam with a rather nice convex contour to it, designed and engineered by William Mulholland. This dam is totally unlike Mulholland's ill-fated St. Francis Dam, which collapsed in 1929 (see Ride 19). This one, 188 feet high and built to last, was completed in 1924 after roughly fourteen months of construction activity and the pouring of 172,000 cubic yards of concrete. All of this is for the statistically minded.

For the aesthetically minded, the lake is surrounded by a "path" as wide as two automobile lanes. The pavement is smooth, except in a few places where some 1929-vintage pine roots have made a successful escape attempt from the wooded area bordering the lake. There's a 12-foot-high chain-link fence surrounding the lake. It is perched on top of a 2-foot-high concrete wall, and it's crowned by some nasty-looking barbed wire. Although the fencing arrangement isn't what you'd call attractive, it is surprisingly acceptable. On most days a few deer are visible behind the fence, as well as a whole bunch of obese squirrels and all manner of hyperactive bird life.

It is this dam, whose top surface is open to bicycle traffic, that supposedly cracks in the movie *Earthquake,* and it is on the shores of this lake that a body is discovered in the movie *Chinatown.* It's unlikely that anything so exciting will happen to you on your circumnavigation. This is the only one of the Department of Water and Power's twenty-four reservoirs that is open to the public, and surprisingly, there isn't a single graffito in sight.

Now, I suppose that you're going to want to know how to get to this little piece of paradise. If you want to put your bike on a rack and drive to the loop road, there are two ways, but I like the approach from Barham Boulevard on the north side of the area; it's simpler. Take the Hollywood Freeway to the Barham exit and go east on Barham to Lake Hollywood Drive. After 0.8 mile turn left on Tahoe Drive. After 0.4 mile turn right on Canyon Lake Drive. Your first right will be a steep downhill with the lake in the foreground and the downtown skyline a distant backdrop. Park anywhere along the hill; be sure to turn your wheels in toward the curb. At the bottom of the hill, the loop road begins. You can go around clockwise or counterclockwise. I recommend the clockwise direction, so that you'll see the Hollywood sign, and the shoreline will be on your right. The road is winding, as it follows the shoreline far below. Racing speeds are not recommended, although you should be able to move at a reasonable rate of speed.

Driving to the loop road is the preferred method for riders who want to avoid hills and who want to put on a few leisurely miles on flat terrain in a nice setting. For those who feel that a 3.25-mile flat loop lacks challenge, drive to Travel Town in Griffith Park and park there. Go straight out of the parking lot and take your first left. This will put you on Forest Lawn Drive. You'll pass the famous cemeteries on the left and Warner Bros. on the right. After 1.75 miles you'll come to a busy intersection; this is Barham Boulevard. Turn left to the top of the hill; this is a pretty steep 0.75-mile hill. At the top there's a traffic light at Lake Hollywood Drive. Turn left and follow the above instructions for driving there. The entire distance is a steep uphill, and you may wish you'd driven it. This is fewer than 5 miles from Travel Town, and if you only do one loop around the reservoir, you'll have a little under 15 miles under your waistband, but half of them will be quality miles, with a capital Q. You can extend the ride by doing more than one loop, a highly recommended ploy.

For Further Information

Department of Water and Power (818) 909–3000

Getting There

To get to the Travel Town parking lot, see "Getting There" for the Griffith Park rides.

To get to Lake Hollywood for a ride around the lakeshore, take the US–101 (Hollywood) Freeway to the Barham Boulevard exit. Take Barham Boulevard about 0.2 mile to the traffic light at Lake Hollywood Drive, and turn right. Take Lake Hollywood Drive to the lakeshore, or follow the route in "Directions at a Glance."

Rose Bowl and Huntington

Location:	Western San Gabriel Valley, northeast of downtown Los Angeles
Mileage:	26
Approximate pedaling time:	2¼ hours
Terrain:	One or two noticeable, but short, hills
Traffic:	Light to moderate
Things to see:	Descanso Gardens, Rose Bowl, Huntington Library, Art Gallery and Botanical Gardens, Caltech, and acres of palatial homes

This ride tries to satisfy everyone, although I'm fully aware of the pitfalls inherent in such a venture. When you try to satisfy everyone, you run the very real risk of satisfying no one. But, damn the torpedoes, full speed ahead! With the risks in mind, this ride has some flat riding, some hills, and an opportunity to smell the roses, literally. For those who want to get right down to the crux of the ride—those of you who eat the dessert first if it's put on the table with the main course—you can drive directly to the Huntington, a library, art collection, and botanical garden in San Marino. It is located at 1151 Oxford Road.

For those who are planning to ride there and stop off for a foot tour of the Huntington, I strongly suggest that you bring walking shoes and a good bike lock. Your trusty steed will be left unattended for an extended period, and there are few feelings worse than finding your bike missing when you return.

Start this ride at the Descanso Gardens parking lot, where there's plenty of free parking, some of it tree-shaded. Descanso is located in La Cañada Flintridge near the junction of the SR–2 (Glendale) Free-

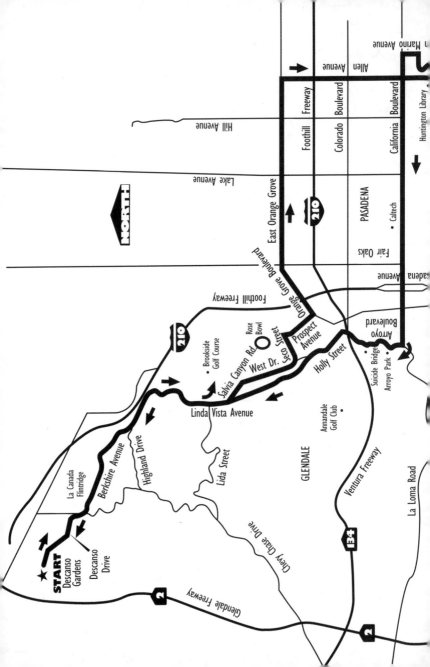

DIRECTIONS at a glance

0.0	Right from Descanso Gardens parking lot onto Descanso Drive
0.8	Right onto Chevy Chase Drive
1.0	Left onto Berkshire Avenue
3.4	Left onto Highland Drive
3.7	Highland becomes Linda Vista Avenue
6.5	Left onto Salvia Canyon Road
6.8	Bear right onto West Drive
7.4	Left onto Seco Street
7.7	Right onto Prospect Avenue
8.1	Left onto Orange Grove Boulevard
8.8	Orange Grove becomes East Orange Grove Boulevard at bend to right
11.1	Right onto Allen Avenue
12.6	Straight into Huntington Library and Art Gallery grounds
12.9	Left onto Oxford Road
13.3	Right onto Orlando Road (at the T)
13.4	Left onto San Marino Avenue
13.6	Left onto California Boulevard
17.1	Right onto Arroyo Boulevard (at the T)
17.9	Left onto Holly Street
18.3	Right onto Linda Vista Avenue
22.5	Right onto Highland Drive
22.8	Right onto Berkshire Avenue (at the T)
25.2	Left onto Chevy Chase Drive
26.0	Left into Descanso Gardens parking lot

way and the I–210 (Foothill) Freeway at 1818 Descanso Drive.

Before you depart for the Huntington, a few words about **Descanso Gardens**. The site of the gardens was deeded to José Maria Verdugo, a Spanish soldier, in 1784 by Pedro Fegas, governor of California, a man who should be noted for his generosity. Not much happened on the land until 1937, when E. Manchester Boddy, owner of the *Los Angeles Daily News*, purchased the site and named it Rancho del Descanso (Farm of Rest). He planted what is purportedly the largest ornamental camellia garden in the world on the 165-acre parcel. The land now sports more than 100,000 camellia plants of 600 different varieties. In addition, there's a spectacular, well-labeled, 6,000-variety rose garden and acres of azaleas under ancient oak trees. A leisurely walk along the meandering, tree-shaded paths is strongly recommended. There's also a Japanese garden and associated teahouse with pools of refreshing-looking water and a small brook flowing through the shady seating area. It's a great place to "take tea" and to spend a few minutes after touring the gardens or contemplating the ride.

Hospitality House, built in 1939 as the Boddy residence, is also worth visiting, particularly for its special Christmas decorations. There's also a real stream with real water that meanders through a California live oak forest. (There are two major varieties of California oak trees: coast oaks lose their leaves in winter, and live oaks keep their leaves year-round.) For cyclists with foresight, there's a beautiful picnic area. There's a tram tour at 1:00, 2:00, and 3:00 P.M. daily (except Mondays) and hourly from 11:00 A.M. to 3:00 P.M. on weekends.

Incidentally, in December the camellias are just coming into full bloom, and the roses are beautiful. In January the camellias are in full bloom and the winter annuals throughout the gardens are at their best. Descanso Gardens is open daily (except Christmas Day) from 9:00 a.m. to 4:30 p.m. Admission is $1.50, except on December 16 and January 20, when it is free. (Admission is also free on the third Tuesday of each month.) Parking is free.

To begin the ride turn right out of the parking lot and coast downhill on Descanso Drive to Chevy Chase Drive (about 0.75 mile). Turn right on Chevy Chase, and a slightly uphill 0.25 mile later, turn left on Berkshire Avenue. From the moment you leave Descanso until you're well into Pasadena, you'll be riding through a decidedly high-rent district. On the right side of Berkshire are several homes in the 10,000-square-foot-plus category, and one in particular that gives a new meaning to the phrase "a man's home is his castle"; the First Armored Cavalry would have difficulty delivering mail there, much less capturing it.

Turn left on Highland Drive after cruising Berkshire for 1.4 miles. Highland soon (0.3 mile) becomes Linda Vista Avenue. Linda Vista ("beautiful view" in Spanish) lives up to its name: it has some great views and the area is most pleasant for bike riding. For those who are into speed, Linda Vista is as good as it gets. Stay on Linda Vista for 2.8 miles. Turn left on Salvia Canyon Road, which cuts off at an angle and drops you on West Drive on the grounds of the **Rose Bowl.** The stadium seats 104,700. It was built in 1902 and has been the site of the famous New Year's Day game between East and West since then. Brown University played in the first Rose Bowl game, lost, and has never returned. Columbia University is the only other Ivy League school to have played there. They lost, too.

Incidentally, on the second Sunday of every month, there is a flea market with entry through the main gate (under the Rose Bowl logo sign). This flea market is the granddaddy of them all, featuring everything from junk to genuine antiques. Although it is frequently called a "swap meet," the only thing you can swap there is cash for goods on display. There's an entry fee, but it is an interesting experience and probably worth the few dollars' admission. (You may want to buy something at the flea market, so I recommend that you drive there after finishing the ride. There's parking for 100,000 people, and since the flea market attracts only about 2,000, there'll be plenty of space for you and your treasures.)

Stay on Salvia Canyon for 0.3 mile and on West Drive for 0.6 mile. Turn left on Seco Street, and after 0.3 mile, turn right on Prospect Avenue. Stay on Prospect for 0.4 mile, which will include one tough, but fairly short, hill, and take a left on Orange Grove Boulevard.

Orange Grove is a thoroughly commercial street, a world apart from the exclusive residential areas you passed through before the Rose Bowl. If you're ultrasensitive to traffic, you can proceed on side streets, but be prepared to get lost. I concede that there are worse things than getting lost, and Pasadena's traffic may be one of them.

After 0.7 mile Orange Grove bends to the right. At the bend it becomes East Orange Grove. Stay with it until you get to Allen Avenue in about 2.25 miles. Turn right on Allen Avenue, and ride directly into the **Huntington's** manicured grounds after about 1.5 miles, in the course of which the character of the street changes abruptly several times from commercial to residential to suburban. You will have traveled about 12.6 miles from Descanso Gardens. There are few rides anywhere that have a wider variety of scenery in such a short distance.

The Huntington is one of the nation's great cultural and educational centers. It's located on just over 200 acres of beautifully landscaped grounds. The botanical gardens cover 130 of those acres, so you can see that there's a good deal of walking to do. Guided tours are available, and while they're very educational and pleasant, especially in nice weather, the pace is excruciatingly slow. The twelve-acre **Desert Garden** is the largest outdoor garden of its type in this country, and probably the world. The **Japanese Garden** features a "drum bridge" and a fully furnished Japanese house, as well as a bonsai collection and raked gravel gardens. The **Rose Garden**, whose blossoms I alluded to above, illustrates the history of the rose. (While Descanso's rose garden is *much* more extensive and showy, its purpose is to display great variety; Huntington's purpose is to illustrate the culture and evolution of the rose.) The two **camellia gardens** are the world's largest, according to the Huntington's P.R. department, although I had always thought Descanso's had that claim to fame sewed up—I guess it's a close and spectacular race. Not to be missed as well are the **Herb**, **Jungle**, and **Palm Gardens.**

Henry E. Huntington established the foundation that bears his name in 1919. Hank was a tycoon whose fortune grew from railroad and real estate ventures in southern California at the turn of the century. Talk about being at the right place at the right time—with the capital to take advantage of it all!

The **Library** is a must-see, complete with a Gutenberg bible, a manuscript of Chaucer's *Canterbury Tales*, and a "double-elephant" folio edition of Audubon's *Birds of America.*

The **Huntington Gallery**, which was originally the Huntington residence, contains an enormous collection of British and French art of the eighteenth and nineteenth centuries, including Lawrence's *Pinkie* and Gainsborough's *Blue Boy.*

The Huntington is open from 1:00 to 4:30 P.M. Tuesday through

Sunday. It is closed on Mondays and major holidays. No picnicking is allowed on the grounds. In a delightful departure from the usual stuffy museum rules, photography is permitted everywhere, but no flash shots are allowed, and tripods, even teeny ones that go in your jersey pocket, are *verboten*. There is a self-service restaurant on the premises, as well as a regular restaurant where you can even partake of English, moderately high, tea, Friday through Sunday. The Huntington is one of the few places in L.A. where it appears to be relatively safe to leave your bike for an extended period with a light cable and lock. Oh, yes, there is a $10 entry fee at the entry drive. It's well worth it.

For a change of pace, and to return by a somewhat different route, exit the grounds on Oxford Street, and turn left there. Turn right at the T and left on San Marino Avenue, a fairly tricky maneuver involving two YIELD signs. Turn left again on California Boulevard, a reasonably attractive street with single-file riding conditions. You'll soon pass right through the grounds of the **California Institute of Technology (Caltech)**, although, except for the general beige/gray ambience, there isn't much to see. Caltech was founded in 1919 as Throop University, whose aim was to instill an appreciation for manual labor. Today Caltech is a center for scientific study, with heavy emphasis on astronomy, geology, and the physical sciences. It is frequently likened to Boston's Massachusetts Institute of Technology, but MIT turns out engineers, whereas Caltech turns out scientists. Both camps, usually with a somewhat arrogant sniff, insist there's a fundamental difference.

Stay on California Boulevard until you get to its end at a T (about 3.5 miles) at Arroyo Boulevard. Turn right on Arroyo, and take it under the freeway complex to a left onto Holly Street (about 0.8 mile). You'll pass along **Arroyo Seco** and **Arroyo Park** on the left and pass under **Suicide Bridge** before arriving at Holly, which is near the Rose Bowl. (Suicide Bridge is so named because it was supposedly a favored jumping-off place for the formerly rich after the crash of '29. There is some disagreement as to whether anyone actually took the plunge from the bridge, but the moniker stuck.) Take Holly 0.4 mile to its T with Linda Vista Avenue, where you'll turn right. After 1.4 miles you'll pass Salvia Canyon Road, the point where you turned off to the Rose

Bowl on the outbound leg. A ring road with various names circumnavigates the Rose Bowl. If you still have energy, you might want to go completely around the Bowl counterclockwise. It's a nice flat ride, and you can't get lost. Just ignore the street names and keep the Bowl on your left. If you're in a contrary mood, the circumnavigation can be done with equal ease in a clockwise direction by turning left at the bottom of Salvia Canyon hill and keeping the Bowl on your right. Either way, when you return to Salvia Canyon, climb the hill to Linda Vista and turn right; then you'll be back on the basic route.

The remainder of the ride is the reverse of the outbound route, providing different views of the spacious mansions and vistas.

For Further Information

Descanso Gardens (818) 790–5571
Huntington directions (to get there) (626) 405–2274
Huntington information (626) 405–2100
Huntington Sunday reservations (mandatory) (626) 405–2273
Rose Bowl information (626) 793–7193
Rose Bowl Swap Meet and Flea Market (626) 587–5100

Getting There

Descanso Gardens

Take the I–210 (Foothill) Freeway to the Verdugo Boulevard exit. Follow Verdugo Boulevard to Descanso Drive; go left for 1 block to Descanso Gardens.

You also can take the I–5 (Golden State) Freeway to the SR–2 (Glendale) Freeway to the I–210 (Foothill) Freeway and follow the above instructions from there. When exiting the SR–2 Freeway onto the I–210, follow signs to the south.

Rose Bowl

Take the SR–134 (Ventura) Freeway to the Colorado Boulevard exit. Follow signs to the Rose Bowl.

You also can take the I–210 (Foothill) Freeway south toward Pasadena and exit to the SR–134 (Ventura) Freeway, heading toward Glendale. Take the first exit (Holly Street) and follow signs to the Rose Bowl.

Huntington Library and Art Gallery

Take the I–210 (Foothill) Freeway to the Hill Avenue exit. Follow Hill Avenue south to Colorado Boulevard. Go left on Colorado to Allen Avenue. Go right on Allen into the Huntington grounds.

Santa Monica/Westwood

Location:	West of Beverly Hills at the Pacific Ocean
Mileage:	22
Approximate pedaling time:	1¾ hours
Terrain:	Well-paved, smooth roads, with one fairly easy hill
Traffic:	Light to moderate
Things to see:	San Vicente Boulevard and the residential area of Brentwood; Santa Monica, including Palisades Park and the Municipal Pier; Wilshire Boulevard; the Federal Building; downtown Westwood; UCLA campus; Sawtelle National Cemetery; Wadsworth Veteran's Hospital and grounds

Westwood is the home of UCLA (University of California at Los Angeles). Contiguous with the UCLA campus is Sawtelle National Cemetery, which is similar in concept to the larger and more famous Arlington Cemetery in Virginia/Washington, D.C. And then there's Santa Monica, one of the most beautiful and politically liberal cities in the United States. Santa Monica sports a gorgeous, palm-lined beach; a pier worth exploring, from which the Race Across America (RAAM) began for several years; and Palisades Park, which is one of those little-known but must-see places that tourists usually miss. This ride is an easy excursion through several geographic and cultural areas that are a cross section of everything southern Californian.

Santa Monica is bounded by the city of Los Angeles on three

0.0	Right from San Vicente Boulevard onto 26th Street
0.1	Left onto La Mesa Way
0.2	Counterclockwise around circular garden; left onto La Mesa Drive
0.7	Right onto San Vicente Boulevard
3.3	Left onto Ocean Avenue (at stop sign; *caution*: cross-traffic does *not* stop)
5.7	Right onto Santa Monica Pier; make U-turn and return to Ocean Avenue
6.1	Right onto Ocean Avenue
6.7	Left onto Pico Boulevard
6.8	Left onto Main Street
7.4	Right onto Colorado Avenue (at T)
8.0	Left onto Lincoln Boulevard
8.9	Right onto Wilshire Boulevard
15.1	Left onto Westwood Boulevard
15.7	Enter UCLA campus
16.0	Left onto Circle Drive (poorly marked or unmarked)
16.3	Right onto Gayley Avenue
16.7	Gayley becomes Montana Avenue
17.8	Left onto Sepulveda Boulevard
18.8	Right onto Constitution Avenue (go under freeway and through PEDESTRIANS AND BICYCLISTS ONLY gate)
19.6	Left onto Bringham Avenue (at T)
19.6	Right onto San Vicente Boulevard
22.3	End of tour at 26th Street

sides. Los Angeles goes by other names, to be sure: Pacific Palisades on the north, Brentwood on the northeast, Sawtelle on the east, Mar Vista on the southeast, and Venice on the south, but L.A. by any name is still Los Angeles. For bicycling purposes, Santa Monica is bounded on the north by San Vicente Boulevard, on the east by 26th Street, on the south by Colorado Boulevard, and on the west by

Ocean Avenue or the Pacific Coast Highway (PCH/SR–1).

Within the actual, as opposed to bicycling, boundaries of Santa Monica live 90,000 people. If the local media are to be believed, about 89,700 are political liberals somewhat to the left of Karl Marx; the remaining 300 are landlords, who, until the early eighties, could be seen twirling waxed handlebar moustaches while posting eviction notices. Ordinances restricting the mustachioed minority have given rise to rather heated debate and a semipermanent sign on Ocean Avenue reading SANTA MONICA—SOCIALIST CESSPOOL. Socialist Santa Monica may be, but a cesspool it ain't. Start this ride by parking your car on **San Vicente Boulevard** around 26th Street. This is around the 13000 block. This street is a good beginning, because westbound it marks the beginning of Santa Monica. On the south side of the street, just east of 26th Street, is the West Side Bakery, which serves excellent breakfast-type food and wonderful bread.

Thus fortified with bread and breakfast, head west on San Vicente Boulevard. The center divider, which is about 50 feet wide, is planted with coral trees; it has a couple of well-worn paths near the curbs, where people like to run.

The coral trees, incidentally, were in very bad need of care in 1986, and the city of Santa Monica, knee-jerk liberalism momentarily failing it, decided to cut them down. Private businesses adopted individual trees and saved them, and today they're in better shape than ever. The street also is lined with magnificent magnolia trees along the north and south curbs.

An alternate, recommended, route to going straight down (west) San Vicente Boulevard is to turn right (north) at 26th Street and left at the first street, La Mesa Way. La Mesa Way becomes La Mesa Drive at a circular garden that would double as a traffic circle, if there were any traffic, which there never is. You loop around the garden counterclockwise and follow La Mesa Drive, a narrow street lined with what have to be the world's largest rubber trees. The homes along La Mesa are huge and beautifully landscaped and maintained; if you skip La Mesa, you will have missed a real sightseeing experience. In less than a mile the street bends south and drops you back on San Vicente Boulevard at 19th Street.

Continue right (west) on San Vicente Boulevard to the end at Ocean Avenue. This is 3.3 gradual downhill miles from the start at 26th Street.

Immediately after you turn left on Ocean Avenue, **Palisades Park** is on your right. This is a 2-mile-long city park atop a 150-foot-high cliff (palisade, if you insist). The park, for most of its length, is only about 75 feet wide. If you stop and look over your left shoulder, you'll see an apartment house with a permanent sign on its southwest corner; the sign depicts a hammer and sickle and bears the words SOVIET MONICA RENT CONTROLLED BUILDING. There is more than a little resentment among landlords toward Santa Monica's rent-control laws, some of the most stringent in the country. In any event, Palisades Park is a beautiful stretch of greenery overlooking one of the world's most beautiful beaches. On a clear day one can easily see Point Dume at the north end of crescent-shaped Santa Monica Bay and Rocky Point on the Palos Verdes Peninsula at the south end. While Los Angeles vaunted smog does occasionally intrude into this paradise, limited visibility is usually due to an offshore cloud bank that visits daily from April through July, and frequently during the other months, as well.

Santa Monica, which lies east and south of you, was discovered in 1769 by Gaspar de Portola, whose mission, no pun intended, was to establish a series of missions along the California coast. Santa Monica Bay reminded Father Juan Crespi of Saint Monica's tears. This requires a considerable stretch of the imagination, but I suppose anything is possible, and no one has come up with a better explanation of the name. In 1828 Francisco Sepulveda, an early Spanish pioneer whose name graces Sepulveda Boulevard, one of the longest and busiest thoroughfares in town, received a grant to raise cattle along the shore. Santa Monica began as a railhead in 1877, and by 1896 the area's beach had become a cooling-off destination for hot Angelenos. Raymond Chandler immortalized Santa Monica as "Bay City."

Palisades Park stretches along Ocean Avenue, from Adelaide Drive on the north to Colorado Avenue on the south. A footpath, bordered by two rows of *Washingtonia* fan palms, winds through the park for its entire length. There is a Visitor Assistance stand near Arizona Street that dispenses free maps and information. Near it is the world's largest *camera obscura*. The "lens" is focused on Ocean Avenue, and it's fascinating to watch the passing scene in full color, though inverted, from what is in fact the inside of a camera. The lens, incidentally, is actually a hole in the wall about 2 inches in diameter, with no glass whatsoever.

(*Note:* Substantial numbers of homeless people loiter in Palisades Park. Panhandling is strictly *verboten,* even in liberal Santa Monica, and is punishable by a night in the hoosegow; on the other hand, some of these unfortunate people would welcome a night of incarceration and they may approach you for a handout, especially if the weather is threatening. Just say, "No.")

A left turn at Montana Avenue will take you to a quintessential yuppie shopping area. For all of its boutiques and occasional sidewalk cafés, it is an undistinguished place, not worth the substantial hill climb.

At the foot of Wilshire Boulevard is a **statue of Saint Monica.** This statue has appeared in numerous films and commercials as a way of showing that the picture was shot in Santa Monica. The same may be said of the sign over the entrance to the **Santa Monica Pier,** which is a block farther south.

About 2.4 miles from the turn onto Ocean Avenue is the Santa Monica Pier. A new and improved pier opened in 1993, replacing a big chunk that was destroyed in 1984's winter storms. Bikes are still allowed on the pier; it still has a carnival atmosphere, and it still sports a fully restored carousel. The carousel alone is worth the trip. Give it a "whirl," or at least take a close look at the carved figures.

The original pier, named Shoo-Fly Landing, was built in the 1870s to handle heavy shipping. Among its first cargoes was tar from the La Brea Tar Pits, which was used to pave the streets of San Francisco. Around 1875 the Los Angeles and Independence Railway replaced the landing with a 1,700-foot-long wharf and a depot that provided passenger access to steamers. In 1894 the Long Wharf was built. At 4,720 feet it was, well, long. It was torn down in 1920. The entrance to the pier is worth a visit, too, if for no other reason than its fame.

Just south of the pier and north of Pico Boulevard is an amusement park that opened in 1997 but is a throwback to the "good old days." The place is a lot of fun, very informal, and reminiscent of a small county fair. Bikes—walked, not ridden—are welcome, but a bike is really a drag at an amusement park. So put this down as yet another place to be revisited later, *sans bicyclette*. This park, incidentally, replaces Pacific Ocean Park, a similar venture owned by CBS and closed about thirty years ago.

After riding 0.6 mile south on Ocean Avenue you'll come to Pico Boulevard. Turn left on Pico, and left again after 0.1 mile onto Main Street.

If you were to turn right onto Main Street, for the next mile, or so, you'd be overwhelmed with the essence of yuppiedom. There are literally dozens of upscale boutiques, coffeehouses, snack bars, and who knows what. Places like Banana Republic, Starbucks, Ann Taylor, Ben and Jerry's, and Il Fornaio. At Rose Avenue, the Venice border, the whole ambience suddenly dies and is replaced by something quite different, even bizarre, reminiscent of the rebellious 1960s. On Rose Avenue, a few yards left of the Main Street intersection, is the **Rose Cafe**, which has a bike rack around the back and very nice patio for enjoying a snack. Prices are moderate, but since this isn't the place for a full meal, anyway, the total tab is within reach of anyone who had the means to bicycle to Santa Monica.

But, since you turned left on Main Street, the **Santa Monica Civic Auditorium** and **City Hall** will be on your right. These are handsome, white, rather modern structures. The Civic Auditorium is truly a multiuse building, with constantly changing events, ranging from American Indian art displays to a fairly prestigious regional dog show.

Main Street comes to a T intersection with Colorado Avenue after 0.6 mile. Staring right at you is **Santa Monica Place**, an enormous shopping center. At one time Santa Monica Place was *the* place to shop, but age has caught up with it, and now it's just *a* place to shop. Rumor has it that it will soon undergo a multi, multi, multi-million-dollar face-lift and reconstruction, but probably not before 1998.

Turn right on Colorado Avenue, and ride for 0.6 mile to Lincoln

Boulevard. Turn left on Lincoln, and ride through downtown Santa Monica 0.9 mile to **Wilshire Boulevard**. Turn right on Wilshire. You will soon pass under *The Wave*, a piece of modern sculpture that straddles the street. It has been called Santa Monica's civic coat hanger. Whatever it is, it sure ain't a wave. Wilshire Boulevard stretches from the heart of downtown Los Angeles to the statue of Saint Monica. If you are an adventurous sort, you might want to ride the full length of this justifiably famous street. On weekends it's an easy and fascinating ride, about 20 miles each way. Bits and pieces of Wilshire Boulevard are covered on other rides in this book, though, and if you do them all, you'll cover about 75 percent of its length—the most interesting 75 percent.

Continue on Wilshire for 5.6 miles. Just after crossing Sepulveda Boulevard, one of the busiest intersections in town, you'll see the **Federal Building** on your right. This is where everything remotely connected with U.S. government action and inaction is protested.

Turn left at Westwood Boulevard, 6.2 miles from the turn onto Wilshire Boulevard. Westwood is slightly uphill, but it shouldn't cause any discomfort. On the right is **Gourmet Row**, sporting a muffin shop, a 7-11, a McDonald's, a Mrs. Field's, and a couple of other eating establishments that change with alarming frequency. The food at all of these places is just what you'd expect, and you're certain to see a few bicyclists outside of them.

Westwood is home to **UCLA**, and the streets will be clogged with college students. At night the place comes alive, because Westwood is *the* place to see a movie. Parking is a nightmare.

Proceed up (north) Westwood Boulevard. The entry gate to UCLA is 0.6 mile from the turn from Wilshire to Westwood. Go 0.3 mile farther and turn left on Circle Drive. This is not very well marked, but if you miss the turn, you'll get a nice tour of this rather urban campus. If you turn left (west), you'll come out of the campus on Gayley Avenue, even if you miss Circle Drive. Turn right on Gayley at the T intersection, which comes up after 0.25 mile. Gayley Avenue is a steep uphill climb, with the UCLA campus on the right and fraternity houses on the left. Take heart—this is the only real hill on this entire ride. At the top of the hill, Gayley Avenue becomes Montana Avenue, and you have a really nice downhill all the way to Sepulveda Boulevard. (The distance from the turn onto Gayley to the left turn onto Sepulveda is 1.5 miles.)

Sepulveda Boulevard southbound goes downhill, with the I–405 (San Diego) Freeway on an embankment high above you on the right. (If you turn right, instead of left, in about a mile you will come to the turnoff to the **Getty Center**, a superb art museum. In fact, thanks to a multi-*billion* dollar trust fund bequeathed by J. Paul Getty, of Getty Oil fame, the **Getty Museum**, which opened in late 1997, is inarguably the richest, most well-presented, most visitor-friendly, largest, art museum in the world; it put Los Angeles on the world's art map, and a visit is an absolute must. As it turns out, a bicycle is probably the best way to visit the Getty. If one drives, one calls for a (scarce) parking reservation; upon arrival, after parking, one is whisked up the mountainside to the museum by tram. If, however, you arrive by bike, you park it somewhere inside the guarded, gated grounds, with no reservation necessary, and you get whisked up to the museum in the same tram as the motorists who had to wait days or weeks for parking clearance.

Continue south 1.0 mile on a mild downhill to Constitution Avenue. At the intersection with Constitution, there's a traffic light that is always green for Sepulveda. On the left is **Sawtelle National Cemetery**, one of 133 such cemeteries in the United States, 16 of which are full, so get your reservation in now. Sawtelle National Cemetery is identical to Arlington in concept and function, but it lacks the latter's publicity and glamour—if one can say that a cemetery has glamour. Bikes can and do take tours of the cemetery, and there is access to the UCLA campus through the cemetery grounds. On the right is an underpass (under the freeway). Turn right and go through the underpass.

If you're lucky, the gates will be open. If you're unlucky, look to the right, and you'll see an opening in the chain-link fence with a sign that reads PEDESTRIANS AND BICYCLISTS ONLY. Go through the opening, and you'll find yourself on the grounds of the **Wadsworth Veteran's Hospital.** On the right, hidden from view, is the **Jackie Robinson Stadium**, the UCLA baseball stadium; on the left is an oil well, working its rocker off to reduce the national debt. Go straight ahead 0.2 mile. The road goes up a *steep* hill to the right and up a very mild incline to the left. Ultimately, both roads end up in the same place. Go left, and at the top of the hill, at the stop sign, cross the street.

The BICYCLISTS ONLY sign at the entrance to the grounds gives the impression that cyclists are welcome. Well, they aren't exactly *welcome*, but they are tolerated. The hospital grounds are patrolled, seemingly, by platoons of police cruisers. Running a stop sign is a federal offense, punishable, one gets the impression, by a number of years of hard labor in Leavenworth.

You'll be surrounded by old, but recently renovated, hospital structures. Some of the buildings, like the gingerbread Victorian church, date back to the nineteenth century. There are little depots at the side of the road that look like miniature bus stations. In fact, they were waiting points for the trolleys that ran through the premises until the fifties.

Go straight through the hospital grounds, turning left where you have a choice, and after about 0.75 mile from the entrance, you'll be on strangely spelled Bringham Avenue. Turn left and immediately turn right, and you'll be in a posh shopping section of **San Vicente Boulevard**, the Los Angeles end. Continue straight ahead, and after a couple of traffic lights, you'll pass the posh **Brentwood Country Club** on your left and beautiful, well-maintained homes on your right. The coral trees in the center median make their appearance around Bundy Drive, and you'll reach 26th Street after 2.7 miles.

Before you get to 26th Street, you'll pass some noteworthy places. A couple of blocks to the left at Gretna Green Way is the town house occupied by Nicole Simpson and her children when she was murdered in June 1994. The place has since been sold and is occupied by someone else, so I won't give the full address, even though it appeared in the newspapers daily for what seemed like years. Likewise, the Mezzaluna Restaurant, which had a starring role in the O. J. Simpson trial, was located at San Vicente and Westgate Avenue, and is now another place entirely. A couple of blocks farther along, if you turn right on Bristol Avenue, you can get to O. J. Simpson's home on Rockingham Avenue; I've done it by Trek in roughly ten minutes, so all the debate as to whether

O. J. could have done it by Ford Bronco in that amount of time seems to me to be kinda moot. O. J.'s home has been sold and is now occupied by someone else; if you really, really want to see the place, look up any day's report on the trial for the address. Anyhow, if one continues up Bristol Avenue across Sunset Boulevard, you'll come to a very nice area, indeed. L.A. Mayor Richard Riordan lives on Bristol just north of Sunset. Because of term limits, he may not still be mayor when you read this, and this is his private home, not the city mansion, so his address will remain a not-too-well-kept secret.

Getting There

Take the I–405 (San Diego) Freeway to the Wilshire (West) Boulevard exit. (Wilshire-West goes toward Santa Monica; Wilshire-East goes toward Westwood and UCLA, so if your destination is Westwood, use the Wilshire-East exit, but be forewarned that except on early weekend mornings, parking is nearly impossible.) Turn right on San Vicente Boulevard, which soon bends to the left, and in a couple of miles you'll be at 26th Street.

South Bay Bicycle Trail

Location:	From north of Santa Monica to the Palos Verdes Peninsula
Mileage:	44.6
Approximate pedaling time:	4½ hours
Terrain:	Flat
Traffic:	None on the bikeway; a few short city-street detours with moderate traffic; tricky places where the bikeway passes through parking lots; some traffic in the form of skateboarders, roller skaters, walkers, joggers, and mimes (yes, mimes)
Things to see:	Beaches, beaches, beaches; beautiful people; weird people; Venice; King Harbor; Redondo Beach Pier; piers, palms, and power plants

The South Bay Bicycle Trail, also known as the Santa Monica Bikeway, holds a fascination for all bicyclists, although they have a wide range of feelings about it. Some love it, and some hate it, but very few can just take it or leave it. My interest was piqued, after a number of years of benign mental neglect, when I read that it had been extended northward from Santa Monica to Temescal Canyon and Will Rogers State Beach, where Temescal Canyon Road intersects with the Pacific Coast Highway (PCH). A bikeway along 22 miles of palm-lined beach is a visual treat, no matter what other attractions there may be, and the views alone are probably reason enough to put up with the nonbicyclists and sand-in-the-bearings. Add in places like Venice the beautiful people playing not-so-good volleyball and the continuous temptation of junk food, and you've got an irresistible combination.

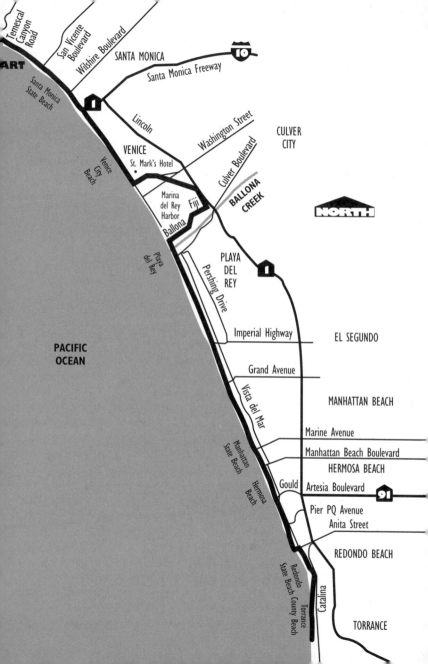

The best reason to take this book along with you is that the land-marks along the bikeway are generally unidentified. In fact, they're a total mystery. For 22 miles there are no mile markers, you don't know what town you're in, how far you've gone, how much bikeway is left, or anything else that you take for granted on the city streets. Mountain bicyclists may be used to not knowing which town or even county they're riding in, but it's unnerving to a "roadie."

So, as a public service, here is a description of the bikeway from one end to the other and back, something akin to, but a little less dramatic than, Magellan's 'round-the-world cruise. The bikeway, which was built in the late sixties, isn't actually a continuous strip from end to end; there are a couple of short, but annoying, breaks. Officially, the bikeway extends from Temescal Canyon, which is a few miles north of the Santa Monica Pier, to the northern edge of Palos Verdes Peninsula. It can, of course, be ridden from south to north, as well as north to south. In fact, you're arguably better off starting in the south, because there's better parking there. (Parking, incidentally, costs $4.00 or $5.00 in parking lots all along the bikeway. You can save this fee by parking a half mile or so east of the beaches and riding your bike to the bikeway.)

The concrete bikeway is 12 feet wide, except where noted below. In most places it is well swept, and it is marked BIKES ONLY all along its length. In most places bikes are defined as anything with feet or wheels. In Redondo Beach there's a PED ONLY lane that seems to have a beneficial effect, leaving the bikeway free for wheeled vehicles, the most dangerous of which are rollerblades, with skateboards coming in a distant second. In general, the difference between the two is that the skateboarders usually have some degree of control.

The bikeway is patrolled by real police who wear navy-blue shorts and white T-shirts and carry big guns. They ride four-wheel all-terrain vehicles when they're not on foot. In other towns along the way, police are similarly attired and armed and ride mountain bikes.

Only about half or fewer of bikeway riders wear helmets. I guess most feel that the worst that can happen is that they'll take a header into the sand. The odds are that that's what *would* happen if you were to fall, but that isn't the worst that can happen, since there are 12 feet of concrete to fall on, too. *Use a helmet on the bikeway.* The odds of an accident are fairly high, considering the traffic density and its peculiar composition. There are many distractions along the bikeway, and a moment's inattention can separate you from your bike. For these reasons, the bikeway is not an express route from or to anywhere. It's an experience, and it should be savored at 12 mph, give or take a couple of mph. In fact, in 1992 Huntington Beach imposed a 10-mph speed limit on the bikeway, and I know of at least two people who've gotten $108 speeding tickets to show for it.

I also recommend that you leave your bike shorts, chamois and all, at home; wear swim trunks, instead, as you will probably want to take a dip here and there along the way. If you have a choice of bikes, bring one with sealed bearings. Do not do this ride alone, if you can avoid it; you'll need someone to watch your bike while you detour for snacks and junk food. The half-life of an unlocked bike here is on the order of six seconds. Also, it's more fun to share the things you'll be seeing with someone else who has an appreciation for beauty and the stranger things in life.

The start of the bikeway, certainly the world's most famous bike lane, is a rather inconspicuous sign at the beach's parking lot and a painted arrow on the pavement. You can actually ride on a bikeway-like stretch of macadam for a quarter mile or so north of that point, but it comes to an ignominious dead end in the sand, so all measurements for this ride are from the official beginning at the BIKE PATH BEGINS sign at Temescal Canyon Road.

The initial pavement is asphalt with a painted yellow dashed stripe down the center. It hugs the western side of the parking lot.

The beach at Temescal Canyon is **Will Rogers State Beach.** Will Rogers was, of course, a major Hollywood personality. He came to Hollywood in 1919 as a trick roper and became known as the Cowboy Philosopher. His home, 187 lush acres at 14235 Sunset Boulevard, built in 1928, is now the **Will Rogers State Historic Park**; it was donated to the state by the Rogers family in 1944. Will Rogers State Beach is in the 16000 block of the PCH. It is a 3-mile-long stretch of fine white sand. The water, should you be so inclined, is good for swimming, diving, surfing, and bodysurfing. Keep your eyes peeled for surfperch, halibut, and bonito. More likely to be seen by bicyclists are gulls, sanderlings, pelicans, and willets.

Temescal Canyon State Park is located at Temescal Canyon Road and Sunset Boulevard. The Spanish word *temescal* is derived from the Aztec for "bathhouse" (a reference to the sweat houses used by the California Indians). The twenty-two-acre park offers swimming, hiking (trails into the hills), Temescal Creek with waterfalls year-round, and, most important of all, *parking!*

At 0.75 mile the bikeway's concrete pavement begins. It remains concrete from here on, except when the bikeway passes through the beach-side edge of parking lots. Along this stretch on most weekdays during the production season, you'll see the TV show *Baywatch* being filmed. There are amazingly few spectators, and the production crews seem to tolerate a few bicycling gawkers fairly well. The key characters, usually in bathing suits, barely (pun intended) wander about between "takes," seemingly oblivious to said gawkers. While the filming itself is an exercise in boredom, watching the cast and crew before and after shots and during breaks is not. If you're lucky enough to hit this stretch of bikeway at the "right" time, you'll come away from the experience with a whole new outlook on television personalities. Dawdling for a couple of hours may be tempting, but I urge you to retrieve your eyeballs and proceed with the ride.

At the 1.0-mile mark is the exit for Chautauqua Boulevard, which leads to the top of Pacific Palisades and northern Santa Monica. There's a pedestrian tunnel that leads to the east side of the PCH; from there you can climb a short, rather steep hill to Ocean Avenue in Santa Monica. At about 1.3 miles a look over your left shoulder will reveal palm tree–lined **Palisades Park** on the bluff high above the beach. Every few hundred yards for most of the length of the bikeway are eating establishments and rest rooms. At the north end of the bikeway, most of the gourmet-food purveyors seem to be Perry's Pizza and More.

About 2.5 miles from the beginning of the bikeway, there's a bike and boogie-board rental place. Palm trees dot the left margin of the beach, and the roller skater traffic picks up. The beach here, which is

part of **Santa Monica State Beach**, is very wide (a quarter mile or so), with fine, white sand.

At 2.8 miles is the **Ocean Avenue walkway overpass**. This is another convenient way to get up to Palisades Park and Santa Monica (or from there down to the beach). At the 2.9-mile mark there is a sharp bend to the right around the massive Santa Monica Pier parking lot; soon after, there's a bend to the left, and at 3.1 miles you pass under the **Santa Monica Pier**, a dank and smelly (in an oceanic kind of way) place. There are palm trees here and there in clumps, and there are clumps of bike racks, too. At the risk of being repetitious, if you're going to park your steed for longer than one second, be sure to lock it.

In the 1870s Shoo-Fly Landing was built on the site of the present Santa Monica Pier. Tar (*brea* in Spanish) was taken from the La Brea Tar Pits (literally the "tar tar pits") to the landing for shipment to San Francisco, where it was used to pave the city's streets. A series of wharves and piers were built on the site over the years. A storm in 1983 polished off all but a few yards of the last pier; a new one, under construction since 1988, was completed in 1993. The present pier has a fine carousel and amusing shops. You can ride your bike out to the end; riding beyond the end is discouraged.

If you decide to pass under the Santa Monica Pier, take your first left; this will put you near the heart of town.

A few words about **Palisades Park**, perched high above the bikeway, on top of the cliff to the left. It sprawls along Ocean Avenue between Adelaide Drive on the north end and Colorado Avenue on the south, a distance of 2 miles. The park is only 25 yards wide at most, and hugs the very edge of the eroding cliffs overlooking the beach. The views are unbelievable, and the lush semitropical vegetation is something easterners dream about. Santa Monica, one of the most politically liberal cities this side of Moscow, has taken a laissez-faire approach to homelessness, public waste elimination, drunkenness, and other ills of society, and Palisades Park isn't the pristine place it used to be. A trip down the length of the park is certain to put you near this element of society, but it's still well worth it.

The Pritikin Longevity Center, formerly Synanon, is located 4.6

miles from the start. It's the big, ugly brick building just after the pier; the bikeway skirts its western flank. Mention of the word "fat" within 100 yards of Pritikin's headquarters is strictly forbidden.

At 5.2 miles you'll pass through a rest area, with a fast-food joint, benches, and palm trees. This is how Easterners envision southern California. In Venice bikes are prohibited from being ridden on **Ocean Front Walk,** which is where the action is. The bikeway is very winding through the Venice area (at 6.4 miles), and if you're in no hurry, you might want to walk on Ocean Front Walk and soak up the atmosphere, of which there is plenty. **Venice Pier** comes along at 7.3 miles. You can rent a bike there. The **Venice Pavilion,** at the foot of Windward Avenue, has a picnic area, an auditorium, and seemingly continuous roller skating and skateboarding demonstrations. The performances are done by both male and female athletes of widely varying degrees of competence while in various states of undress. If you can rip your eyeballs from the activity, you may notice various **murals** depicting life in Venice. Speaking of murals, there are a couple of notable ones on the buildings along the way. On one of the walls of the **St. Mark's Hotel** at 25 Windward Avenue is a re-creation of Botticelli's *Birth of Venus.* This particular version, painted by a local artist named Cronk, depicts Venus wearing gym shorts and roller skates. Well, this *is* Venice.

A few words about Venice: In 1904 cigarette mogul Abbot Kinney (yes, Virginia, there is a street named after him in Venice) purchased 160 acres of swamp where Venice now stands. His intention was to create a "Venice of America." In the process a Grand Canal, two networks of smaller canals, and a lagoon were dug. Gondolas and gondoliers to propel them were imported from Italy, and arched bridges were placed here and there over the canals. Kinney made a valiant effort to make Venice, California, a high-brow mecca, but by 1920 the crowds came primarily for the roller coaster, casinos, and bathhouses. Simultaneously, but unrelated, Abbot Kinney died (in 1920), just as the local sewage system was proving to be inadequate; the canals became filthy, and by 1930 the amusement park was gone, and all but four of the canals had been filled in and paved. Oil was discovered in Venice in 1929, and thereafter, rather unlovely derricks dotted the decaying residential landscape. By the sixties Venice had become the beatnik/hippie capital of California, if not the world.

Today Venice Beach, which stretches 3 miles between Marine Street and Spinnaker Street in Venice, is still a beautiful stretch of sand. The swimming and surfing are still good, and there's still a **fishing pier** at the foot of Washington Street. (It's 1,100 feet long and closed to bicycles, although you can walk its length with your bike. It was completed in 1965 and seems to be withstanding the sea's ravages better than its several predecessors.)

Ocean Front Walk must be seen to be disbelieved. It was built in 1905 by Abbot Kinney, and today it is a string of shops, sidewalk vendors, exhibitionists, restaurants, T-shirt stands, roller-skate rental emporiums, sword swallowers, buskers, and bums.

At Venice Pier the bikeway vanishes, and you'll find yourself on **Washington Street,** another reason to wear a helmet when touring the bikeway. You'll cross some of Venice's canals, which are still none too savory, although at this writing there's a multimillion-dollar project out for bid to raise the level of savoriness. On the right are some curved high-rise apartment houses. Between them and you is a lagoon loaded with ducks, and if you look closely, you'll spot some rabbits, as well. Some of the rabbits look pretty exotic, but the ducks appear to be just ducks. Soon after you see the lagoon, be prepared for a right turn (at 8.2 miles). Suddenly you'll find yourself on a nice bike path paralleling **Admiralty Way.** There's a parcours, in case you want to vary your exercise, and there's a walkway to keep pedestrians and other undesirables off the bike path. Cross Admiralty Way at 8.9 miles; there's a bike-height crossing button, the use of which will *eventually* reward you with a green light. Cross into the Marina del Rey Public Library parking lot, and almost immediately turn left; if you don't, you'll vault a low chain-link fence and sail gracefully over your handlebars right into the drink.

Cross Bali Way—be very careful, there's traffic from both directions. Wind your way through a working boatyard and a couple of new and used yacht dealerships with their associated repair shops. Through all this the bikeway remains 12 feet wide, but it's really just two solid stripes of yellow paint with a dashed yellow line down the middle. For riding hazards you will have traded skaters for a few cars and an occasional boat (towed by a car, one presumes). Cross Mindanao Way at 9.3 miles; the bikeway now parallels Admiralty Way. At 9.4 miles the bikeway turns right along Fiji Way, and soon you'll be on Fiji Way itself. On the right, at 10.0 miles, is **Fisherman's Village**, featuring a distinctive lighthouse among other things. Watch for distracted drivers. At 10.2 miles curve left and bear right onto a dedicated bikeway—in fact, *the* bikeway. It will take you out onto a long finger of land, sandwiched between **Ballona Creek** and the **Marina Entrance Channel**. Ballona Creek is where the UCLA crew does its thing and has its boathouse. There are numerous UCLA crew "banners" painted on the banks of the creek.

Ballona Lagoon derives its name from the city of Bayona (pronounced bye-yona) in northern Spain. Bayona was the ancestral home of the Talamantes family, which was granted land under the name Ballona de las Carretas. The surrounding wetlands were developed into what is now Marina del Rey (Spanish for "king's yacht harbor"—very roughly translated) in the sixties. This is a favored haunt of L.A.'s yuppies and home to many, if not most, LAX-based female flight attendants. Gone are the Gabrielino Indians who formerly occupied the wetlands. **Marina del Rey Harbor**, at 375 acres of land and 405 acres of water, and so thick with yachts that you can almost walk across it, is one of the largest artificial harbors in the world. **Admiralty Park**, which you'll pass, is a really nice stopping-off point for a view that is as southern Californian as it gets.

The **Ballona Wetlands** just south of Marina del Rey were formed during the last Ice Age. Thirteen-acre **Del Rey Lagoon Park** at 6600 Esplanade, off Culver Boulevard in Playa del Rey, contains some of the last remaining wetlands, not to mention a baseball diamond, basketball courts, and a small-boat launch.

At the end of the finger of land along Ballona Creek, turn left over a concrete bridge (11.0 miles), and turn right immediately after crossing it. You're now back on the bikeway. The west end of **Los Angeles International Airport** (LAX) runways are to the east at 12.9 miles. The sand all around is **Dockweiler State Beach**, a 255-acre beach, established in 1947 to honor Isadore B. Dockweiler, a state park commissioner. The beach is at the very end of the runways, and you can count the rivets on the planes as they climb into the sky. There are numerous little-used fire pits and picnic facilities. In view of the deafening noise and tons of aluminum passing 200 feet over your head, the lack of use isn't all that surprising, and one wonders whether this is really such a great tribute to Dockweiler.

To the left, off the bikeway and west of Vista del Mar Drive, which parallels the beach, are the **Airport Dunes**. These are remnants of the El Segundo Dunes that once covered 36 square *miles*. These dunes represent the only sizeable remaining coastal strand plant community between San Luis Obispo County and the Mexican border. These are plants that grow only along the coast like ice plants and coreopsis. Homes were built here during the sixties, but they were situated immediately under the takeoff flight paths of jets departing LAX, and the city of Los Angeles purchased and demolished them in the seventies. LAX, incidentally, is the world's second or third busiest airport, with a landing or takeoff every forty-five seconds or so. So, it's no wonder that the homeowners were anxious to sell. The question is why they bought in the first place. Although streets and sidewalks remain, the dune ecosystem is recovering nicely. About forty acres in the south have never been developed and are in an undisturbed natural state. The dunes are home to numerous endangered species of flora and fauna that exist only in this habitat. I have personally seen a fox and innumerable rabbits in the sandy fields, but I understand that the fox is not native to the area. The fauna, I imagine, are all deaf.

Back on the bikeway you'll see there are two sets of smokestacks ahead. The red-and-white ones belong to the city of Los Angeles' Scattergood power plant. You'll come abreast of them at 14.7 miles. The white stacks with the black tops are southern California Edison's El Segundo power plant, which you'll pass at 15.5 miles. Both plants are oil-fired, and there are sometimes tankers offloading a few hundred yards from shore. This section of bikeway was destroyed by the ocean a few years ago, but it's now in great shape again. In the event that the bikeway is again wiped out by a storm, a suitable detour will be arranged and marked for you by the Powers That Be.

The city of **El Segundo** is to the left; LAX is at the north edge of

El Segundo. El Segundo (which means "the second" in Spanish) was named in 1911 for Standard Oil Company's second oil refinery in California. Some 1.6 acres of the El Segundo Dunes are located within the confines of the refinery, which is still operating and which is one *big* facility!

The city of **Manhattan Beach** begins after the SCE plant. There are no signs anywhere to let you know which community you're passing. **Manhattan Pier**, part of **Manhattan State Beach**, is at 17.4 miles. If these volleyball courts were laid end to end, they'd stretch to the Spalding factory. This is a favorite weekend playground for volleyball players, and the bikeway understandably gets congested with onlookers at times. This is also the site of the fabled **Muscle Beach**, where male bodybuilders strut their stuff.

The bikeway is actually on the site of the defunct Pacific Electric Railway tracks. The beach itself is absolutely fabulous, with gentle surf and a hundred yards or more of pure, fine white sand. Most of the sand on the beach came ashore naturally after the construction of a breakwater just to the south in Redondo Beach.

Manhattan Pier today, after a long, boring history that includes man's relentless building and the sea's relentless dismantling, has shops and restaurants ranging from mediocre to fantastic. It also houses the **Roundhouse Marine Studies Lab**, which contains displays of marine life, marine biology, and oceanography. Classes also are offered. The pier has parking and fishing. At the right spot and at the right time of year, you might spot California gray whales migrating to or from their Mexican breeding grounds and their summer homes off Alaska.

At 17.9 miles there's an END BIKEWAY sign. Don't believe it. Turn right, go down the steps, and turn left. I suggest that you walk your bike down the steps, since you have to share the pavement here with pedestrians and other nonmotorized users. At 19.0 miles (at 14th Street) you'll come to the **Greg Jarvis Memorial Bicycle Rest Stop**. Jarvis, you may recall, was one of the crew members on the ill-fated *Challenger* space shuttle. He was also an avid bicyclist. This is presumably an area where you have to walk your bike, although I've never seen anyone actually doing it.

You are now in the city of **Hermosa Beach**. (*Hermosa* means "beautiful" in Spanish.) The city was developed in 1903 with the coming of the Pacific Electric Railway. You'll find parking, the ever-present volleyball courts, swimming, and surfing here. Surf fishing is also popular here, with catches of surfperch and shovelnose guitarfish common. What one does with a shovelnose guitarfish, a type of ray, I have no idea, but I assume it's so named for its appearance rather than its digging or musical abilities. Hermosa Beach, incidentally, has a pier, too. This one, built in 1965, replacing a couple of storm-removed predecessors, is nearly a half mile long! It has parking, fishing, and lots of seagulls. Watching the pelicans is kind of fun, too. Don't stand under lampposts, as bombing is a favorite hobby of gulls.

At 19.8 miles the bike route ends and you're out on the street again (Harbor Drive), this time in **Redondo Beach.** Redondo Beach dates from 1881, when a rate war between transcontinental railroads brought thousands of people to southern California. Henry Huntington's Pacific Electric Railroad was extended to Redondo Beach in 1903, and then the boom was really on! In 1905 Huntington bought 90 percent of the city's land and formed the Redondo Land Company. Huntington held surfing exhibitions featuring Hawaiian surfer George Freeth, whose performances at Redondo Beach were probably the first instances of surfing in California.

When you come back from Harbor Drive, you'll have to be very careful to spot the entrance to the bikeway. There are KING HARBOR banners along the street, and there's another SCE power plant on the east side of Harbor Drive. The bike lane is not marked well, and since there's curbside parking, you should be extra careful. At 20.4 miles the bikeway jogs up on the sidewalk and passes through the complex at **Redondo Beach Pier.** It's the strangest bike-lane configuration I've ever seen. You actually go through the parking building! Watch the BIKE PATH signs. For a few feet, maybe 100, you'll have to walk your bike. Pay attention to the WALK YOUR BIKE signs, as the cute cops in the cute shorts and T-shirts give out not-so-cute tickets for violating the walk-your-bike law. At the south edge of the pier, you can resume riding your bicycle.

There's a Peruvian restaurant under the Redondo Beach Pier that serves Inca Cola, a popular drink in Peru that tastes like Fleer's Double-

Bubble chewing gum, and there's a Japanese place that carries Poccoli Sweat, which is a very distant relative of Gatorade. Also on the Redondo Pier is the **Ken and Bob** (former KABC radio "Drive-Time" personalities) **Walk of Fame**, with its starfish rivaling the brass counterparts in Hollywood. Now that Bob Arthur has retired, I imagine the Walk of Fame will pass into history.

There are modern apartment houses atop the low palisades on Esplanade Street on the left (east), sand immediately to the right, and **Palos Verdes Peninsula** straight ahead.

King Harbor was built in 1939. Because of underwater geology, the resulting wave action caused severe erosion around the harbor. In 1958, to curb the erosion, the breakwater was extended. King Harbor now has boat slips, parking, rest rooms, and restaurants. A massive fire in 1989 destroyed what had been the most extensive pier/restaurant/recreational complex along the bikeway. Reconstruction was completed in 1996.

Back on the bikeway you'll cross **Redondo State Beach**—eighty-five-acres of beautiful, clean sand—and the usual volleyball courts, rest rooms, food stands, and the like.

Contiguous with Redondo State Beach is **Torrance County Beach.** The latter sits on the western flank of the city of Torrance, a community founded in 1911 by Jarred S. Torrance, whose goal was to establish an ideal residential and industrial town. He nearly succeeded. The beach itself is a gorgeous stretch of white sand, and the bikeway comes to a permanent end at 22.8 miles, without so much as a whimper or even a sign to herald your accomplishment. There's a very steep ramp leading to Esplanade Street. The really courageous can go directly to Palos Verdes Drive and tour the **Palos Verdes Peninsula.** Just above the north end of the beach is a nice grassy park at Paseo de la Playa and Calle Miramar; it has a garden and picnic facilities. (Final Spanish lesson for the day: *paseo* means "park" or "walk," as in a walkway, and *playa* means "beach.")

Although you can take city streets back to Santa Monica, you'll pass through very congested and downright ugly areas, so I recommend that you return via the bikeway; the reverse trip looks *completely* different. By the time you get back to your car, you'll have had one full day, and you can bask in the knowledge that as accessible as the bikeway is, few Angelenos have ever ridden from one end to the other and back.

For Further Information

Dockweiler State Beach (310) 322–5008
Hermosa Beach (310) 372–2166
King Harbor—Harbor Master (310) 372–1175, ext. 239
Manhattan State Beach (310) 372–2166
Roundhouse Marine Studies Lab—Course information
    (310) 379–8117
Santa Monica Pier Office (310) 458–8689
Temescal Canyon State Park (310) 454–5591
Whale-watching Charter Boat information (310) 374–4015
Will Rogers State Historic Park (310) 454–8212

Getting There

Temescal Canyon Road dead ends at Pacific Coast Highway about 1.5 miles north of the Santa Monica city line. From most places the quickest route is to take the I–405 (San Diego) Freeway to the I–10 (Santa Monica) Freeway. Take the I–10 to its end, where it becomes Pacific Coast Highway. Continue on PCH past the heavy shoreside development to the Temescal Canyon Road intersection. The Temescal Canyon parking lot at Will Rogers State Beach is on the left.

If you are approaching from the western San Fernando Valley and you don't mind some fairly hairy canyon driving, follow Topanga Canyon Boulevard (SR–27) for 11 miles from Woodland Hills to PCH. (Topanga Canyon Boulevard crosses the US–101 (Ventura) Freeway and Ventura Boulevard in Woodland Hills at the western edge of the San Fernando Valley.)

If you are visiting from Ventura County, you can take a beautiful shoreside drive along the PCH all the way to Temescal Canyon, or you can take the US–101 (Ventura) Freeway to Las Virgenes Canyon Road, which ends at PCH at the campus of Pepperdine College. Turn left on PCH and you'll come to the Temescal Canyon intersection a couple of miles after passing through the part of Malibu that is the tourist mecca.

Marvelous Malibu

Location:	Malibu, a 19-mile stretch of beach on the west flank of Pacific Coast Highway (PCH), beginning at Santa Monica's northern boundary
Mileage:	44 for each ride
Approximate pedaling time:	3½ hours
Terrain:	Rolling; a few moderate hills
Traffic:	Moderate to heavy, depending on inland weather; passing miles of parked cars can be unnerving, especially during the summer on weekends; there are good shoulders in most places on PCH, and the pavement is nearly all good
Things to see:	Beach, after beach, after beach, each with its unique ambience; seasonal porpoise and whale sightings; seasonal beautiful people; year-round celebrities; Pepperdine University

It takes two rides to "do" Malibu. Both rides start and end at the same place, although you can cut the second ride short by starting where the first one leaves off. If you do the rides early in the day on weekends, you won't be bothered very much by traffic, which quite honestly can be horrendous, especially in the section between Trancas Canyon/Zuma Beach and Topanga Canyon. If you return to your car late, you'll have that rare experience in which your bike is a considerably faster means of transportation than a car; Pacific Coast Highway becomes the world's longest parking lot on weekend afternoons. In any event, the first Malibu ride goes from Topanga Canyon to the Los Angeles/Ventura County line and back to Trancas Canyon. The second ride follows exactly the same route, but the description of the sights along the way begins at Trancas Canyon and takes you back to your car at Topanga. Here goes:

We'll start at Topanga Canyon and ride north to the county line and back—44 miles of the most famous, spectacular, scenic, interesting beachfront in the world, and most of it is cool. It is not, however, flat. There are numerous places along the way on the southbound leg where you can run a few yards into the surf to cool off, and this is highly recommended, although in all the years I've been doing this ride, only once have I ever actually seen anyone get off a bike and take a dip. I'm relying on you to change this. So, if you wear cycling shorts on this ride, dive in! Better yet, wear swimming attire: No one will notice. Or care. Either way, it's best to dry off a bit before resuming your ride, because dripping saltwater on your bike is a definite no-no. (Several beaches, including Leo Carrillo and Zuma, have free showers very near the roadside that'll permit you to wash off surf and sand before resuming your ride.) Oh yes, and bring a good bike lock.

It's best to start this ride early to ensure a cool ride up the coast and to beat the southerly wind that almost always blows in the afternoon. After arriving at Topanga Canyon, find a parking place. If necessary, turn right and head inland on Topanga until you find a suitable spot for your car. Then return to PCH and head north (right) up the coast. After 5 miles of rather heavy traffic, you'll come to famed Malibu. It was on PCH in Malibu that RAAM (Ride Across America) rider Casey Patterson had a close encounter of the broken-bones kind with a pickup truck in 1990.

About 7.5 miles from Topanga, you'll come to **Malibu Canyon** and **Pepperdine University** on the right. The university has one of the most beautiful campus locations of any school anywhere. The university, which was originally located in downtown Los Angeles, was founded in 1937 by George Pepperdine and moved to its present location in 1972. There are 2,600 undergraduate students at the Malibu campus. The school is affiliated with Churches of Christ but is

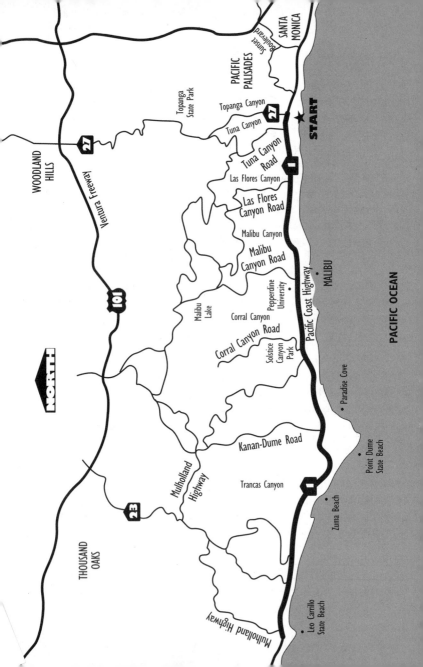

basically nonsectarian in its admissions policies and educational approach. A side trip to the campus will afford unbelievable views of the Pacific Ocean and the shore, all the way to Palos Verdes and out to Catalina Island. You also may see the swimming pool that was the site of the 1984 Olympics water polo competition.

Straight ahead on PCH is a *big* hill. There is a way around the hill, but the detour entails a tricky left turn back onto PCH. The odds of negotiating it safely are right up there with winning the California lottery, so you're probably better off trying to conquer the hill. After reaching the top, you'll be treated to a nice downhill, a much wider road, and lighter traffic, then another hill, and a downhill past **Paradise Cove** and **Zuma Beach**. If you turn left at Western Beach Road and ride a half mile or so along the sand, you'll come to Jim Rockford's (of the TV show *The Rockford Files*) place, or at least the place that was the fictional Rockford's fictional home; it's also the site of the Beach Blanket series of movies and innumerable commercials. This is a private beach, but the entry fee is small, and bike riders have been known to talk their way in without charge, if they promise not to spend the day.

Continuing on PCH, intersecting on the right are Tuna Canyon, Las Flores Canyon, Carbon Canyon, Malibu Canyon, Corral Canyon, Latigo Canyon, Kanan-Dume Road, Trancas Canyon, Encinal Canyon, Decker Canyon, and Mulholland Highway, in that order. If you come to Little Sycamore Canyon, you've gone too far by 1.7 miles. At Trancas Canyon, incidentally, there's an excellent supermarket with everything you'll need for on-the-spot refreshments and a picnic later. I have personally seen several movie stars of the first magnitude there, so keep your eyes peeled. The odds of seeing a celebrity during a twenty-minute rest stop are about fifty-fifty, but you really have to look carefully, as even the most glamorous celebrities don't look particularly glamorous hung over, uncoiffed, and in torn jeans.

A good place to turn around is at the intersection of Mulholland Highway and PCH. This is only a few yards from the county line, and it is directly across the road from **Leo Carrillo State Beach**. The official address is 36000 PCH, Malibu. The traffic at the intersection tends to be a bit fast, so be careful when making the U-turn. Up to this point nearly everything worth seeing has been on the other side of the road. Now by making a U-turn at Mulholland Highway, the points of interest like the blue Pacific are at your right elbow.

The beach was named for movie actor Leo Carrillo, who was also the son of the first mayor of Santa Monica. His most famous (only?) role was as the Cisco Kid's sidekick, Pancho. It is rumored that he never actually saw the beach, but there it is anyway, all 2,190 acres of it, stretching from its sandy shores and spectacular coves to its 1,600-foot elevation a mile or two inland. The beach is a mile long, divided in two by **Sequit Point**, a rocky promontory riddled with caves and tunnels that you're welcome to explore. At the south end of the beach there are good tide pools at low tide, and sea lions are frequently seen on the rocks just offshore. As mentioned earlier, there are showers a few feet off the road.

Nicholas Canyon County Beach is 1 mile north of Decker Canyon Road, across from the **Malibu Riding and Tennis Club**. You can't ride to the shore here, but you can take the stairway from the small, unobtrusive parking lot at the bluff's lip down to a beautiful sandy beach. The parking lot has a couple of portable rest rooms that are remarkably clean.

Next are three state beaches that don't appear individually on maps—at least not maps I've seen. They are part of the **Robert H. Meyer Memorial State Beaches**, which were opened to the public in 1984.

El Pescador State Beach, at 32900 PCH, Malibu, has a small parking lot, picnic tables, and rest rooms high above the Pacific on a bluff. A trail leads down the bluff to a ten-acre beach that sports a variety of seabirds. The beach's name means "fisherman" in Spanish, and the birds are indeed fishing. You won't have much company here, even when Zuma is jammed to the rafters.

La Piedra State Beach, at 32700 PCH, Malibu, is a nice nine-acre swimming and sunning beach below a bluff which has a small parking lot, picnic tables, and rest rooms at the top. Nude bathers, but not bikers, have been spotted here on weekdays, but they're as rare as the movie stars at Trancas—i.e., they exist, but don't expect to see them

often. *Piedra* means "stone" in Spanish, and there are quite a few around, but this beach is a nice, sandy find for anyone willing to clamber down the bluff.

El Matador State Beach, at 32350 PCH, Malibu, covers eighteen acres. It, too, is located at the top of a bluff, but the beach is quite accessible. It's a sandy stretch with boulders protruding from the water here and there, just offshore. From the parking lot, which has picnic tables and rest rooms, you have a panoramic view of the Channel Islands and the nearby coast. Onshore, there is a large stand of giant coreopsis, a shrub that grows chest-high with yellow flowers (in the spring). It's a rare plant, found only on the Channel Islands and for a few yards inland along the southern California shore. Rangers lead educational beach walks, and there are talks on Chumash Indian life at El Matador.

A little farther south, at 31300 PCH, is Broad Beach Road and **Broad Beach**. There are no public facilities here, although Broad Beach is a public beach. Private property adjoins the beach, and you're in danger of trespassing. This is recommended for a dip only if you're virtually on fire—not a likely condition along the coast. Nearly every home on Broad Beach Road is occupied by someone rich and/or famous.

You can "do" all of these beaches in a relatively short time, or you can take all day. As forewarned, in the afternoon, especially the late afternoon, the traffic can become a bother, so it's best to start early and get to Broad Beach by noon. The terrain you'll have covered is fairly hilly, so don't let the low mileage fool you; if you've been pedaling hard between beaches, you'll have had a good workout. The next ride will cover the stretch of PCH from Trancas Canyon to Topanga.

You've now had a first look at Marvelous Malibu, with an emphasis on the beaches north of Malibu proper. The first Marvelous Malibu ride started and ended at the intersection Topanga Canyon Road and PCH, traveled north along PCH's undistinguished right (east) side and, after making a U-turn at Mulholland Highway, took a detailed look at the wonders on the scenic west side. This ride, Another View of Marvelous Malibu, starts at Topanga Canyon Road and PCH, goes up to Trancas Canyon, where the first ride ended, and returns to

Topanga Canyon while soaking in the western views between Trancas and Topanga. (The first step is to park your car on Topanga Canyon in such a way that it's facing the direction you want to go upon your return from the ride. Making a U-turn when you get back to the car will be about as challenging as driving gets; in fact, I can almost guarantee a few gray hairs—assuming you survive.)

Malibu is so famous, it doesn't really need elaboration, but here goes anyway. It's a very recently incorporated area of Los Angeles County stretching 27 miles, from the Pacific Palisades to the Ventura County line. The area has been inhabited for about 7,000 years until recently by Chumash and Gabrielino Indians. In 1887 Frederick and May Rindge purchased the land and commenced a lengthy battle with the state to prevent construction of what is now PCH (State Route 1). May Rindge continued the battle after her husband's death and went so far as to build a private pier and railroad to exclude the Southern Pacific; this crusty lady actually dynamited Southern Pacific construction facilities. She finally lost the battle, and the state completed Roosevelt Highway, now known as Pacific Coast Highway, in 1929. Rindge threw in the towel and began leasing and later selling land to a host of famous people. Various state and county agencies have been reacquiring land since the sixties, and the shore is now a patchwork of public and private property.

Malibu has been an incorporated city since the late 1980s, and although its population has among the highest average incomes in the nation, the city was, and may still be, near bankruptcy. This strange state of affairs is due to Malibu's ongoing war with Mother Nature, who's coming out on top. Almost every year since its incorporation, Malibu has endured some kind of devastating natural phenomenon, including fires, floods, and earthquakes. The fires, in particular, have been damaging because they rob the canyons named above of vegetation that absorbs moisture and anchors canyon soil; moisture in the form of torrential rains then roars down the canyons, across PCH and into the Pacific. The floods take with them everything in their path, and the sodden cliffs on the east side of PCH collapse. Houses, including multimillion-dollar mansions perched at the edge of the cliffs, are reduced to matchsticks and rubble and are washed across PCH. Hapless homeowners on the west side of PCH are inundated with Mercedes-sized boulders and occasionally one of the formerly clifftop homes. Every now and then, the homeowners on the ocean side of the road are pounded by huge waves that demolish property on the not-so-pacific Pacific. Fighting fires and cleaning up after floods has kept the City of Malibu financially strapped.

A mile south of Broad Beach, at 30000 PCH, is **Trancas Canyon,** and diagonally across the road is **Zuma County Beach,** 105 acres of white sand and surf that attracts people from all over the globe. The swimming there is only fair, as there are moderate riptides and the water never really gets very warm. It is, nevertheless, a very popular beach, second only to Santa Monica.

Trancas has a very good supermarket, as mentioned in the previous ride, and making the necessary left turn onto Trancas Canyon Road isn't nearly as daunting as you'd think. Neither is making the necessary left turn back onto PCH, since there's a very obliging traffic light at the intersection.

Zuma Beach has a permanent surfing area. There are at least two good rest rooms and shower facilities a few feet off PCH. There are also the usual hot dog stands for refreshments. This being California, the hot dog stands also dispense such things as pizza and falafel. Beach conditions and other information can be had by calling (310) 457–9891. Zuma is not recommended as more than a pit stop on this ride because of the crowds and traffic. Also, as you ride by, watch out for surfboarders: They generally walk parallel to the road with their big boards held horizontally under one arm. If the surfboarder turns right, you could run smack into the board, spinning the board and its owner around to whack you in the back, a situation that's much funnier to a spectator than to a participant.

Immediately after Zuma is a half-mile hill of moderate, but unwelcome, proportions. Next, you'll come to **Point Dume State Beach** (pronounced "doom" or "doomay" and named after Father Dumetz of Mission San Buenaventura). The point itself is a mass of basaltic lava. The state beach is a rocky shoreline with a thirty-four-acre sandy beach west of the rocks. There are good tide pools and good swimming as well as surfing here. Migrating whales can be seen in the winter months, and just a few weeks before writing this I saw a pod of porpoises playing in the water here. Point Dume can be seen on a clear day from Santa Monica; in fact, it's the northernmost point of land that can be seen from Santa Monica's palisades, so it's something of a landmark. It's also mentioned from time to time in weather reports, as though the climate makes an abrupt change there. It may, in fact, do that, but I've never witnessed anything of the sort.

Paradise Cove is just off the road at 28128 PCH, Malibu. Its claim to fame is that it was the location of *The Rockford Files*. The cove is privately owned but is open to the public for a fee. It has a restaurant, a pier, nice sand, and rest rooms. It is the site of California's first artificial reef, formed in 1958 when the Department of Fish and Game sank twenty old cars. The Coastal Commission reports that the reef has now deteriorated.

Escondido Beach (*escondido* means "hidden" in Spanish) is located at 27200 PCH, Malibu, at the mouth of Escondido Creek, and is accessible by a stairway. While it certainly has its charms, it's not a recommended stop, as it has no facilities. Likewise, **Corral State Beach**, located between Corral Canyon and Solstice Canyon on PCH, is not a bad spot for a quick dip and/or a picnic. Corral State Beach is a well-known grunion spawning beach, and rumor has it that offshore fishing is excellent.

Malibu Creek State Park is located at 28754 PCH, Malibu. The state park actually encompasses more than 5,000 acres of woodland and mountains on the inland side of PCH. The beach itself is marked by the flow of Malibu Creek into the Pacific. Steelhead trout were spotted in the creek in 1992 for the first time in many years, denoting, it is said, the cleanup of the creek water and the ocean water. Malibu Creek State Park could be the subject of a whole ride in itself, although there isn't much pavement within its boundaries.

Malibu Lagoon State Beach is located at the intersection of Cross Creek Road at the north end of Malibu Colony. It's a 166-acre area that includes **Malibu Bluffs**, **Malibu Lagoon**, the **Malibu Lagoon Museum**, and the **Malibu Pier**, as well as a 35-acre sandy beach. The lagoon is brackish and is a fun wading spot, accessible (barely) by walking your bike. The museum and pier are best passed up by bike, but do take note of them for a later, motorized, visit. After seeing the weekend traffic, you'll probably want to postpone your motorized visit until after Labor Day, but do keep the area in mind, because it's truly beautiful, historic, and fascinating. Incidentally, in late September and October the shrubs around Malibu Creek are filled with monarch butterflies, which are worth seeing, too. Near the pier are numerous fast-food and other food emporiums, in case you missed the picnicking opportunities. A left turn into the fast-food places can be made, if you're cautious—and lucky. A bit south of the pier, at 22548 PCH, is the **Zonker Harris Accessway**, the first public accessway to the beach. Named after the sun-worshiping "Doonesbury" character, it was opened in 1980.

The last beach before Topanga Canyon and your car is **Las Tunas State Beach**. *Tuna* means "prickly pear" in Spanish, and the beach is, in fact, named for the prickly pears growing in profusion along the shore. This is also not a recommended stopping point, because of the heavy traffic. Besides, by now you're probably anxious to get into the air-conditioned comfort of your car.

For Further Information

Chumash Indian life at El Matador (818) 888–3440
Corral State Beach (grunion) (310) 457–9891
Malibu Creek State Park (818) 880–0350
Robert H. Meyer Memorial Beaches (818) 880–0350
Zuma Beach (310) 457–9891

Getting There

Take the I–10 (Santa Monica) Freeway to its west end, where it becomes Pacific Coast Highway (PCH). Take PCH north to Topanga Canyon Road (SR–27). Turn right on Topanga Canyon Road, and find a parking place.

Alternatively, take the U–101 (Ventura) Freeway to Topanga Canyon Boulevard (SR–27) South, which is at the western edge of the San Fernando Valley. In about 11 miles, just before reaching PCH and the Pacific Ocean, find a parking place.

Marilyn Monroe Memorial Tour

Location:	Eastern San Fernando Valley
Mileage:	22
Approximate pedaling time:	2 hours
Terrain:	Flat
Traffic:	Light to moderate; a couple of hairy intersections
Things to see:	All the old haunts of Marilyn Monroe's prefame life

And now, for something completely different. Enough of this stuff about seeking out clean, cool air. Enough about good hills and rest stops. Enough about great scenery and the health benefits of getting there. Marilyn Monroe would be celebrating her seventy-something birthday about now, and in recognition of the fact that nothing has ever connected her with bicycling, not even one cheesecake photo, we're going to ride through her old haunts. Marilyn was, as very few people know, one of the original "Valley Girls," maybe even the quintessential Valley Girl. Nothing has ever linked Valley Girls with bicycling either, so we have a really clean slate.

Of course, things have changed in the Valley since Marilyn was here. After all, she lived at 14743 Archwood Street in 1937. That was a long time ago by anyone's standards, and by the standard of Valley history, it's in nearly the same class as the conversion of the Indians at the Mission San Fernando. In all candor, if Marilyn were still with us, she probably wouldn't be caught dead in the Valley, although lots of the rich and famous do live there. But in 1937 she was only eleven and probably had little to say about it. Actually, according to the *Daily News*, which ran a feature on her in 1987 on the twenty-fifth anniversary of her passing, Marilyn loved the Valley.

I first saw the Valley in 1959, from the vantage point of Mulhol-

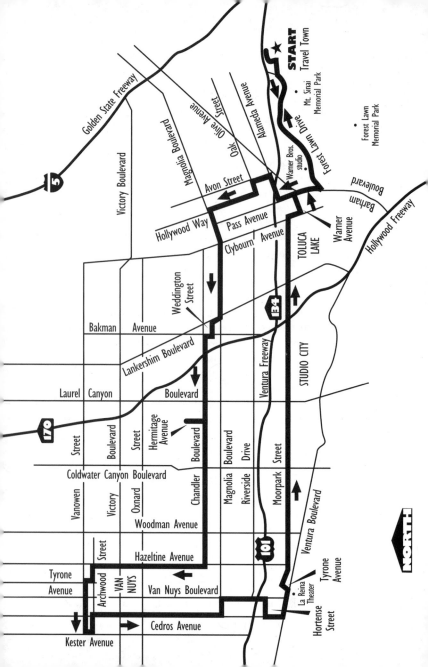

DIREC-TIONS at a glance

0.0	Straight out of Travel Town parking lot onto unmarked road
0.2	Left at stop sign onto Forest Lawn Drive
2.2	Right onto Barham Boulevard
2.6	Bear left at billboard onto Pass Avenue
2.9	Right onto Alameda Avenue
3.3	Left onto Avon Street
3.5	Left onto Oak Street
3.7	Right onto Hollywood Way
4.5	Left onto Magnolia Boulevard
6.2	Right onto Lankershim Boulevard
6.4	Left onto Weddington Street
6.5	Left onto Bakman Avenue
6.6	U-turn on Bakman Avenue
6.8	Left onto Chandler Boulevard
8.2	Right onto Hermitage Avenue
8.3	U-turn on Hermitage
8.4	Right onto Chandler Boulevard
10.7	Right onto Hazeltine Avenue
12.5	Left onto Archwood Street
12.7	Right onto Tyrone Avenue (at T)
12.8	Left onto Vanowen Street
13.6	Left onto Kester Avenue
13.7	Left onto Archwood Street
13.9	Right onto Cedros Avenue
15.9	Left onto Magnolia Boulevard
16.3	Right onto Van Nuys Boulevard
17.0	Right onto Hortense Street
17.2	Left onto Cedros Avenue
17.4	Left onto Ventura Boulevard
17.8	Left onto Tyrone Avenue
17.9	Right onto Moorpark Street
18.6	Right onto Clybourn Avenue
18.8	Left onto Warner Avenue
19.0	Right onto Pass Avenue

land and Sepulveda; the place was pretty much all farmland, with a few residential areas spotted here and there, mostly in the eastern sections. One of the first things any newcomer to the Valley does is climb up to Mulholland Drive, usually in a car, for the view of the Valley on the north and Los Angeles on the south. Marilyn did that a lot, dreaming about becoming famous.

A good starting place is our old friend, Travel Town in Griffith Park. It has plenty of free (and shaded) parking, and it's close to a number of freeways. Go straight out of the parking lot and turn left at the stop sign. In a few minutes you'll pass **Forest Lawn Cemetery**. It is said that Marilyn, who is interred in the cemetery herself, frequently went on outings there, seeking out the resting places of famous movie stars. You can do this, too, but I'd suggest you make a separate trip for it.

After a couple of miles on Forest Lawn Drive, you'll see the **Warner Bros. studio** on the right. When you get to the end of the street, turn right. This is Pass Avenue, or Barham Boulevard, or Olive Avenue, depending on which map you consult. When you get to the corner of the studio's building, where the street bears right, bear left; watch for traffic coming from the right, which is definitely Olive Avenue. As soon as you make the turn, heading north, you'll be on Pass Avenue. After 0.25 mile, turn right on Alameda Avenue. **Sorrentino's Restaurant**, which until 1990 was on the southwest corner of Pass and Riverside, was one of Marilyn's regular lunch spots. Sorrentino's was torn down and is now the Southern California Sony Service Center, with a very elaborate Kinko's copy center sharing the site.

Take the second left onto Avon Street. Marilyn lived there for at least one year, possibly as long as three years. Turn left on Oak Street, right on Hollywood Way, and then left on Magnolia. Much of this area consists of rejuvenated, revitalized, recycled movie studios, and

many of the residents are employed (or wish to be employed) in the burgeoning East Valley–based entertainment industry. Continue on Magnolia to Lankershim Boulevard. Turn right; after 2 short blocks, turn left on Weddington Street. Take your first left on Bakman Avenue. The school on the left is the **Lankershim School.** In 1938 Norma Jean won awards here for track and field and the high jump. She became known, in the Lankershim School at least, as "Norma Jean the jumping bean." Go (back) north on Bakman to Chandler (a left, a right, and a left onto Chandler Boulevard.) Continue on Chandler to the second right after Laurel Canyon. This is **Hermitage Avenue.** Marilyn lived at 5254 for a year with her first husband, Jim Dougherty, a high school sweetheart whom she married when she was sixteen.

Go back to Chandler and continue west to Hazeltine (about 2.3 miles). Note the unused railroad tracks separating the north from the south side of Chandler. These were the tracks of the late lamented Red Cars, which ran until 1960 and provided good rapid transit at a time when nobody was interested in good rapid transit. But I digress. Turn right on Hazeltine, and after about a mile, at the first right after Oxnard Street, you'll see **Bessemer Street.** Marilyn lived near the corner on the north side in 1944. Continue north to the sixth left, past busy Victory Boulevard (about 0.8 mile). Turn left on **Archwood Street.** Go to 14223, one of three houses Marilyn lived in on Archwood Street, all on the north side.

Go to the end of Archwood; take a right onto Tyrone Avenue and then a left onto Vanowen Street. Turn left onto Kester Avenue and take your first left after that. Voila! You're on Archwood again. Marilyn lived at 14743 in 1937 and 14747 in 1943. She moved a lot in 1943, when, incidentally, she packed parachutes at a plant, probably Lockheed, where the Burbank Airport is now located. Legend has it that she was photographed for a wartime women-at-work article under the direction of none other than Ronald Reagan. But I digress again. Continue east on Archwood to the end, and turn right (south) on Cedros Avenue. After 1 block you'll come to **Van Nuys High School.** It was here that she met Jim Dougherty, a nonbicycling jock (a football player, actually) and student president.

Continue south on Cedros a couple of miles to Magnolia; take a left and then your second right onto Van Nuys Boulevard. After crossing under the Ventura Freeway, take your first right onto Hortense Street. It is rumored that Walt Disney got the name for Hortense Horsefly from this street, but in any event, Marilyn Monroe lived in a one-bedroom apartment with a Murphy bed at 4254 **Vista del Monte Avenue**, the first street on the right. Number 4254 is now a new townhouse, but you can use your imagination.

Turn left on Cedros (again) and left on Ventura Boulevard. The **La Reina Theater** is/was at the southeast corner of Cedros and Ventura. I say "is/was" because the exterior of the structure is still standing, preserved as a model of an art deco movie palace. The interior, alas, gave way to 1990s' boutiques without a trace of chewing gum on the floors. It was at this theater that Marilyn saw her first movies and became enamored of the stars and the Hollywood way of life. She was, to say the least, a regular patron of the La Reina, and it was a major influence on her life. And yours. If it weren't for that theater's influence, you might be taking an entirely different bike ride.

Turn left on Tyrone and your first right after that onto Moorpark Street. Moorpark is a relatively painless route back to your car. Stay on Moorpark for 5.7 miles or so, to the very end at the T with Clybourn Avenue. You'll pass right by Bob Hope's house in Toluca Lake, which has nothing to do with Marilyn Monroe, but it's a point of interest anyway. (It's on your right as you pass Arcola Avenue.) Turn right at the end of Moorpark (Clybourn Avenue), and turn left at Warner Avenue. This will take you back to the movie-studio at the confluence of Warner/Pass/Olive. If there is a commuter-discouraging barrier at Warner and Pass/Olive, walk your bike around it. Turn right and then left on Forest Lawn Drive, and you can't miss Travel Town. You'll have covered around 27 flat, urban miles and have seen that in her early years, at least, Marilyn Monroe wasn't so different from anyone else.

Getting There

Travel Town is located at the northeast corner of Griffith Park. From points east and west of Griffith Park, take the SR–134 (Ventura) Freeway to the Victory Boulevard exit. Within 50 feet of the exit is a T intersection with Zoo Drive. Travel Town is to the right. Follow the signs.

From the north or south, take the I–5 (Golden State) Freeway to the Griffith Park/Los Angeles Zoo/Autry Western Heritage Museum exit, and follow the ZOO DRIVE signs north and then west, past the museum to Travel Town.

Beverly Hills

Location:	West of Hollywood; east of West Los Angeles
Mileage:	15 with the tour of homes of the rich and famous; 10 without the homes tour
Approximate pedaling time:	1½ hours for the 15-mile version; 1 hour for the 10-mile version
Terrain:	Flat, with a few gradual grades and (optional) easy hills
Traffic:	Generally light; occasionally heavy
Things to see:	Rodeo Drive and the other posh streets of downtown Beverly Hills; Hansel and Gretel's house; Beverly Hills Hotel; homes of the decidedly rich and fabulously famous; Greystone Mansion; Sunset Strip

It's hard to talk about Beverly Hills without alluding to the homes of famous people. It's more than alluding to them; it's showing off and bragging that you know that Mr. and Mrs. Stupendously Famous live right in that there mansion. In point of fact, Beverly Hills, and its even wealthier neighbor Bel-Air, are loaded with people who are, well, loaded. Many are, in addition, famous. But they move around a lot, so the mansion of a famous person today may be the home of someone who is merely rich tomorrow. (In spite of this, I will point out where a few famous folks *used* to live; that's a lot safer from the accuracy angle, and more considerate from the privacy angle, than pointing out where certain famous people live at this writing.)

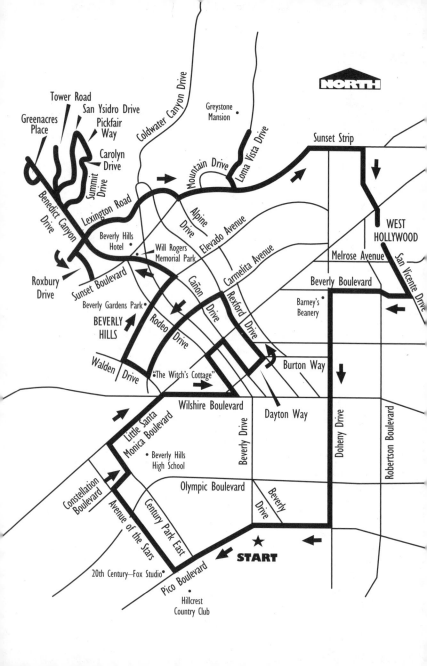

DIRECTIONS at a glance

0.0 North onto Avenue of the Stars into Century City
0.6 Right onto Constellation Boulevard
0.8 Left onto Century Park East
1.0 Right onto Little Santa Monica Boulevard (at the T)
1.3 Right onto Wilshire Boulevard
1.8 Left onto Rodeo Drive
2.1 Right onto Little Santa Monica Boulevard
2.2 Right onto Cañon Drive
2.4 Left onto Dayton Way
2.5 Left onto Rexford Drive (at the T)
2.8 Left onto Carmelita Avenue
3.5 Right onto Walden Drive (Hansel and Gretel House is on the southeast corner of Carmelita and Walden)
3.7 Right onto Elevado Avenue
4.3 Left onto Cañon Drive

For Riders Skipping House Tour
4.6 Right onto Sunset Boulevard

For Riders Doing House Tour
4.6 Cañon becomes Benedict Canyon Drive (at Sunset Boulevard)
4.9 Left onto Lexington Road
5.0 Left onto Roxbury Drive
5.2 U-turn on Roxbury Drive
5.4 Right onto Lexington Road
5.5 Left onto Benedict Canyon Drive
5.7 Right onto Summit Drive
6.2 Left onto Carolyn Drive
6.3 Left onto Pickfair Way
6.5 Left onto San Ysidro Drive (at the T)
6.9 Right onto Tower Road
7.0 U-turn on Tower Road
7.1 Cross San Ysidro Drive

7.2	Right onto Benedict Canyon Drive
7.5	Left onto Greenacres Place (Harold Lloyd's driveway); immediate U-turn
8.0	Left onto Lexington Road
8.4	Right onto Alpine Drive (at the T)
8.5	Left onto Sunset Boulevard
8.8	Left onto Mountain Drive
8.9	Right onto Loma Vista Drive
9.2	Left into Greystone Park (Doheny mansion) driveway
9.5	Left onto Loma Vista Drive
9.6	Right onto Mountain Drive
9.9	Left onto Sunset Strip

(Mileages on left are for those who skipped famous-homes tour.)

(5.5) 10.2	Sunset Boulevard becomes Sunset Strip— leave Beverly Hills
(5.8) 10.5	Right onto San Boulevard
(7.3) 12.0	Right onto Beverly Boulevard
(7.8) 12.5	Left onto Doheny Drive
(9.2) 13.9	Right onto Pico Boulevard
(10.1) 14.8	End of ride at Avenue of the Stars

The thing that impresses out-of-towners most about Beverly Hills is not the sheer wealth that resides there but the size of the city—its hundreds and hundreds of acres (3,647 to be exact) of mansions. The "poor" section of Beverly Hills is actually middle class and is exceedingly small relative to the section that's on the right side of the tracks. It is said that 90 percent of all the Rolls Royces sold in the United States are garaged in Beverly Hills. Another 8 percent are probably in neighboring Bel-Air. No matter—this is a unique city that has to be seen to be believed.

It was not always so. At the end of the nineteenth century, what is now Beverly Hills was bean fields—hundreds and hundreds of acres of beans. The population was comprised of working-class Mexican laborers, except for one Chinese family named Seng that cultivated vegetables in "Chinaman Canyon," near what is now Schuyler Road. Then oil was discovered, just east of present-day Beverly Hills, and Burton Green, Charles Canfield, and Max Whittier bought Rancho Rodeo de las Aguas. Their interest wasn't in beans but in oil, and in 1905 they drilled about thirty wells. The only ones to produce significant amounts of black gold were a couple of wells in the extreme southern section of the property, near where Twentieth Century–Fox stands today.

The purchase price of $670,000 was too steep for bean farming, and oil development was out, so the triumvirate did the only natural thing left in California: They became real estate developers. The original boundaries of Beverly Hills were Whittier Drive on the west, Doheny Drive on the east, Wilshire Boulevard on the south, and Sunset Boulevard on the north. A trolley, whose tracks ran along Santa Monica Boulevard until 1989, connected the new development with Los Angeles to the east and Santa Monica and Venice to the west. The city was named for Beverly Farms, Massachusetts, because Burton Green, it is said, read that William Howard Taft had visited Beverly Farms, and Green was Taft's number-one admirer.

One of the area's five original model homes still exists at 515 North Cañon Drive. Another thing that sets Beverly Hills apart from its rivals is that the parkway strip of each and every street is planted with trees, the same species on both sides of each street for its entire length. What is more, this urban forest, or arboretum, is maintained and manicured, creating an unmatched ambience.

There is no "best" place to start a tour of Beverly Hills because of city-wide parking restrictions, so I'll recommend a workable one. Start on a side street near the corner of Pico Boulevard and Avenue of the Stars.

Just west of the intersection is the southern entrance to the **Twentieth Century–Fox Studio**. This studio has been in financial difficulty off and on, mostly on, since the making of *Cleopatra* almost bankrupted the company in 1963. As a result of that fiasco, the studio formed a joint venture with ALCOA (Aluminum Company of America) that involved selling off the lion's share of the back lot and establishing **Century City.** In a few moments you will turn north (the only way possible) on Avenue of the Stars and tour Century City.

But first, take a look toward the south. There you'll find the **Hill-crest Country Club.** For many years Groucho Marx petitioned to join the prestigious club, always to be turned down. When the board of directors finally agreed to admit Groucho, he replied, "I wouldn't belong to any club that would have someone like me as a member."

Proceed north on Avenue of the Stars. For 0.4 mile the Twentieth Century–Fox Studio will be on your left (note the oil wells); on the right you'll pass some luxurious apartment houses. A couple of blocks east is Beverly Hills High School, the only public school in the nation with its very own oil well, income from which goes a long way toward providing certain amenities that are unheard of in oil-less educational institutions. Soon after you cross over Olympic Boulevard, you'll come to the still-spectacular **Century Plaza Hotel** on the left and the **ABC Entertainment Center** on the right. The skyscrapers here will look familiar. They've been in the news and have been featured on innumerable television shows and movies. (*Die Hard* with Bruce Willis was filmed at the **Fox Plaza Building** at 2121 Avenue of the Stars.) It is said that there are more lawyers in these buildings than in all of the United States combined west of the Mississippi.

After 0.6 mile from the start on Avenue of the Stars, turn right on Constellation Boulevard. After about 0.2 mile, take your first left onto Century Park East. Another 0.2 mile will put you at a T intersection with Little Santa Monica Boulevard; turn right. (Big Santa Monica Boulevard is a few feet farther north and has horrendous traffic; Little Santa Monica Boulevard is a quiet country lane by comparison.) A couple of tenths of a mile along on the right side is the **Friars Club**, the exclusive haunt of the performing part of the entertainment industry.

After about 0.3 mile from the turn onto Little Santa Monica Boulevard, turn right on **Wilshire Boulevard.** The famous stores and other buildings along this section of the street are too numerous to list here. To your right (south) are several acres of the poorer section of town—actually, not poorer, just less prestigious. At the corner of Rodeo Drive and Wilshire, along Wilshire, you will see the **Beverly Wilshire Hotel, Ambercrombie & Fitch** (at 9424), **Tiffany** (at 9502),

Bonwit Teller (at 9536), **Saks Fifth Avenue** (at 9600), **I. Magnin** (at 9634), and **Neiman-Marcus** (at 9700). The Beverly Wilshire Hotel, incidentally, is where much of *Pretty Woman* was filmed, and Julia Roberts is reported to be a regular in the café to this day. You will feel quite out of place in bike clothing, however, so don't even think about stopping there for a cup of coffee and some celebrity watching.

Turn left after 0.5 mile onto **Rodeo Drive**. In some circles this is the most talked-about street in America. It, too, changes with the times as points of interest come and go, but some names, probably destined to be around a while longer, jump out at you—e.g., **Giorgio** (at 273), **Van Cleef & Arpels** (at 300), **Hermes** (at 343), **Gucci** (at 347), and **Cartier** (at 372). After 0.25 mile of unsurpassed luxury, turn right at Little Santa Monica Boulevard. Take your first right (after about 0.1 mile); this will put you on Cañon Drive (south-bound). Take it 2 blocks (0.2 mile) to Dayton Way, where you turn left. Take Dayton Way 2 blocks (0.1 mile) to its end at a T intersection with Rexford Drive. Turn left on Rexford, and continue across Little and regular Santa Monica boulevards.

Before you cross the Santa Monicas, you will see the famous **Beverly Hills Post Office**, zip code 90210. It is probably the only post office in the United States with valet parking. The equally famous **City Hall** is on the right, sporting its ornate dome, as is the newly refurbished **Public Library**, which is well worth a visit. City Hall also houses the (in)famous Beverly Hills Police Department. The Hills are alive with the sound of traffic tickets being written. There seems to be a Beverly Hills police car everywhere. This is almost certainly the most heavily patrolled town in America, and the police have a reputation for being a bit hardnosed. The late Zsa Zsa Gabor's run-in with Beverly Hills' finest comes to mind.

Immediately after you cross the Santa Monicas, you will see **Beverly Gardens Park** stretching into the distance east and west of you. This park contains an extraordinary display of California botany. A side trip the length of the park is recommended. Placed here and there on temporary exhibit are the works of modern sculptors. These have been controversial, from time to time, though when you visit, the artworks may be mundane. Make no mistake, though: If you see a

rusted-out 1955 pink Cadillac sticking grill-first into the ground, this is not a derelict car; it's a work of art. The city council says so.

Take your first left (after 0.25 mile) onto Carmelita Avenue. Ride on Carmelita for 0.7 mile to Walden Drive. As you cross Bedford Drive, a block down (south) is **Clara Bow's home** (at 515 Bedford). (Clara Bow was before even my time, but she turned twenties' Hollywood upside down as the "it" girl. She is reported to have given "it," or showed "it," or demonstrated "it" to dozens of Hollywood's best-known men in the house at 515 Bedford.)

On the southeast corner of Carmelita and Walden, you will see the most unusual house in all of Beverly Hills—and that's saying something. It's known as "**The Witch's Cottage**" or "**Hansel & Gretel's House**," depending on whom you talk to. Either way, it's something out of Grimm. One story says that it's actually the original headquarters of the Irvin Willat Studio in Culver City, moved to its present site in 1931. It must have been a small and impractical headquarters, and the current residents admitted in a newspaper article published a few years ago, that it's a small and impractical house. It was put on the market at the height of the Los Angeles real estate boom of the 1980s for at $2.9 million, but it didn't sell, proving that something is only worth what someone is willing to pay for it. At this writing in late 1997, the house is again on the market, this time for $1.4 million, by the second owners who have occupied it continuously for more than thirty years.

The other story is that it was built in the mid-twenties as a set for a silent version of Hansel and Gretel, and it was moved to the present site for its present use. This explanation makes a little more sense, because the house makes a better witch's house than office. I chatted with one of the owners of the house (who was as pleasant as could be and was certainly no witch) several years ago during a gawking break. She told me that while they are inured to people staring at the property and taking pictures of it, it is just plain impolite, and legally, it is trespassing to hop the fence for a closer look or for a snapshot or for any other reason. In short, watch your manners and leave these people be.

Turn right on Walden and ride 0.2 mile to Elevado Avenue; turn right. After 0.6 mile on Elevado, turn left on Cañon Drive. Cañon Drive is quintessential Beverly Hills, with 10,000-square-foot mansions lining the street, which has 100-foot-high California Sand Palms and 60-foot Mexican Sand Palms alternating in the parkways.

Ride 0.25 mile to an utterly confusing six-way intersection of Cañon, Beverly, and Lomitas. Dead ahead is a perfectly wonderful park, **Will Rogers Memorial Park**, an equilateral triangle, with Cañon Drive along its left (west) side, Beverly Drive forming its right side, and unseen Sunset Boulevard along its northern edge. From this vantage point, you can see the **Beverly Hills Hotel**.

The Beverly Hills Hotel was built in 1913 amidst the bean fields. It has 350 rooms, including 20 luxurious bungalows, where the entertainment industry crowd goes to get away from it all or to make deals. The hotel's twelve acres of manicured gardens are, well, indescribable. The hotel is also the site of the world-famous **Polo Lounge**, where, believe it or not, ordinary folks can have a great, though somewhat pricey, lunch. And yes, you *will* see celebrities there. Bike-clothed clientele are probably discouraged, and it is questionable what the reaction of the valet parking attendants would be if you were to roll up to the main entrance. (The hotel, which is now owned by the Sultan of Brunei, was reopened in 1997 after a several-hundred-million-dollar renovation.)

Howard Hughes lived at the hotel in his prerecluse days, as did Marilyn Monroe. In fact, when Marilyn was fired for habitually being late on the set, it was at the Beverly Hills Hotel that she overslept. It was at this hotel that Elizabeth Taylor and Richard Burton waged their well-publicized and vociferous intramarital war, and it was in the hotel's pool that Esther Williams glided through the water to fame. The *L.A. Times* ran a possibly apocryphal story that when the wake for hard-drinking John Barrymore was held at the ballroom, equally hard-drinking Errol Flynn snatched Barrymore's body from the mortuary and brought it to the hotel so that Barrymore could be present at his own farewell party.

Cross Sunset Boulevard on Cañon Drive (which passes to the *left* of the park). The distance from the southern point of the park to Sunset is 0.1 mile.

This next section of the ride is for those who want to visit the former homes of some of the rich and famous. There are a couple of hilly sections that come up after the homes on Lexington Road. To avoid these and still get your socks knocked off by some sights, turn right on Sunset Boulevard. The hill-climbing sightseers will rejoin the ride on Sunset Boulevard in a little while. For those heading toward the homes of famous people, I believe that all have died or otherwise moved from these addresses; nevertheless, it can be fun to visit them.

Cañon Drive becomes Benedict Canyon Drive at Sunset Boulevard. Turn left on Lexington Road, and take your first left (after about 0.1 mile) onto Roxbury Drive. In order, from the house closest to Lexington, you'll pass:

1023	Agnes Moorhead	1002	Jack Benny
1020	Ira Gershwin	1000	Lucille Ball
1004	Peter Falk	918	James Stewart

Make a U-turn and go back to Benedict Canyon (about 0.25 mile).

The next few points of interest involve some hills, but they're doable, especially since you have a mission: to see some *really* spectacular and famous places. Turn left and proceed one block (0.25 mile) to Summit Drive, where you will make a right. **Tom Mix** lived at 1018 in the twenties. He was an initialer. He put his initials on everything. Look closely and you'll see *T.M.* in the mortar and cement everywhere—the gates, the lintel, the driveway. I understand that the interior of the house is bizarre. For example, it is said that when Mix's horse, Tony, went to the big corral in the sky, T.M. converted the tail into a bellpull. There were two parlors, one in movie-cowboy style for T.M., and one for the fourth Mrs. Mix, a former cowgirl movie actress, in pseudo–Louis XVI style.

At 1033 Summit Drive is **Ronald Colman's** former home, one he bought from **Corinne Griffith** in the mid-thirties. Its Tudor style fits nicely with the veddy British Colman's persona. He "dated" actress **Benita Hume**, who owned the house directly behind his. It is said that during the courtship he installed a door in the back wall, so that they could visit each other without being observed. In 1938 Hume married Colman, and she moved in, thereby lessening the wear and tear on the rear entrance.

At 1085 Summit Drive is **Charlie Chaplin's** 1923 home. It's pretty much hidden from view by more than seventy years of landscaping. It is said that Chaplin was very frugal—some would say cheap. To save money on construction, he reportedly used studio craftsmen to construct many parts of the home. Studio workers, accustomed to building sets that have to look good on camera but that only have to last sixty days or so, did their usual work, and neighbors dubbed the place "Breakaway House." **George Hamilton** bought the place, presumably reinforced, in 1982, and put the *H* on the gate.

At 1143 Summit Drive is the former **Pickfair**, legendary home of **Mary Pickford** and **Douglas Fairbanks, Sr.** In the twenties and thirties, sitting on fourteen luxuriously landscaped acres and occupied by the nation's favorite couple, it was arguably the most famous home in America. If you can name a famous personage of the twenties, the odds are better than even that he or she stayed at least overnight at Pickfair. There are stories of the magic couple being duped into inviting fakes to spend the night—a secretary from Santa Monica, for example, who presented herself as Princess Romanoff. Behind all this glamour, however, was the fact that Doug was a womanizer and Mary, well, Mary liked to have a drink, or two, or three, or four. By the mid-thirties their careers were in the dumper, and they were divorced in 1936. Mary subsequently married actor Buddy Rogers, who moved into Pickfair. By the time Mary died in 1979, all but three acres had been sold off to developers, and **Jerry Buss**, owner of the Los Angeles Lakers, the Los Angeles Kings, and the Forum, moved in. Buss made extensive changes to the structure, fell upon hard times, and sold the joint in 1990. The new owners, **Pia Zadora** and her husband, had it torn down, and Pickfair was replaced by a mansion befitting 1990s New Money.

You have traveled 0.5 mile on Summit Drive. Turn left on Carolyn Drive; go 0.1 mile to a left turn on Pickfair Way. Go 0.2 mile to a T intersection with San Ysidro Drive. Turn left again. At 1155 San Ysidro Drive is the former home of **Fred Astaire**, who lived there from the early thirties until his death in 1990. When you come to Tower Road, after 0.4 mile, turn right. If you make a short detour to the right, you will see **Juliet Prowse**'s abode at 1136 Tower Road,

Artur Rubinstein's place at 1139, and Spencer Tracy's former home at 1158. Make a U-turn and backtrack across San Ysidro Drive to Benedict Canyon Drive, where you turn left. The total detour to Spencer Tracy's home to the left turn onto Benedict Canyon Drive is under a quarter of a mile.

When you get to Benedict Canyon Road (0.1 mile), you'll have to make a Management Decision. If you turn right in 0.8 mile, you'll come to Cielo Drive. Almost immediately on the left is 10050 Cielo, where the **Charles Manson** "family" murdered Sharon Tate, Jay Sebring, Voytek Frykowski, and Abigail Folger in 1969. Tate was married to **Roman Polanski** at the time. He has since left the country, and presumably the house, and has become involved in legal difficulties, a description of which would give this book an "X" rating (now NC-17, which somehow doesn't sound quite as bad).

You can continue up Cielo Drive to Bella Drive to Falcon Lair at 1436, home of **Rudolph Valentino**. This is a rather tough and unrewarding climb, though, so I recommend that you coast back down to Benedict Canyon Road. Turn right on Benedict Canyon, and about 0.3 mile after the turn, you'll come to Greenacres Place. A right turn there will put you on a driveway leading up to the massive gates of an Italian Renaissance–style mansion: **Greenacres**, former home of **Harold Lloyd**. Lloyd occupied the place beginning in 1928. It is said that his taste was exquisite and that the twenty acres of surrounding land were beautifully landscaped and included a nine-hole golf course. **Jack Warner**, of Warner Bros. fame, had the house next door. Warner's property also included a nine-hole golf course, and it is said that from time to time, Warner and Lloyd would put up a temporary bridge over their shared fence, so that they could play a full eighteen holes. Lloyd died in 1971. In 1990 his estate was purchased by entertainment mogul David Geffen for $47.5 million. This was the highest price ever paid for a private residence in the United States until 1998 when Thunderbird Lodge was purchased in Lake Tahoe for $50 million.

Continue down Benedict Canyon Road 0.5 mile to Lexington Road, and turn left. This is still a decidedly high-rent district! After 0.4 mile on a pine tree–shaded, gently rolling, curved street, Lexington ends at a T intersection with Alpine Drive. Turn right on Alpine and continue about 0.1 mile to **Sunset Boulevard**; turn left.

It has been said that Sunset Boulevard is the quintessential street of Los Angeles, stretching 27 miles from downtown to the ocean. It traverses a broad spectrum of terrains and cultures, from the downright grubby, to the decidedly strange (Sunset Strip), to the audaciously wealthy. This part, in Beverly Hills, is decidedly the latter. The streets branching off to the right (south) present mile after mile of the plain wealthy, while on the left are immense estates that make the housing on the south look like so many cracker boxes—giant, economy-size cracker boxes, but unimpressive, nevertheless.

If you'd like an interesting detour, 0.3 mile after turning onto Sunset Boulevard, turn left onto Mountain Drive. After 0.1 mile take your first right onto Loma Vista Drive. Cross Doheny Road; in 0.25 mile you'll come to **Greystone Park** on the left. Edward Laurence Doheny, Sr., was an Angeleno who became fabulously wealthy in the oil biz. His wells, visited on Ride 5, were among the first in Los Angeles. In the twenties Doheny became embroiled in the Teapot Dome scandal that rocked the nation. (It seems that Albert Fall, Secretary of the Interior, took an itsy-bitsy bribe, a mere $100,000, to lease U.S. government land in the Elk Hills, 90 miles north of Los Angeles, to Doheny for oil drilling.) Doheny built Greystone at a cost of $4,000,000 in 1928, when a buck was a buck. In fact, the $4,000,000 bought a 46,500-square-foot, 55-room, steel-framed "cottage," sheathed in reinforced concrete; even the roof is concrete. The entire structure is faced in gray Arizona stone, and the roof is veneered with slate, furthering its grayness. It sits on sixteen acres of gorgeously landscaped land and is probably the most grandiose home, other than Hearst's San Simeon, west of the Hudson. The grounds are open to the public, although you'll have to walk your bike. The house is opened periodically for tours. Inquire at the gate.

Retrace your steps and turn left (east) on Sunset Boulevard. About 0.3 mile from the turn onto Sunset, you'll come to the famous sign that simply reads BEVERLY HILLS. It's facing the other way, because you're exiting Beverly Hills, but you'll recognize it anyway. Actually, there are several of these signs, but this one is *the* one on Sunset Boulevard. Immediately afterward, the street changes character completely, and you know you ain't in Beverly Hills anymore.

You're now on "**Sunset Strip**." Sunset Strip is actually still Sunset Boulevard, but it is a narrow strip of land the width of the street and the buildings on either side of it that is not part of any city. In legal parlance, it's unincorporated and therefore not subject to the city laws of Los Angeles up the hills on the left (north) or West Hollywood down the hills on the right. The strip is patrolled by the Los Angeles County sheriff, and it is under county jurisdiction. It is festooned with garish billboards touting recording stars and wannabe stars. It is figuratively Hollywood. In the "good old days," it was home to Ciro's and several other nightclubs; in the sixties it was Hippie Heaven and home to the Whisky-A-Go-Go. 77 *Sunset Strip*, a seventies TV show, featured the façade of Dino's Restaurant. Now-defunct Dino's, in turn, featured Dean Martin's caricature in neon, and Kookie Burns, forever combing his hair, was the TV show's parking attendant. The strip isn't what it used to be, and although you know that you're not in Beverly Hills, Los Angeles, or Kansas, for that matter, you're also not on the strip of the glamorous forties and fifties, the outrageous sixties, or the exciting seventies. You're on the merely different strip of the eighties and nineties. To be sure, the Tower Records store is still a twenty-four-hour hub of offbeat activity, and at this writing, the Playboy logo is still on 9000 Sunset Boulevard, but it isn't the same. At #9229 is Bar One, a super-exclusive private club with a big-shot, entertainment-industry, members-only guest list and no sign on the door. And at #9015 is the Rainbow Bar and Grill, where John Belushi ate his last supper, a bowl of lentil soup. A block after San Vicente, at the corner of Horn Avenue, is Wolfgang Puck's restaurant, Spago.

Approximately 0.3 mile after leaving Beverly Hills and entering Sunset Strip, turn right (south) on San Vicente Boulevard. Make sure your brakes are in good order; it's a *steep* downhill. After 0.4 mile you'll cross Santa Monica Boulevard. Immediately after crossing you'll see the **Pacific Design Center** on your left. Dubbed "The Blue Whale," this is a striking building sheathed in an almost fluorescent royal-blue tile. Within its walls are many, if not all, of Los Angeles furniture wholesalers. Good furniture and accessories. Bad furniture and accessories. If you own a stick of furniture in Los Angeles, its wholesale relatives were displayed here. Directly opposite the Blue Whale are **West Hollywood Park** and **the Public Library**, nice enough resting spots, but for a real rest and experience, continue onward for a few minutes.

After 1.0 mile on San Vicente, you'll cross **Melrose Avenue** and Santa Monica Boulevard at a wide and confusing intersection. Melrose has become a mecca for shoppers who want to pay extra for their possessions. Very artsy stuff can be had along Melrose's uninspiring store-lined curbs for retail plus 10 or 20 percent. While there are some good galleries and boutiques along this up-and-coming street, there are also more phonies than in most of the boardrooms of Hollywood. Nevertheless, if you've heard of Melrose, and you want to soak up some of its atmosphere, take a short detour to the left, and enjoy. (At #8585 is **The Bohdi Tree**, a bookstore, where Shirley MacLaine discovered in the early eighties that she'd been someone or everyone else at one time or another.)

Immediately on the right at the intersection of Santa Monica Boulevard, at #8447, to be exact, is the world-famous **Barney's Beanery**. It's an old dump, prominently and justifiably featured in any compendium of Los Angeles dives. Its walls are covered with license plates from around the country; it has pool tables with Tiffany shades; it has poor lighting and questionable service. But it also has great chili, burgers, fries, and about 6 million brands of beer. A stop is mandatory, even if you don't buy a Barney's Beanery T-shirt.

Continue down San Vicente to Beverly Boulevard (another 0.5 mile or so) and turn right. Stay on Beverly Boulevard 0.5 mile to Doheny Drive; turn left. You'll be on Doheny Drive for 1.4 miles, during which you'll cross such famous thoroughfares as Santa Monica Boulevard, Wilshire Boulevard, and Olympic Boulevard. You'll be surrounded by very expensive apartment houses, though Doheny will seem unimpressive after the luxury you've been immersed in all day. Beverly Hills is on the right and West Hollywood is on the left.

Pico Boulevard, where you turn right (west), is even less impressive. It's one of the older streets in town, although most of the buildings date back only twenty years or so. Near the corner of Peerless Place is the **Simon Wiesenthal Center and Museum**, which commemorates the murder of 6,000,000 Jews by the Nazis during World War II.

After 0.9 mile on Pico Boulevard, you will come to the Avenue of the Stars, where you started out 15 miles ago. If you don't want to re-visit several of these places by car, I'll eat my helmet on the hard-shell without condiments!

For Further Information
~~~~~~~~~~

Barney's Beanery (213) 654–2287

Getting There
~~~~~~~~~~

The best way to get to the starting point is to find Pico Boulevard on a map, and follow it east or west, depending on where you're coming from, to Avenue of the Stars. This usually means taking the I–405 (San Diego) Freeway to the Pico Boulevard exit and heading east a few miles.

An alternative for those coming from the south is to get on the I–10 (Santa Monica) Freeway and take it to the Robertson Boulevard exit. Turn left on Pico Boulevard and you'll be at the starting point in short order.

Palos Verdes Peninsula

Location:	Southeastern corner of Los Angeles
Mileage:	34
Approximate pedaling time:	2¾ hours
Terrain:	Flat, with one big hill
Traffic:	Light, except for heavy traffic on Sepulveda Boulevard and Pacific Coast Highway
Things to see:	The entire Palos Verdes Peninsula is a highlight of any visit to Los Angeles; it features a beautiful mountainous interior, striking residential areas, gorgeous seascapes, secluded coves and beaches, and a lighthouse

Palos Verdes is located at the southwestern corner of the Angeleno bicyclist's world. To the south, in Long Beach, there'll be traffic and oil refineries, if not dragons. You can't go farther west—not on a bike, anyway. So, Palos Verdes has become a sort of exotic bicycling destination, a frontier to be examined and conquered. The peninsula is bounded on the north by Santa Monica Bay, on the west by the open Pacific Ocean, and on the south by San Pedro Bay. It emerged during the Pleistocene Age when the sea floor uplifted; it became connected to the mainland through continued uplifting and sedimentation of the Los Angeles Basin. Fortunately, this all occurred before humans appeared on the scene. Humans now occupy the thirteen distinct marine terraces that make up the peninsula, with San Pedro Hill topping it all off at 1,480 feet. In the early nineteenth century, the Palos Verdes Peninsula was a ranch belonging to the Sepulveda family. In the 1920s it was subdivided into estates. Presently, the peninsula con-

	0.0	South on Pacific Coast Highway (PCH) at south end of Sepulveda Boulevard (at Artesia Boulevard, which is the boundary between Manhattan Beach on the north and Hermosa Beach on the south)
	3.9	Right onto Palos Verdes Boulevard
5.2		Bear left onto Palos Verdes Drive North (automatic)
9.9		Right onto Palos Verdes Drive East
16.2		Right (automatic) onto Palos Verdes Drive South
21.0		Becomes Palos Verdes Drive West (at Point Vicente Lighthouse/Coast Guard Reservation)
25.8		Left onto Palos Verdes Boulevard
30.5		Left onto Pacific Coast Highway (PCH)
34.4		End of ride at Artesia Boulevard

sists of San Pedro, a part of the city of Los Angeles—its harbor—and the independent cities of Palos Verdes Estates, Rancho Palos Verdes, Rolling Hills Estates, and Rolling Hills.

It can get quite warm on the inland side, and there is a substantial, though pretty, uphill section; on the ocean-facing side, the climate is quite moderate, though plagued by early-morning fog much of the year.

The directions for the ride, once you get your car parked satisfactorily, are simple. First, find Sepulveda Boulevard. Sepulveda must be one of the longest streets in the entire country. It runs at least 50 miles from the northern San Fernando Valley to Hermosa Beach. Park your car at the Hermosa Beach end. Sepulveda becomes Pacific Coast Highway at the junction of Artesia Boulevard, at the border of Manhattan Beach and Hermosa Beach. At this point Sepulveda is not particularly attractive; okay, it's *ugly*, but there are some fast-food places along the way that will beckon irresistibly on your return. Follow Pacific Coast Highway (PCH to its friends) south to Palos Verdes Boulevard, a distance of 3.9 miles; turn right. This is still not what anyone would call an attractive landscape, but try to look at it from the point of view of a visiting Iowan; this is pure southern California, and you'll notice plenty of out-of-state plates in the passing parade (one more reason to be extra-careful).

After 1.3 miles Palos Verdes Boulevard becomes Palos Verdes Drive North, which immediately turns inland (eastward) as it passes the **Palos Verdes Golf Course**. You are now well into the city of **Palos Verdes Estates**. (More about this later.) You will notice that the neighborhood has changed for the better. After about 4.7 miles of rather nice riding, turn right on Palos Verdes Drive East, which climbs sharply past the **Palos Verdes Reservoir**. The scenery is quite beautiful, but the climb is long and fairly difficult, so you may not appreciate it until later. Eventually you'll reach the top and be rewarded by a spectacular, but relatively safe, downhill to the point where the road becomes Palos Verdes Drive South, 6.3 miles from the turn onto Palos Verdes Drive East. Take this road to the right (you'll do it automatically, anyway), and enjoy the vistas off to the left.

The water is the Pacific Ocean, specifically the **Catalina Channel**. Catalina and a couple of other Channel Islands should be clearly visible in the distance. The land on both sides of the road is the city of **Rancho Palos Verdes**. The ocean is a tantalizing 0.6 mile, as the sea gull flies, to the south. (Peninsulas do that—disorient you—since they're three-sided and curvy.) Exactly a mile after joining Palos Verdes Drive South, you'll come to Paseo del Mar on the left. If you follow this street toward the water, in the 600 block you'll come to a steep trail down to **Flat Rock Point**. Flat Rock Point sports a very rocky beach and is the end of **Bluff Cove**, a picturesque, sheltered indentation in the shoreline. The bluffs for which it is named line the shoreline as far as the eye can see and beyond. These bluffs are quite unstable, and here and there you'll spot pieces of road at the water's edge that used to be at the top of the palisades. The kelp beds immediately offshore harbor all manner of marine life, and this is a favorite area for scuba diving. You probably shouldn't go all the way down to the trail as it is very steep and makes for a difficult return; stop at the overlook in the 1300 block and enjoy the view of Bluff Cove, the Channel Islands, and the beach cities to the north from there.

If you look at the right place and at the right time, the remains of the freighter *Dominator* can be seen in the water off Lunada Bay at Rocky Point. The *Dominator* ran aground and sank in a winter storm in 1961.

The city of Rancho Palos Verdes lies between Palos Verdes Estates on the north and San Pedro on the south. It was established as a posh residential community in the late forties and was incorporated in 1973. History in this area is a very modern thing. Even geology, with the palisades retreating almost daily, is new.

After riding 2.4 miles from the point where you joined Palos Verdes Drive South, you'll be abreast of **Portuguese Bend.** Ride another 0.8 mile and you'll come to a deep ravine leading down to a cove between **Inspiration Point** and **Portuguese Point.** This is **Smugglers' Cove,** which earned its name from the activities that went on there during Prohibition. The riding in this area is nothing short of phenomenal. The road is excellent, and the views of the ocean are picture-postcard gorgeous. Immediately after passing Portuguese Point, you'll come abreast of the **Abalone Cove Ecological Reserve,** formerly Abalone Cove County Beach. It still appears as a county beach on most maps, even though it has been an ecological reserve since 1978. The area includes the beaches, tide pools, and nearby ocean. The bluffs are 180 feet high here, with several trails leading down to the tide pools and water. This is, in fact, one of the best tidepool areas in Los Angeles County. (There are also good tide pools 30 miles north along the Malibu coast.) If you are unfamiliar with tide pools, here's a brief description:

A tide pool is a pool of seawater that remains behind in rocks and places where rocks form dams along the shore at low tide. The pools are usually no more than a foot deep, and they're interesting because of the vast array of sea critters that inhabit them. The showiest is probably the starfish, which comes in several colors. Sea urchins, sea cucumbers, snails, and crabs also abound in these pools. If you are so inclined, you can actually pick these guys up and watch them react; too much handling is stressful to any one creature, but there are so many specimens that few are ever handled to excess.

Abalone Cove sports the ruins of a 1930s resort, whose old clubhouse (not in ruins) is now used as a lifeguard headquarters.

After Portuguese Bend and Abalone Cove County Beach, you'll pass **Point Vicente**. There is a trail down to the beach, well marked as POINT VICENTE FISHING ACCESS. There are rest rooms down there, but unless you *really* have to go, wait a few minutes; there are more conveniently located facilities available just ahead. This is the site of the now-defunct Marineland, which operated from 1954 to 1987. Marineland featured shows similar to those now presented at San Diego's Sea World. Like Sea World, Marineland had a marine-animal medical-care facility.

Point Vicente Park and Lighthouse come up on the left shortly after the fishing access. The park is located high on the bluff overlooking Point Vicente. It has a very good museum with a relief map of the Palos Verdes Peninsula that will fascinate you after your climb over the mountain that makes up the bulk of the peninsula's landmass. There are excellent displays illustrating the geology of the area, as well as its fauna and flora, onshore and offshore. Rest rooms are available; there are also picnic tables, and for a later visit, parking. The 1926 lighthouse is open to the public on Tuesdays and Thursdays, and a guided tour can be arranged.

The name of the road changes to Palos Verdes Drive West somewhere along here, probably at Point Vicente Park—but not to worry, there's no way to go wrong. The road surface is a bit rough in places, but it is wide, and traffic shouldn't be a problem. (I hesitate to say that a road is rough or smooth, because resurfacing of roads is scheduled by various communities at mysterious intervals. A road that is rough today may be smooth as a baby's bottom by the time you get there. Conversely, a smooth road at this writing may crumble by the time you ride on it.)

A good alternate route to Palos Verdes Drive West is Paseo del Mar, a narrow road that hugs the bluff tops. In fact, if it hasn't tumbled down into the ocean, I recommend it. **Malaga Cove** is just off Paseo del Mar, east of Via Arroyo in Palos Verdes Estates. Local kids call this place Rat Beach. It's a very popular swimming and commercial-shooting beach. On a bluff high over the water, there's a gazebo from which a path leads down to the beach and the **Roessler Memorial Swimming Pool**, a free, public pool. The top of the bluff features a great deal of cactus and Indian paint brush, in season. The offshore kelp beds provide a habitat for vast quantities of sea life.

You've ridden only 10.0 miles from the beginning of the hill climb to the point where you again reach Palos Verdes Boulevard. At this point, there's an excellent Italian gourmet sandwich shop hidden behind the supermarket. You can return to your car via the same route that got you here, or you can take the South Bay Bikeway back. (Get off the bikeway at Beryl Street and go east to PCH.) Either way, you will have seen the geographical, geological, and sociological wonders that bring visitors by the tens of thousands to southern California each year. You will have had a pretty good workout, and you will have beat the heat.

For Further Information

Malaga Cove Beach information (310) 378–0383
Point Vicente Lighthouse tours (310) 377–5370

Getting There

Take the I-405 (San Diego) Freeway to the Artesia Boulevard exit. Go west on Artesia Boulevard to SR-1. (It's called Sepulveda Boulevard on the right and Pacific Coast Highway on the left.) A parking space can usually be had in the Manhattan Mall on the northeast corner of the intersection.

18 Masochists' Mirth on Mountainous Mulholland

Eastern Mulholland Drive • The First Western Mulholland Drive • The Second Western Mulholland Drive

Location:	From Universal City to Sherman Oaks From Woodland Hills to Agoura From Mulholland Drive and Las Virgenes Road to Leo Carrillo Beach
Mileage:	26, 28, and 49, respectively
Approximate pedaling time:	2 hours, 2½ hours, and 4 hours, respectively
Terrain:	Hilly; some steep, long, challenging grades
Traffic:	Light, except as follows: a. Ventura Boulevard is likely to be congested during the week and at certain times and places on weekends; b. virtually ideal riding all of the time; only one or two places where one shares the road with any appreciable amount of traffic; c. traffic on Pacific Coast Highway on weekends may be heavy but is manageable anytime and is likely to be light during the winter and on weekdays
Things to see:	From east to west: hillside homes of the rich and possibly famous; fabulous views of the San Fernando Valley; the Wild West; Los Angeles as it was in the nineteenth century (using a little imagination); great beaches

Mulholland Drive/Highway Overview

The following three rides cover Mulholland Drive, whose name in the western rural areas is Mulholland Highway. One ride covers the eastern end of the road, and there are two versions of the western extension. If one strings together the latter two, they come to about 77 miles. No one, to my knowledge, has ever done Mulholland from one end to the other by bike in one day. For one thing, there's a long stretch in the middle that is still unpaved. Also, all Mulholland Drive miles are hilly miles. My recommendation, therefore, is to do the eastern section on one day, the first western ride on one day, and the other western ride a few days later.

Mulholland Drive is a long road. It runs 16 or so paved miles, from Cahuenga Pass in the Hollywoodian east to Sepulveda Pass in the Encinan middle. Then, with little fanfare, it picks up pavement again near Topanga Canyon in Woodland Hills, and it continues all the way to Pacific Coast Highway (PCH) at Leo Carrillo State Beach, a distance of about 32 miles. Hilly miles. Scenic miles. Historic miles. People come from as far away as Burbank to see this road. Actually, nearly all of the land along the road from the Pacific to points considerably inland is being acquired by the National Park Service (NPS), and people from all over the country are beginning to discover it.

Eastern Mulholland Drive

Mulholland Drive begins its westward journey at the Hollywood Freeway/Cahuenga Boulevard Overpass. This is near Lake Hollywood; it's also near the intersection of Barham and Cahuenga Boulevards. It's probably best to park your gas guzzler near that intersection, ride to the overpass, and turn right onto Mulholland Drive. You will find that **Cahuenga Pass** is the low point of a saddle in the Santa Monica Mountains. This is a roundabout way of saying that you'll be faced with a heck of a steep hill immediately upon turning onto Mulholland Drive. There are six switchbacks or partial switchbacks in the first mile. The views become more and more spectacular as you rise above

Universal City. About 5.7 miles from the starting point, Laurel Canyon Boulevard crosses Mulholland Drive.

If you follow Laurel Canyon to the left (south), you'll come to Hollywood. It's a narrow, winding road with fairly heavy traffic, especially on weekdays at rush hour. ("Rush hour" is roughly from 6:30 to 9:30 A.M. and 4:00 to 7:00 P.M.—we have long hours in Los Angeles!)

If you follow Laurel Canyon to the right (north), you'll end up in North Hollywood, which is in the San Fernando Valley. If you decide that Mulholland Drive is too much of a grind, in spite of its magnificent vistas, you can take Laurel Canyon Boulevard down into North Hollywood; turn right on Ventura Boulevard, which becomes Cahuenga Boulevard. Follow Cahuenga to Barham Boulevard to find your car. Ventura Boulevard, many agree, is an interesting street in itself. This part of it is included in Ride 6.

Continue westward and, it seems, upward, on Mulholland Drive. **Laurel Canyon Park** is a good rest spot. It begins about 0.3 mile from the intersection with Laurel Canyon Boulevard and is located on the left (south) side of the road. Unwittingly, you have been passing numerous celebrity homes; the chances are pretty good that a home with a view is a home owned by someone you've heard of. Speaking of views, I hope you've brought along a camera, as the views from Mulholland Drive are spectacular. (The nighttime views are even more spectacular, and a trip in the car following this part of the ride is unforgettable!)

At 8.5 miles from the start, you'll come to an intersection with Coldwater Canyon Boulevard on the left. The last viewpoint from Mulholland Drive before reaching Coldwater Canyon—an overlook with the San Fernando Valley spread out at your feet—is the spot where Marilyn Monroe purportedly lost her virginity in the forties. Actually, Mulholland Drive continues to be something of a lovers' lane. Marilyn was not the first, and certainly not the last, to have a tryst on Mulholland Drive. Real estate development and fairly frequent L.A. Police and private patrols have put a crimp in the romantic goings-on, but at times it's still hard to find a parking place at the better scenic overlooks.

The road swoops downward to the right immediately after the in-

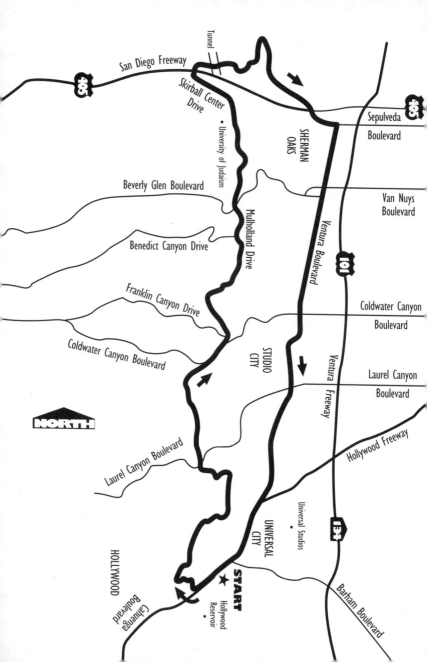

DIREC-TIONS at a glance

0.0	South on Cahuenga Boulevard
0.5	Right onto Mulholland Drive
16.6	Left onto Skirball Center Drive (at the traffic light—do *not* cross the bridge)
17.1	Right onto Sepulveda Boulevard (at the T)
20.3	Right onto Ventura Boulevard
26.4	Ventura becomes Cahuenga Boulevard (at Lankershim Boulevard)
26.9	Left onto Barham Boulevard and the end of the ride

tersection with Coldwater Canyon Boulevard. About 0.8 mile from the intersection and immediately after completing the right curve, carefully make a left turn. Following the main traffic to the right will take you down the hill to **Sherman Oaks** in the San Fernando Valley. Mulholland Drive continues with light traffic, and an unwanted hill, to the left. If you want to quit, now is a good time. Coldwater Canyon Boulevard is a pretty good road down into the valley. You can turn right on Ventura Boulevard, and eventually you'll arrive back at your car.

Turning left onto Coldwater Canyon Boulevard will send you into the heart of Beverly Hills (see Ride 16). The above statements about rush hour on Laurel Canyon apply to Coldwater Canyon in spades.

Continuing on Mulholland Drive to the left after Coldwater plunges into the valley, the road rolls up and down at elevations between 1,200 feet and 1,400 feet above sea level. The vistas continue, sometimes on the right, revealing the San Fernando Valley, and sometimes on the left, revealing Hollywood, downtown, and perhaps Beverly Hills.

At the 10.0-mile mark is the entrance to **Franklin Reservoir**, which is located in Franklin Canyon. This is a surprisingly heavily wooded area, reachable on a well-graded dirt road. It's a great place for picnics, if some movie company hasn't taken the place over for a location shoot. Several collateral dirt roads lead down into the Franklin Reservoir area. These are privately owned roads dating back to the thirties, when the *Saturday Evening Post* gave away lots as subscription prizes. Unfortunately for the winners, there was no access to the lots, and over the years most of them were confiscated for unpaid taxes. Today there is access, although the property remains, by and large, undeveloped. The value of a one-third-acre lot today is in the area of $500,000, it is said. It is also said that something is worth only what someone is willing to pay for it. From the undeveloped nature of the area, it's apparent that no one is yet willing to pay $500,000.

About 13.2 miles from the start of Mulholland Drive, you'll come to an intersection with Benedict Canyon Drive. This is a very narrow road that plummets into Beverly Hills and Bel-Air. It's quite a nice biking road, and it passes through some unbelievable real estate, but the return to Mulholland Drive is a killer!

About 0.4 mile farther along, you'll come to Beverly Glen Boulevard. To the right (north) it snakes its way down to Van Nuys in the San Fernando Valley; to the left it winds down to the campus of UCLA (University of California at Los Angeles). Westwood and UCLA are covered in Ride 12.

At about the 16.0-mile mark, you'll come to Roscomare Road on the left. This is a welcome sight, because from here on, it's all downhill. Roscomare Road passes along a crest of the mountains flanking Sepulveda Canyon and through some of the best neighborhoods in Los Angeles and Bel-Air—and that's saying something!

Mulholland Drive begins a very steep downhill soon after passing Roscomare Road. On the left is the new campus of the **University of Judaism**, and straight ahead is a nice-looking bridge that seems to say, "Cross me!" Don't do it. Turn left at the traffic light at the near end of the bridge. The bridge is, in fact, Mulholland Drive, but you are now at the end of the eastern part of the Mulholland tour. Incidentally, it was on that bridge in 1978 that Frank Sinatra's kidnapped son was exchanged by his kidnappers for a large, undisclosed amont of money.

The left turn at the traffic light puts you on Skirball Center Drive. Mulholland Drive actually continues for a couple of miles on the other side of the bridge, but it dead-ends in a poorly graded and un-maintained dirt fire road, and the only way to get back is to double back. Of course, if you want to be able to say that you rode every inch of Mulholland Drive, you should proceed over the bridge, go to the end of the pavement, double back, turn right on Skirball Center Drive and do the two western segments of the Mulholland Drive ride detailed below. If you do continue over the bridge you'll come to the church where Ronald Reagan attended services regularly until his recent illness, and you'll pass several of the most prestigious private schools in Los Angeles.

Otherwise, assuming you turn left down the hill, take a right over the I-405 (San Diego) Freeway bridge. A right at the T will put you on Sepulveda Boulevard. Sepulveda is a very long road—more than 40 miles long. If you'd turned left, it would put you in West Los Angeles, very near to UCLA to the east and a few miles from Santa Monica and the Pacific Ocean to the west. As it is, you're now climbing again to the crest of the Santa Monica Mountains. The crest, at 1,400 feet, is 0.8 mile ahead at the face of the tunnel; yes, tunnel! The tunnel, which was blasted through the mountain in 1929, is well lighted and is 0.2 mile long. It's downhill from the south entrance all the way to Sherman Oaks in the San Fernando Valley. The road is wide and smooth. Unfortunately, this is also an alternate route to the San Diego Freeway, so it gets a bit hairy during rush hours. On weekends, though, it's sheer bliss for bicyclists. Normal top speed going down is about 30 mph. The hill is about 3.8 miles long, ending at Ventura Boulevard, where you should turn right.

As you ride along Ventura Boulevard, you'll note its diversity, posh for one mile, depressed for another; high rises in one section, one-story storefronts in another. After 10.0 miles on Ventura Boulevard, the street becomes Cahuenga Boulevard, at the intersection with Lankershim Boulevard. **Universal Studios** is just to the left (north) at that intersection. Your car will be somewhere along the next half-mile, or so, of thoroughly urban street. You will have covered about 31 miles. The ones on Mulholland Drive should count extra!

Getting There

Take the US–101 (Hollywood) Freeway to the Barham Boulevard exit. Park on Barham Boulevard as close to Cahuenga Boulevard as possible. There is usually plenty of curbside parking available.

First Western Mulholland Drive

Start this ride from any point on Topanga Canyon Boulevard south of Ventura Boulevard in Woodland Hills. Ride south (uphill) on Topanga, after parking your gasoline chariot anywhere on Topanga, and turn right on Mulholland Drive. At this point, Mulholland passes through some quasisuburban/rural areas; be careful to turn left when Mulholland does or you'll miss your first hill, and you wouldn't want to do that, would you? At the turn from Topanga onto Mulholland, the altitude, according to the U.S. Geological Survey, is about 850 feet. Just after Old Topanga Canyon Road intersects on the right and, a few yards later, departs southward on the left, Mulholland turns right and starts to climb. This grade, dubbed "Cardiac Hill" by local cyclists, is deceiving. It rises past two tony private schools on the left and a hidden trailer park on the right to 1,500 feet at the intersection of Dry Canyon Cold Creek Road, where, at the time of this writing, some heavy bulldozing and real estate development was underway. The hill will seem hard, because it is, but it doesn't *look* difficult. There are no views from the top, so there's no feeling that you've accomplished anything and no sense of great height.

Old USGS maps show Dry Canyon Cold Creek Road snaking its way along for several miles. Mulholland Drive was paved in the fifties, and hilly as it is, it's relatively straight; with Dry Canyon Cold Creek Road, it forms a sort of dollar sign through the mountains. This explains why Dry Canyon Cold Creek Road seems to enter and exit and cross Mulholland at four or five places. Just to confuse people, road-sign makers have played havoc with Dry Canyon Cold Creek Road. In places it pops up as Dry Canyon Road. In places it's Cold Canyon Dry Creek. In others it's some other permutation of the original name. But not to worry—all of your aerobic exercise on this ride will be on Mulholland Drive, and there are no turnoffs that you need worry about.

While you're panting at the top of Cardiac Hill, lean up against a (stationary) bulldozer, and ruminate for a few moments about William Mulholland, who dreamed up the idea of a Hollywood-to-the-Sea Highway along the crest of the Santa Monica Mountain Range. This section of road wasn't completed until the late forties, although pieces of it were in place in the twenties to provide access to the remote ranches in the area. William Mulholland was a big Los Angeles booster, the man who brought water to the area, gave us the historical basis for *Chinatown* (the movie), and started the city on its way to surpassing San Francisco and San Diego in a number of areas, including population. (Mulholland, the man and the road, are mentioned in some detail on other rides.) Once you've recaptured your breath, you'll be treated to a really nice 2-mile-plus downhill, a 1-mile uphill, a ½-mile downhill, etc. Concentrate on the views of the coastal mountains to the left and not on the rolling hills fore and aft. There are numerous birds, of prey and otherwise, overhead, wildflowers on the sides of the road, and on the road itself, once in a great while, a turkey vulture lunching on a recently deceased varmint.

About 10 miles into the ride, as you sweep down the last hill, at an elevation of 800 feet, there is a scenic turnout on the left. There are plaques showing which mountains are which. The area to your left and straight ahead is part of the Santa Monica Mountains Conservancy (some day, it is hoped, to be Santa Monica Mountains National Park). You'll be tempted to pass up the scenic turnout as you zoom down the well-deserved hill. Stop anyway and take a look. Then continue down the road, a really satisfying downhill swoop, to Las Virgenes Road, elevation 602 feet. Immediately prior to the crossing on the left is a very large campus. This was originally the ranch of King Gillette of razor (and blade) fame. He lived on the ranch in an authentic adobe, built with imported Mexican labor. (Some things never change.) He commenced construction of a magnificent home on the ranch as a gift to his wife, but she died before it was finished. Gillette couldn't bear the thought of living there without her, and he gave the

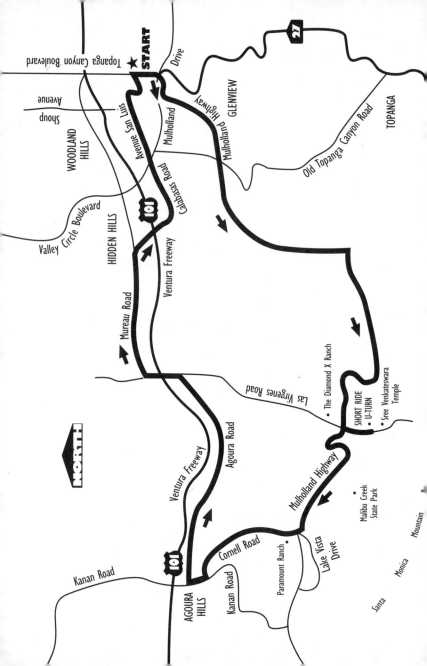

DIREC-TIONS at a glance

0.0	Right on Mulholland Drive from Topanga Canyon Boulevard (SR–27) in Woodland Hills
0.4	Left onto Mulholland Highway
9.8	Left onto Las Virgenes Road (at traffic light)
10.3	Left to Sree Venkateswara Temple (tour temple and return to Las Virgenes Road)

10.5 Right onto Las Virgenes Road

11.0 Right onto Mulholland Highway to return by the same route that got you here, making this a 22-mile ride, or left onto Mulholland Highway

14.2 Right onto Cornell Road (at stop sign)

16.5 Right onto Kanan Road (at T)

16.7 Right onto Agoura Road (fast-food places available on Kanan Road, just north of intersection with Agoura Road)

19.3 Straight on Agoura Road around chain-link fence

21.2 Left onto Las Virgenes Road (on green arrow); use caution crossing freeway entrance

21.8 Right onto Mureau Road

24.0 Left onto Calabasas Road

25.7 Calabasas becomes Avenue San Luis (crosses Mulholland Drive at traffic light)

26.7 Right onto Topanga Canyon Boulevard (SR–27)

27.7 Mulholland Drive on right—end of ride

whole shebang to the Catholic Church. They sold it to another order, who sold it to another; this process was repeated several times, with increasing internecine profits, until the final sale to the Church of the Universal Triumphant (CUT).

CUT is run by Elizabeth Claire Prophet—her real name—who established a new religion based, in part, on her belief that she is the reincarnation of Mary Magdalene, among others. CUT, after a number of years of feuding with the National Park Service (NPS), made apparent peace, but in an unexpected move sold the property to **Soka University**, a Japanese language school. It is a branch of a Tokyo-based religious sect (some would say cult), whose current plans include keeping their enrollment small and renovating all of the structures on the property. There are currently only 50 students there. (Ms. Prophet, meanwhile, has moved to Montana, where she and her followers have become survivalists and are digging in for the inevitable holocaust.)

The Diamond X Ranch to the right (north) on Las Virgenes Road was once the home of movie actor Rex Allen. It is now the ranger station for the NPS. The ranger's office is Allen's former bedroom, still furnished in Mrs. Allen's lavender-flowered wallpaper. There's a large, comfy-looking stone fireplace to warm ranger feet.

Just down the road to the left (south) is **Malibu Creek State Park**, a scenic gem that encompasses **Century Ranch**, the site where the movie and long-running television series *M*A*S*H* was filmed, of which there is nothing left to see. A controversy raged for some time over the construction of a new entrance to the park, which was thought to be the site of Chumash Indian relics. Modern descendants of the ancient Chumash are clashing with authorities over the preservation of such sites, of which there are dozens in the area. It turned out that the supposed relics at the Malibu Creek entrance were shellfish remains discarded at the site by a tailgate-based clam and lobster vendor about twenty years ago. Sigh.

If you turn left on Las Virgenes Road, you'll have to climb yet another steep 0.5-mile hill, but it's worth it. The left turn onto Las Virgenes Road and crossing of the road are controlled by a traffic light. The signal is a "demand light," but it doesn't honor demands by anything having less than two tons of steel. There is a pedestrian button, but it is very inconveniently located, and if your timing is wrong, the light will turn green and red again before you can get back to your bike. This produces a Mack Sennet sort of scenario that is funnier to the observer than to the participant. Your best bet is to wait for a car to trigger the thing, but if traffic is light, as it usually is, you may as well bite the bullet and try the pedestrian button. *Do not run the light:* There's a dangerously blind curve to the right, and cars can come around it unexpectedly at fairly high speed.

After negotiating the left turn near the top of the steep hill you were warned about above, after about 0.5 mile you'll come to the **Sree Venkateswara Temple** on the left. There's a left turn "pocket" lane there. You will definitely want to see the temple. Unfortunately, getting into the left-turn lane is another opportunity to have a close encounter of the most unpleasant kind with a motorist.

(All this talk of high-speed traffic may sound a little peculiar, since Las Virgenes Road is in the middle of the Old West—mountains rising abruptly on both sides of the road, horse ranches everywhere—and the loudest sound is that of woodpeckers pounding their brains out on the native oaks. But Las Virgenes is also the main route between the populous interior and the coast; it links US-101 with the Pacific Coast Highway, and although it's only two lanes wide, it carries more than its share of high-speed traffic.)

The temple, which was under construction for seven years and was finally completed in April 1988, is the largest Hindu temple of this architectural style in the Western Hemisphere, according to the *Los Angeles Times*. It is located on a 4.5-acre site amid California live oak trees and steep hills. Construction was carried out almost entirely by *silpis*, Hindi specialists brought here from southern India, each of whom must pass a demanding seven-year apprenticeship. The architecture is modeled on 10th-century documents known as the *Shastra*. The positions of the nine deities, the cupolas, and the overall dimensions are spelled out in the *Shastra*.

Construction is of brick covered with mortar. There are nine cupolas, each of which encloses a statue of one of the nine Hindu deities. The statues were brought here from India. In addition, there is a multipurpose auditorium and a central meditation hall. The intricate carvings and decorations are astounding!

Although there is a sign prohibiting photography, this apparently refers to photography *inside* the temple. The *Los Angeles Times* ran several pictures in a 1988 article commemorating the opening of the temple.

At this point you may feel that you've had enough of the Wild West and this kind of southern California scenery for the day. If so, return to Mulholland Highway; turn right, and retrace your "steps."

Alternatively, there's another, nicer way back that retraces only 90 percent of your steps:

About a mile beyond the temple on Las Virgenes Road is a left turn onto Piuma Road. If you cross the bridge, you've gone too far. About 0.5 mile from the left turn is a county fire station. Stop there for water and a rest; you'll need both.

Bear left at the fire station; the road soon becomes Dry Canyon Cold Creek Road, which, as mentioned earlier, crisscrosses Mulholland. The terrain is mildly hilly at first; after a while, it becomes quite hilly, then very hilly, and finally, there's a hellacious hill, now known as Shastra's Revenge, a reference to the Hindu temple. After 2.0 miles you'll come to a stop sign at Mulholland Highway. You can turn right and return to your car in about 5.0 miles, or you can stay on Dry Canyon Cold Creek Road and get back to your car in about 7.0 miles. If you turn right you'll climb "Seven Minute Hill" (the west side of Cardiac Hill), which takes most of us mere mortals fifteen to twenty minutes. (The elevation at the top of Seven Minute Hill, where Dry Canyon Cold Creek Road crossed Mulholland the first time, is 1,500 feet.) Either way, you'll have to climb back up there if you ever want to see your car again. If you continue on Dry Canyon etc., you'll cross Mulholland several times, have a slightly easier time of it, be far away from traffic, and generally see countryside that hasn't changed much in seventy-five years (although there is one section of new, million-dollar–plus homes in the section that parallels Seven Minute Hill).

In any event, once you're back on Mulholland, head back to your car the way you came. If you don't push yourself, your charley horses will be gone in a day or so.

If you're going to continue on the first Western Mulholland Drive ride:

Leave the temple the way you came in. Go back to Mulholland Drive and turn left. Climb the hill ahead, keeping a sharp eye on the scenery to the left (south). Before the top (elevation 1,000 feet exactly) the views of 2,000-foot-plus rocks rising from 200-foot bases are spectacular! On your left on Mulholland Highway, just after you turn left, is **Malibu Creek State Park**. (The entrance is back on Las Virgenes Road, just south of the traffic light, but the views are from your current route.) The park, which comprises more than 5,000 acres of craggy mountains and chaparral, is a hiker's paradise. Malibu Creek is the southernmost spawning ground for steelhead trout in North America. For the bicyclist, the views on the left side of Mulholland Highway are almost enough to make one forget the hill(s). The valley visible from the summit was the site of *M*A*S*H*, *South Pacific*, and *The Dukes of Hazard*, all filmed during the time Twentieth Century–Fox owned 2,000 acres in the area. Another swooping downhill and a long, more or less level, stretch will bring you to Cornell Road, elevation 800 feet.

After 3.2 miles on Mulholland Highway, turn right (north) onto Cornell Road, which has several steep, but mercifully short, hills. On a couple of the downhills you can build up enough speed to carry you most of the way up the next hill. Immediately after the turn onto Cornell Road, on the left, is the **Paramount Ranch.** This 400-acre parcel is the NPS's pride and joy. It is the remnant of a 4,000-acre ranch once owned by Paramount Studios and gradually sold off after the forties, as the fortunes of the motion picture business declined. The Paramount Ranch was given to the NPS several years ago, and it is being refurbished so that movies can still be made there. In fact, this is the only place in Los Angeles County where the public can wander among *real* movie sets. (Universal Studios' tour is a theme park, not a real studio tour. The VIP Tour at Warner Bros. *does* take you through real movie sets, but wandering is *verboten*.)

A mile or so from the turn, you'll come upon a section of new, 6,000- to 10,000-square-foot homes. In 1987 there was nothing but sagebrush and prickly-pear cactus here. About 2.3 miles from the turn, you'll come to a T intersection. Turn right (onto Kanan Road). A few yards ahead on the left is a fast-food place, and there are others very nearby. Turn right on Agoura Road (at the traffic light, just this side of the fast-food joint), and proceed through the village of **Agoura**, which, for the most part, retains its twenties, umm, charm. You'll go over a fairly steep, but short, hill and then descend into a nice rural area for a couple of miles.

After 2.3 miles from your turn onto Agoura Road, you'll come to a traffic light whose green cycle—if you get a green at all—is literally two seconds. Agoura Road continues up the hill known as "Moving Hill" dead ahead. In the late 1980s Agoura Road was built, a boon to bicyclists. Within a few months natural springs in the hill on the right (south) side created hydrostatic pressure under the road. Pavement buckled, retaining walls cracked, and the whole hill started a slow slide toward the US–101 (Ventura) Freeway immediately to the north. A water main broke under the roadway, and things *really* got messy. The road has since been patched and through the magic of civil engineering the northward migration has been halted. Proceed over the hill.

Turn left at the T intersection with Las Virgenes Road, and take your first right after going over the Ventura Freeway (SR–134 and US–101). Use extra caution crossing the freeway entrance, as motorists often either fail to see cyclists or take pains to beat them across the entrance. The first right turn after crossing over the freeway is Mureau Road, paved in 1990. Mureau Road goes up over a couple of short but steep hills and winds around to the right (south), crosses over the US–101 (Ventura) Freeway, and bumps into a T intersection with Calabasas Road. At the point where it bends to the right, before the T intersection with Calabasas Road, you'll see a road entering from the left. This leads to the exclusive gated community of **Hidden Hills**. It is possible to run the gate at Hidden Hills and muck about on Jeb Smith Road, Kit Carson Road, and Jeremiah Johnson Road, among others, but it really isn't worth the hassle with the guard, who's only doing his job. Anyhow, turn left on Calabasas Road.

This takes you into the heart of Calabasas (which means "pumpkin" in Spanish). The pumpkins for which the place is named are about 3 inches in diameter and grow wild on the hillsides. They cost about fifty cents apiece in local markets in October. Calabasas is also the home of the **Leonis Adobe**, on the left at 23537 Calabasas Road. This is a very unusual two-story affair, built in 1879 by Miguel Leonis. Actually, the second story was added in 1879 to a one-story adobe that was built in 1844. The place was one posh hacienda in its day. It's open to the public at no charge, Wednesday through Sunday from 1:00 to 4:00 P.M.

Calabasas Road becomes Avenue San Luis at the **Motion Picture**

Country Home and Hospital (at Valley Circle Boulevard), a 256-bed hospital and retirement facility given over to the care of film-industry employees. Founded in 1921 with donations from Mary Pickford and Douglas Fairbanks, the Motion Picture Country Home continues today with donations from Lew Wasserman (chairman of MCA) and numerous others in the film industry. You may have noticed that an inordinate number of celebrities seem to die in Woodland Hills. In point of fact, Woodland Hills is home to relatively few celebrities, but they go in great numbers to the Motion Picture Country Home for their final illness.

Continue over Avenue San Luis's rolling hills. San Luis bends to the right at Shoup and then bends to the left after 2 blocks. Turn right at the traffic light. This is Topanga Canyon Boulevard, and your car should come into view pretty soon. If not, call the police.

Getting There

Take the US–101 (Ventura) Freeway to the Topanga Canyon Boulevard South exit. Cross Ventura Boulevard and park on the right after passing Dumetz Street. Mulholland Drive and this ride begin at the next traffic light.

Second Western Mulholland Drive

Following the route of the preceding ride, get to the intersection of Mulholland Highway and Las Virgenes Road. Take Mulholland west and after 3.2 miles, cross Cornell Road. Continue up (west) Mulholland.

Below road level on the left after crossing Cornell Road is **Malibu Lake**, which is surrounded by exclusive homes. Mulholland continues to climb very slightly through the village of **Cornell**. You will soon come to **Peter Strauss Ranch**, now a state park, formerly known as Lake Enchanto. I could write a whole book on the Peter Strauss Ranch and Lake Enchanto. Suffice it to say that Lake Enchanto resulted from the damming of a creek in the twenties and that its history is checkered. Charles Hinman, the dammer, wanted to build a resort replete with miniatures of spectacular world-class sights—Mt. Fuji, for example. He settled for a petting zoo. A very large swimming pool, with an island, cabanas, and cottages, was built, as was a large terrazzo dance floor. In the forties a dance band broadcast music from the island. Hinman had numerous "personal problems" and was jailed, and Lake Enchanto embarked upon dark days. In the sixties it was taken over by Chief Windfeather, who claimed not only the lake but all of California for the Chumash Indians. He obviously fell short of his goal, and Lake Enchanto was occupied by a succession of religious sects and, briefly, so to speak, by a nudist colony.

Eventually actor Peter Strauss, who had filmed on the site, bought the place and proceeded to clean it up. He discovered that the dam and all structures on the property were in violation of every building code known to man. The dam burst in an unusually heavy shower, and Mr. Strauss sold the site to the Santa Monica Mountains Conservancy to hold for the NPS, until the latter can afford to take it over. In the meantime, it is available for rent for weddings, bar mitzvahs, and company picnics. It is open to the public for guided tours on the first and third weekends of each month.

Continuing around a bend in the road, you'll come to the **Rock Store** on the left. It will look familiar if you've watched any television during the past twenty years. If you're riding on a Sunday, the Rock

Store will be hidden behind 7,000 motorcycles. Actually, it's more like 150, but to a bicyclist, they can be overwhelming. These aren't your Hell's Angels types. By and large these are simply bicyclists with horsepower—accountants, engineers, mechanics, and even a doctor or two with *big* machines and sufficient funds to keep the mechanical monsters in spotless condition. They (the motorcyclists) do look pretty scruffy, but then we cyclists aren't exactly fashion plates either. Do stop at the Rock Store; it's your last chance for fuel and/or water for a long way.

The store is at an elevation of 836 feet. You now begin the toughest climb of the ride: Within 3 miles you'll climb to 1,707 feet, at the intersection of Kanan Dume Road. The scenery on the road and the views from it are unmatched. On the way up is a large red house that must qualify as the ugliest, most out-of-place abode in California. Near the top there's another **viewpoint.** Stop there, soak up the view, contemplate the red house, and let some sweat evaporate. On a clear day, and there are more of them than L.A.'s detractors will admit, you clearly can see the **San Gabriel Mountains**, 60 or more miles away.

After you cross Kanan Dume Road, Mulholland bears right, and you'll climb to 2,026 feet—but who's counting. **Rocky Oaks Park** is on the right. It's noted (surprise!) for its scenic rocks and oaks. It has an amphitheater from whence NPS's astronomy seminars are conducted, and a pond.

In 2.4 miles Mulholland appears to end at a T intersection. Don't be fooled. Take a left, following the sign that reads, STATE ROUTE 23 SOUTH. This is a very narrow road, rough in spots, and occasionally covered with sand and gravel or rocks from a recent rain, so be careful. After 7.5 miles Mulholland turns right. Just before that turn, you'll see a magnificent golf course 1,000 feet below road level. This is reputed to be owned by the Church of Perfect Liberty, but I've also heard that it was sold to Japanese interests. Either way, it's truly spectacular. Also clearly visible are three enormous GTE satellite dishes and, at 32926 Mulholland Highway, the studio of a Finnish sculptor named Eino—he's far too successful to have a last name. Samples of his unsold work, mostly white marble abstracts, are standing on a promontory overlooking the golf course. Eino taught at Pepperdine

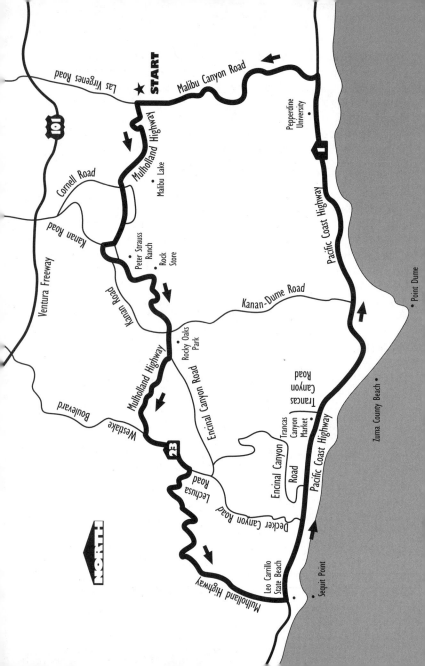

DIREC-TIONS at a glance

0.0	Start at intersection of Mulholland Highway and Las Virgenes Road. Start on Mulholland, going west
3.2	Cross Cornell Road
5.8	Rock Store on left
8.8	Cross Kanan Road
9.8	Right onto Mulholland Highway (at Encinal Canyon Road)
12.2	Left onto Westlake Boulevard
14.1	Right onto Mulholland Highway
21.6	Left onto Pacific Coast Highway (at T)
27.1	Left onto Trancas Canyon Road (Trancas Market rest stop)
27.1	Left onto Pacific Coast Highway from Trancas Market parking lot
38.1	Left onto Malibu Canyon Road (at top of hill; Pepperdine University on left)
43.7	Malibu Canyon Road becomes Las Virgenes Road
45.2	Intersection with Mulholland Highway—end of ride

University and was the track coach for Lasse Virren, a successful Finnish runner in the 1980 and 1984 Olympics. In any event, his works of art, when they're on display, are well worth a stop. Even when they're not on the scene, the view is spectacular.

Pacific Coast Highway is 5.5 miles from the turn. It's all downhill. You'll drop from 1,543 feet to 17 feet through some beautiful countryside to **Leo Carrillo State Beach.** Carrillo was a movie actor, whose claim to fame is primarily as the Cisco Kid's sidekick. For generations the Carrillo family was prominent in southern California affairs, and Leo was wealthy and famous without the movies. The beach boasts some very interesting caves, which have been featured in innumerable movies, but it's not visible from your bicycle. If you can chain your steed somewhere, it's worth a look. Leo Carrillo State Beach extends some miles inland, and for a long way the road overlooks a deep canyon with a stream, before plunging down to PCH. The beach, incidentally, was named in honor of Carrillo's activities on behalf of California's Latinos. He never had anything to do with the beach itself.

Turn left on PCH. Be careful. Automobile speeds are high here, and motorists aren't expecting cyclists to be crossing the road. Once on PCH you'll encounter numerous relatively easy hills, the first of which comes along at Leo Carrillo and isn't so easy. You will be on PCH for 17 miles, much of it very scenic.

Trancas Canyon Market, on the left side of the road, 5.5 miles from the turn onto PCH, is a very good rest and refreshment stop. (PCH up to Trancas is covered by Ride 14.) Trancas Canyon marks the extreme northern boundary of Malibu. There are rest rooms 0.5 mile farther along PCH, at **Zuma Beach.** These are located only a few feet off the road, and if worse comes to terrible and you're doing this ride alone, you can bring your bike into the rest room with you. There is a miserable hill after Zuma Beach, and another one just before Pepperdine University, but by and large the route is quite easy. Turn left on Malibu Canyon Road.

This road, as its name so subtlety suggests, passes through Malibu Canyon on its way to the Mulholland Highway (among other places) and your car, which is patiently awaiting your return. Down below the road, *way down,* is Malibu Creek, which runs all year—no mean feat for a southern California creek. There's a tunnel on the road, but it should cause no problems. (Above the face of the tunnel are the faint remains of "The Pink Lady." This was a 20-foot-high, anatomically correct graffito of an adult female—that was a traffic-stopper in every sense of the word. Her skin, of which there was a great deal, was painted pink. The artist was identified, and as punishment *she* was forced to paint over her masterpiece.)

Although after several miles of climbing it may seem like there will never be a summit, at about the time you see sherpas herding yaks and you hear a chorus singing "Nearer My'God to Thee," there's the top, and from there to your car, past the Hindu temple, it's a wonderful downhill.

For Further Information

Leonis Adobe (818) 712–0734
Malibu Creek State Park (818) 706–1310

Getting There

Take the US–101 (Ventura) Freeway west of the San Fernando Valley
to the Las Virgenes Road exit. Park at the intersection of Las Virgenes
Road and Mulholland Highway. There is a small dirt parking lot near
the southwest corner.

San Francisquito/ Bouquet Canyons and the San Andreas Fault

Location:	Northern Los Angeles County, north of the Santa Clarita Valley, mostly in Angeles National Forest
Mileage:	35 without the San Andreas Fault; 48 with the fault
Approximate pedaling time:	3 hours without the San Andreas Fault; 5 hours with the fault
Terrain:	Hilly . . . a few short, difficult hills and a couple of long gradual climbs, but there is a 16-mile, mostly gradual, downhill that makes up for much of the difficult climbing
Traffic:	Light; this is an almost traffic-free route, although there is a short stretch of annoying traffic at the beginning and end of the ride
Things to see:	Gorgeous scenery; the spectacular Los Angeles water system

Canyon Country, at the risk of offending several thousand readers, is a tough place to ride. During much of the year, it's too hot; during much of the year, it's too cold; much of the time, it's too windy; and it's always hilly. Some would say too hilly. But if you want to get away from it all—"it all" being smog and traffic—there are places in Canyon Country that are second to none.

This ride starts in the Hughes Market parking lot near Valencia Boulevard and Bouquet Canyon Road in Saugus. In the process of getting there, don't be surprised if it's overcast when you get in the car and clears as you enter the Santa Clarita Valley, home of Valencia,

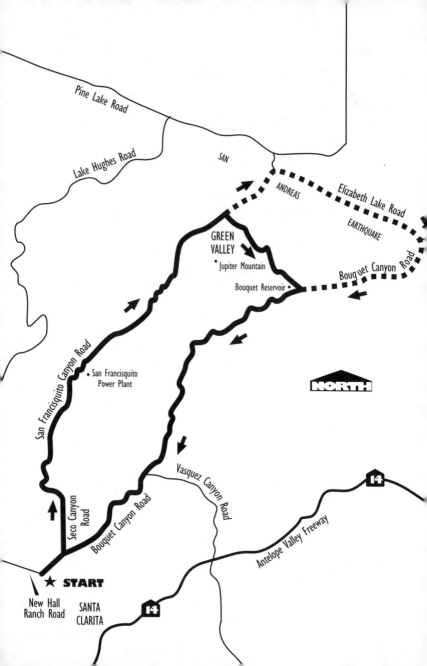

DIREC-TIONS at a glance

0.0	Right out of Hughes Market parking lot onto Bouquet Canyon Road
0.4	Left onto Seco Canyon Road
2.4	Seco becomes San Francisquito Canyon Road
12.4	Right onto Spunky Canyon Road
13.4	Rest stop in village of Green Valley

San Andreas Fault Route

13.4	Left on Spunky Canyon Road to return to San Francisquito Canyon Road
14.4	Right onto San Francisquito Canyon Road
17.5	Right onto Elizabeth Lake Road
24.3	Right onto Bouquet Canyon Road
31.1	Intersection with Spunky Canyon Road on the right; continue straight on Bouquet Canyon Road; those skipping the San Andreas Fault rejoin the ride here
48.2	Left into Hughes Market parking lot and end of ride

Shorter Ride Without San Andreas Fault

13.4	Right onto Spunky Canyon Road
18.0	Right onto Bouquet Canyon Road
35.1	Left into Hughes Market parking lot and end of ride

Magic Mountain, and other such attractions. After unloading your two-wheeled vehicle, turn right (north) on Bouquet Canyon Road.

The rather undistinguished area near the parking lot quickly gives way to an urban residential area. After traveling north on Bouquet Canyon for about 0.4 mile, turn left on Seco Canyon Road, which becomes San Francisquito Canyon Road 2.4 miles after the turn onto Seco. (Caution: There are some new housing developments in this area, and street names may have changed. Seco bends to the left, and just as it becomes San Francisquito, it bends to the right.) Almost immediately upon becoming San Francisquito Canyon Road, the scenery becomes rural; on the left side of the two-lane country road is the **Santa Clarita River**, which from July on becomes the Santa Clarita "River," the quotation marks denoting a marked lack of water. A couple of miles farther along, the road veers away from the river and crosses a creek that runs all year. There are cottonwood trees everywhere and a nice selection of wildflowers (in season), and the canyon walls rise sharply. The terrain remains flat to slightly rolling for 9.0 miles. The most descriptive word for the area is *cozy*, although there are some who might describe it as claustrophobic. Be that as it may, the area is cooler than the surrounding country, greener (where it hasn't been burned over), and downright pleasant. The road surface is excellent.

At approximately the 9.0-mile mark (from the parking lot), you'll reach a hydroelectric generating station on the **Los Angeles Aqueduct**. Water is pumped through enormous pipes over the mountains from the relatively soggy (even in drought years) north to the positively arid south. This station is actually part of a fantastic engineering feat, with the plant generating electric power from the flowing water to drive the pumps that make the water flow in the first place. It's about as close to perpetual motion as a bicyclist on this ride is going to get.

Also at the site is a historic marker commemorating the St. Francis Dam disaster. Never heard of it? This was the second-worst disaster in the "civilized history" of California (a phrase that one of my British friends claims is an oxymoron). The first-worst disaster (for all you catastrophehounds) was the San Francisco Earthquake of 1906. The story, which the marker does not tell, goes something like this:

The St. Francis Dam was once a 185-foot-high giant. Well, Hoover Dam and Glen Canyon are real giants; at 185 feet, though, this one was nothing to be sneezed at. On March 12, 1928, at 11:57 P.M. to be exact, it was reduced to a few concrete chunks as it unleashed 38,000 acre-feet of water (12 billion gallons) into the narrow, rock-walled San Francisquito Canyon. The resulting flood wiped out Powerhouse #2 in the canyon, took out the Edison Saugus Substation, swept through Castaic Junction, and went on to Santa Paula, where it carried off the Willard Street Bridge. The water reached the ocean by dawn, leaving 400 dead in its path.

The dam's designer, and the chief engineer of Los Angeles' Bureau of Waterworks and Supply, was William Mulholland, without whom we wouldn't have Mulholland Drive, the movie *Chinatown,* or water in Los Angeles. Mulholland was a self-taught engineer, and he ultimately built eighteen other dams for the Los Angeles water system, none of which collapsed, so his record could have been worse. The St. Francis Dam leaked from the start, but Mulholland, it is said, thought that all dams leaked a little. He ordered installation of a 2-inch pipe to carry away the seepage, but new leaks were discovered in the opposite wall. Mulholland's assistant, Harvey Van Norman (the Van Norman Dam, which is on high ground overlooking the San Fernando Valley, partially collapsed in the February 9, 1971 earthquake), accompanied Mulholland to the dam site just hours before the collapse and declared it safe. After the disaster it was discovered that the schist walls to which the dam was anchored were exceedingly weak and crumbled into mud in the presence of water!

As you pedal upstream, about 1.5 miles from the historic marker are weathered chunks of concrete and reinforcing steel, now almost buried. These are the last remnants of the dam. On the west side of the road is a footpath leading to the top of a small rise. From there you can see the path of the water, and to the southeast you can see the grassy valley that was the reservoir.

After this respite the road emerges from the narrow walls of the canyon and begins the long climb to **Green Valley** and beyond. The road hugs the west side of the canyon, and the scenery becomes decidedly less lush—in fact, downright dry. You'll have your last major climb at the point where the pipes of the Los Angeles Aqueduct cross the road. Nearby are power lines that nearly always make a very distinctive sound as the wind whooshes through them. In truth, the sound is downright weird, and at night it would make your hair stand on end.

After traversing a plateau for a mile or so, you'll come to the intersection of Spunky Canyon Road (about 12.4 miles from the parking lot). Turn right for a blessedly downhill mile. On your right is a **general store** in the midst of the little village of **Green Valley**. This is a good place for a rest stop. The altitude is about 3,400 feet. Sorry, no rest rooms, but it's a nice place otherwise, staffed by very friendly folks who are used to bicyclists. After a welcome break you'll have a decision to make. You can retrace your "steps" to San Francisquito Canyon and turn right there to go to the San Andreas Fault, or you can continue on Spunky Canyon.

If you retrace your steps and turn right, you'll be faced with a humongous hill. I set my personal speed record of 56 mph coming down that hill. You'll go over the top, just as you get nosebleeds and altitude blackouts. Well, maybe it's not that bad, but when you reach the top, it'll be a welcome sight! On the other side there's a downhill that levels out and halts at a T intersection with Elizabeth Lake Road. Turn right at that point, and you'll find yourself on a very lightly traveled rural road in a narrow valley.

This is the **Leona Valley**, and Elizabeth Lake Road is right on the San Andreas Fault. I mean *on* the fault! Surprisingly, there's nothing to indicate that this is *the* fault. No trembling ground, no shattered buildings, not even a sign. Take your first right (Bouquet Canyon Road), and climb another humongous hill. After reaching the crest (there really *is* a crest), you'll be treated to a few miles of really nice downhill. Spunky Canyon Road intersects from the right, and you'll see **Bouquet Reservoir.** You will have added about 13 miles to the shorter version of the ride.

If you decide to skip the San Andreas Fault and continue along Spunky Canyon Road instead, you'll soon come to a real grind of an uphill. It goes up into conifer country, to an elevation of about 4,000 feet. Just when you expect to hear that heavenly choir, you are rewarded with a steep downhill that brings you alongside **Bouquet Reservoir,** a rather attractive part of the L.A. water system. Turn right at Bouquet Canyon Road, a T intersection (about 5.0 miles from the store), and after another steep uphill climb, you'll have 16 miles of gradual downhill through Bouquet Canyon. (The long version of the ride joins up with the short version at the T intersection.) There are numerous campsites on the right (west) side of the road, bordering a nice little stream that seems to have plenty of trout. (I say this because on nearly every ride during the fishing season one sees people with strings of one-pounders. They are probably not paid to parade

220

alongside the road, so I assume that there's good fishin' in that thar crick.) The downhill ride is shaded and cool, although the pavement is a bit rough in places. Traffic is usually very light, but pay attention to motoring campers, as bicycles seem to be invisible to them after a day in the great outdoors. At the end of the canyon is a **Visitor Center** and an abrupt emergence into a still-rural, but more open-space kind of world. The ride back to the parking lot is basically downhill.

Getting There

To start this ride, you have to get to the corner of Valencia Boulevard and Bouquet Canyon Road in Saugus. This is easily done from the I–5 (Golden State) Freeway, from whence you take the Valencia Boulevard exit east to Bouquet Canyon Road. At Valencia and Bouquet turn left, cross the bridge, and take your first right (Newhall Ranch Road). On the left there's a Hughes Market in a large shopping center. Park somewhere in the lot. After unloading your two-wheeled vehicle, turn right (north) on Bouquet Canyon.

Santa Clarita Valley/
Canyon Country

Location:	Extreme northeastern Los Angeles County, north and east of the San Fernando Valley
Mileage:	33
Approximate pedaling time:	2½ hours
Terrain:	Excellent roads, but several hills that will get your attention
Traffic:	Light
Things to see:	William S. Hart Park, Pioneer Oil Refinery, Cowboy Walk of Fame, the Way Station, Magic Mountain, Vasquez Canyon, Sand Canyon, Placerita Canyon, Oak of the Golden Dream, Disney's Canyon Country outdoor sets

Canyon Country is a rather ill-defined region in the northeast corner of Los Angeles County. It is separated from the Los Angeles megalopolis by the San Gabriel Mountains, some of which rise to 10,000 feet or more. The area you will be riding through is the Santa Clarita Valley. Bicyclists frequently ride from the city of Los Angeles into Canyon Country via the Sierra Highway, which is at the northeastern-most corner of the San Fernando Valley. Cyclists also visit the Santa Clarita area via Little Tujunga (pronounced tah-hung'-a) Canyon; these cyclists have a masochistic streak and legs like tree trunks. Even the Sierra Highway riders have to have the strength to cope with "Little Nasty" and "Eternal Hill" (formerly "Refinery Hill"). This ride avoids the rigors of Little Nasty and Eternal Hill. For the majority who like a few hills, Canyon Country and this ride have plenty.

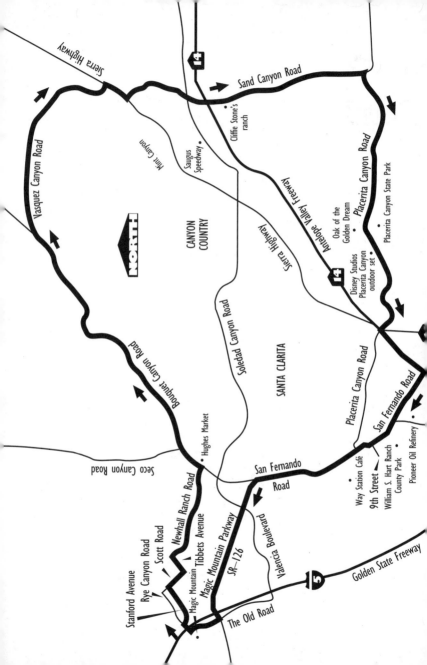

On the northwest corner of the intersection of San Fernando Road and Sierra Highway, behind the gas station and to the west of it on the flank of Eternal Hill, is **Eternal Valley Memorial Park**. This is actually an expanded pioneer cemetery that dates from the 1860s. At the top of Eternal Hill was a refinery that operated for more than sixty years and was an olfactory beacon and further challenge to the lungs of countless cyclists. The refinery was closed and dismantled in 1990, after receiving seventeen air-pollution citations in one year. The value of the refinery's product, diesel fuel, was less than the cost of fixing the problems, and the place was rendered defunct. Not to worry, there's a new refinery at the intersection of Sierra Highway and Placerita Canyon that you'll be seeing later. It opened for business in late 1990, after a couple of years of environmental hassles; it seems to be odorless, and it generates electric power from excess steam produced by the refining process.

Start out by heading north (straight ahead) on San Fernando Road. San Fernando Road is a very long, very gradual downhill. Its slope is barely discernible, but nearly everyone thinks they've become extraordinarily strong, as they breeze effortlessly along the road at 20 mph or more. Your first stop is the **Pioneer Oil Refinery** (SRL 516) in Pico Canyon, just west of San Fernando Road. After 0.9 mile turn left on Pine Street. The restored refinery is 0.5 mile west of San Fernando Road on the left. The first oil wells ever drilled in California are also nearby. They were dug in 1876 and produced 150 barrels per day. The oil was carried away from the wellhead in leather bags to the first refinery in California (SRL 172), which is located in nearby Newhall, an old town now annexed by the city of Santa Clarita. (Signs point the way to these places of interest.)

You are now in the town of Santa Clarita. This particular section of the town was once known as Newhall, but in a referendum in 1989, the towns of Newhall, Saugus, and Valencia were incorporated into the new city of Santa Clarita. The name Santa Clarita has never really stuck, however, and old-timers continue to use the old names.

Backtrack to San Fernando Road, and after 0.2 mile, on the left, you'll come to the **William S. Hart Ranch County Park.** Construction of the ranch was begun in 1910 by a previous owner and completed by Hart in 1928. William S. Hart was a cowboy movie actor well before my time, although his name is well known and remembered in these parts. The park features the ranch house with 253 acres of chaparral-covered hills and rangelands, original furnishings, Indian art, and a really nice nature trail. The home, which Hart dubbed "La Loma de los Vientos" (Hill of Winds, or I guess, Windy Hill), also contains a truly impressive collection of Charles M. Russell sculptures and paintings. Bear in mind that this really was the Wild West in the twenties and thirties, even though it's only 30 miles or so from downtown Los Angeles. Admission to the park is free. The official address is 24151 Newhall Avenue, but it can be reached only from San Fernando Road.

A word about *chaparral* (Spanish for explosive). This is the brushy shrubbery you see wherever development has not yet taken place. Chaparral is highly drought resistant, a necessity in this area, since average annual rainfall is only around 14 inches. (A true desert gets 10 inches or less of precipitation, but 14 inches isn't exactly a rain forest.) Typically, the chaparral "greens up" during and after the brief winter rains and then dies back and lies dormant during the long, hot, dry season. The dried branches typically have a high vegetable-oil content; at some point during the dry season, some nut inevitably tosses a match into the chaparral, and one of southern California's famous brushfires begins. On any ride into the canyons, you'll notice vast burned-over areas, the result of these arsonists. The chaparral recovers quite quickly from the recurring fires, but wildlife is slower to return, and destruction of homes is fairly common. Sometimes, depending upon location, it is impossible to obtain fire insurance; it is then impossible to obtain a mortgage. So, many of the homes destroyed in brushfires are unprotected by insurance and are a total and devastating loss to their owners.

Moving onward to more pleasant subjects: After you pass the entrance to the William S. Hart Park (or even go in), look to the left. You'll see the beginning of the **Cowboy Walk of Fame**, a poor-person's Hollywood Walk of Fame, with a distinctly Western flavor. It has plaques set in the sidewalk commemorating various famous cowboys—movie cowboys, mostly. The plaques are, if anything, nicer than Hollywood's, but most of the movie cowboys are so long gone that only a few names will be familiar. Within a few blocks you'll be in the heart of beautiful downtown Newhall, elevation about 1,300 feet, population around 15,000 (before becoming part of Santa Clarita). It's typical old small-town southern California.

At the corner of San Fernando Road and 9th Street, on the left (west), is the **Way Station Café**. This place is a must-stop for gluttons. It's a fifties-, or perhaps forties-style California café, with all kinds of junk on the walls, juke-box satellites at the counters and booths, and the best darn home fries and pancakes this side of, well, maybe Denver. The service is lightning fast and slightly gruff in an inoffensive way, the portions huge, and the prices mighty low. It is not the kind of place you'd want to visit at the beginning of a ride, but at the tail end, that's another story.

After riding 2.8 miles from the entrance to William S. Hart Park, turn left at the busy intersection with Magic Mountain Parkway. After 2.8 miles turn right on The Old Road (no choice). At the intersection of Magic Mountain and The Old Road is Marie Callender's restaurant. Straight ahead on Magic Mountain Parkway, you'll see—surprise—**Magic Mountain**. This is a 260-acre amusement park owned by Six Flags. It has several of the biggest and bestest roller coaster rides in the entire world. There's the Colossus, Shock Wave, Ninja, Viper, Psyclone, and others. Several do loop-the-loops; some do them while you stand! Some are just gut-wrenching. Do not enter Magic Mountain after eating at the Way Station! The most prominent landmark is the 384-foot Sky Tower, which is visible from time to time during much of this ride. The park also has live shows, musical entertainment, water shows, and a petting zoo. An unlimited ticket for an adult without a discount costs about $20. Discounts are available through several supermarkets, and from time to time through newspaper coupons and other promotions. Kids under 48 inches tall and geezers fifty-five and older get in for half price.

After turning right on The Old Road, which was the main road before the freeway (I–5) was built, ride 0.5 mile to a right turn on Rye Canyon Road. Take your first right (on Stanford Avenue) after about 0.1 mile. After about 0.8 mile turn right on Scott Avenue. This is the heart of the up-and-coming light-industrial area that will give the Santa Clarita Valley its financial vitality in the years to come. The area has innumerable, well-designed, attractive, one-story light-industrial buildings, some of them with very familiar names, some of them struggling start-ups. Scott Road becomes Newhall Ranch Road after it intersects with Tibbetts Avenue, a private road. About 2.5 miles from the turn onto Scott Road, you'll come to the intersection of Bouquet Canyon Road. If you want a rest stop, the **Hughes Market** in the shopping center across the street has an excellent bakery and deli. There's also a Wendy's near the Bouquet Canyon Road curb.

Turn left (north) on Bouquet Canyon Road. Bouquet Canyon, incidentally, was originally named Cañon del Buque by General Beale, but the general apparently had a bad ear for languages, and he called it Bouquet. (*Buque* in Spanish is pronounced boo-kay and probably is someone's surname—I can't find it in a dictionary.) Be that as it may, continue north on Bouquet Canyon Road for 5.5 miles. This will take you through some typical, somewhat older, sections—fifteen years old, or so—of the town of Santa Clarita. The road is somewhat rolling, although the hills are nothing to worry about. By the time you come to Vasquez Canyon Road, you'll know you're truly in the Wild West. Turn right on Vasquez Canyon Road.

During the 3.8 miles that you're on Vasquez Canyon Road, you'll cross some of the most desolate territory in southern California. The chaparral-covered hills are so dry that even the indestructible chaparral doesn't look healthy. This was the hideout for several big-name banditos of the nineteenth and early twentieth centuries. Not the least of them was Tiburcio Vasquez, a noted bad guy of the 1860s. I've always said that if *I* ever murder anyone, Vasquez Canyon is where I'll throw the body. There are now several homes along the road, one very large place in particular, thereby reducing the number of body-disposal sites. Nevertheless, you'll be able to envision the bandits charging among the hills on their horses, doing bad deeds. You'll be rewarded near the end of Vasquez Canyon Road with a screamingly fast downhill on straight, smooth pavement. The road ends at a T intersection with Sierra Highway in Mint Canyon, (which looks rather uncanyonlike).

Vasquez Rocks, also known as Robbers' Roost, is a geologic formation between Mint and Soledad canyons, west of Acton. Named for Tiburcio Vasquez, the jumble of rocks was used by him and others since his time as a hideout. Vasquez was caught in the Santa Monica Mountains and executed in San Jose in 1875. Interestingly, Vasquez Rocks lie right on the San Andreas Fault. The SR–14 (Antelope Valley) Freeway, which opened in 1963, passes right through the rocks and presumably will need some touching up when the fault slips again.

Turn right on the Sierra Highway at the T intersection, and ride blissfully downhill for 0.5 mile. Then turn left on Sand Canyon Road.

(There is another *big* hill on Sand Canyon Road. If you want to avoid it, continue straight on Sierra Highway for 3.0 miles; turn left on Soledad Canyon Road, and ride for 2.1 miles; then turn right on Sand Canyon Road.) If hills don't bother you too much, take Sand Canyon Road past the intersection with Soledad Canyon Road. Soledad comes up after 1.8 miles. There are a couple of places to eat and drink at the southwest corner of the intersection; they're pretty lackluster, but your trip over Vasquez Canyon and Sand Canyon can make you thirsty, so a stop may be in order.

Incidentally, a couple of miles to the west on Soledad Canyon Road is the **Saugus Speedway**. This is a locally famous place for stock-car racing and legal off-track betting. It is also the site of tremendous swap meets every Sunday. These are bigger, and some say better, than those held at the Rose Bowl on the second Sunday of each month. In any event, immediately to the rear of the Saugus Speedway are some railroad tracks, and it was right behind the back stretch that, in 1911, the last train robbery in the United States took place.

Continuing south on Sand Canyon, you'll pass right by the late **Cliffie Stone's ranch**, 0.75 mile or so after the intersection with Soledad Canyon. (Cliffie Stone, for the uninitiated, was an old-time Country and Western singer—more Western than Country.) All along Sand Canyon Road, woodpeckers, mostly redheads, bang their brains out on the power poles. Near the tops are round holes that serve as nests, and the activity in the spring is feverish.

Toward the end of Sand Canyon is a magnificent, gated housing tract, where a man's home is literally as well as figuratively his castle. Minimum price: $1,000,000. Minimum size: 10,000 square feet on two to five acres. Major complaint: too much noise from the gold mine that operates a quarter mile away at the foot of the hill behind the property.

After 3.1 miles (from Soledad Canyon Road), turn right onto Placerita Canyon Road. (If you go straight ahead on Sand Canyon, it becomes Little Tujunga Road, which is a killer—gorgeous, but a killer!) There is a series of hills on Placerita Canyon Road, but the first one is the hardest, and it's not all that bad. About 1.7 miles from the turn is the entrance to **Placerita Canyon State Park**. *Placer* (the "a" in placer is pronounced like the "A" in shaft) is Spanish for "gold mine"; in Californian usage, it's the kind of gold mining that involves panning. *Placerita* means a "small *placer* mine," and it was here in Placerita Canyon that gold was discovered in California in 1848, not at Sutter's Mill in 1849, as usually reported. The strike at Sutter's Mill set off the Gold Rush, but it wasn't the first. Gold, as mentioned above, is still mined in Placerita Canyon, and just beyond the entrance to the park, on the right, is the **Oak of the Golden Dream**. (You can reach the Oak by bike by entering the park and going through the tunnel under Placerita Canyon Road.)

Placerita Canyon State Park is a 314-acre preserve with lots of chaparral and stands of California live oak. The canyon and park are very picturesque, with the San Gabriel Mountains forming a dark backdrop. The park has a nature center and a self-guided tour on well-marked trails.

The Oak of the Golden Dream is so named because an early settler, it is said, fell asleep under the oak tree and dreamed that there was gold nearby. When the dreamer awoke he was hungry, and he pulled up some wild onions growing at the edge of the stream gurgling past the oak tree. What do you think he found clinging to the onions' roots besides onions? Right—flecks of gold. As far as I know, no one ever got rich from Placerita Canyon's gold, but there's evidently lots of it still there. All you gotta do is take a nap under the tree.

The official address of the park (which is only a formality, as there are no other landmarks in the canyon) is 19152 Placerita Canyon Road.

About 0.5 mile beyond the park's boundary, on the right (north), is the **Disney Studios Placerita Canyon outdoor set**. It is pretty well hidden from most vantage points, so you'll have to keep an eye out for it, but once you see it, you'll recognize the streets and buildings. The set is nestled in a several-hundred-acre forested valley; someday its value as a movie set will be less than its value as a housing tract, and it will bite the dust. At the moment, though, this area is quite remote, and development seems unlikely.

Five miles after turning onto Placerita Canyon Road from Sand Canyon Road, you'll pass under the SR–14 (Antelope Valley) Freeway, and you'll come to the Sierra Highway again. Straight ahead on the right side of Placerita Canyon Road is the new refinery mentioned earlier. The hills are dotted with oil wells.

Turn left onto Sierra Highway; climb the short hill, and coast down the other side to San Fernando Road, 1.1 miles from the turn. You should recognize the **Carl's Jr.** on the left, and with any kind of luck your car will be where you left it about 33 miles ago.

For Further Information

Magic Mountain (805) 255–4111 or (818) 367–5965
Placerita Canyon State Park (805) 259–7721
William S. Hart Ranch County Park (805) 259–0855

Getting There

Take the I–5 (Golden State) Freeway to the SR–14 (Antelope Valley) Freeway and get off at the first exit, which is San Fernando Road. Immediately after you leave the freeway, you may park along the street; if you'd prefer a parking lot, there's a Carl's Jr. less than 0.1 mile ahead on the right. This particular Carl's Jr. is a favorite with cyclists, because it is well located for riders returning to the San Fernando Valley from Canyon Country. It has unlimited soft drinks, a reasonably healthy menu, and clean rest rooms—all in all a good place to start out and rest up.

Hidden Valley

Location:	Northwestern Los Angeles County
Mileage:	36
Approximate pedaling time:	3 hours
Terrain:	Rolling, with two or three noticeable hills
Traffic:	Light on mostly rural two-lane roads, except in the city of Thousand Oaks and the immediate vicinity of the ride starting point
Things to see:	Simi Valley, Conejo Valley, and Hidden Valley; Lake Sherwood and Westlake Lake; California Lutheran University; Ronald Reagan Presidential Library

This is a great day-tour that tends to get overlooked by out-of-town visitors, because Hidden Valley is, well, hidden. There are, in fact, three valleys on this tour: Simi Valley, Conejo Valley, and Hidden Valley. Another feature that can't go unmentioned is Lake Sherwood. In fact, the ride goes by two lakes, Westlake Lake being the redundant other. This ride is not easy; it is moderate to difficult, depending on what kind of shape you're in. There are several hills that will get your attention, regardless of your condition, but be assured that cyclists are climbing these hills all the time, and I'd be very surprised if you didn't pass a whole bunch of them on your ride.

A good place to start is on Los Angeles Avenue in the city of Simi Valley. There's a shopping center at the northwest corner of Madera Road and Los Angeles Avenue. The southeast corner of the parking lot, next to the ARCO-AM/PM station, is a frequent parking place for

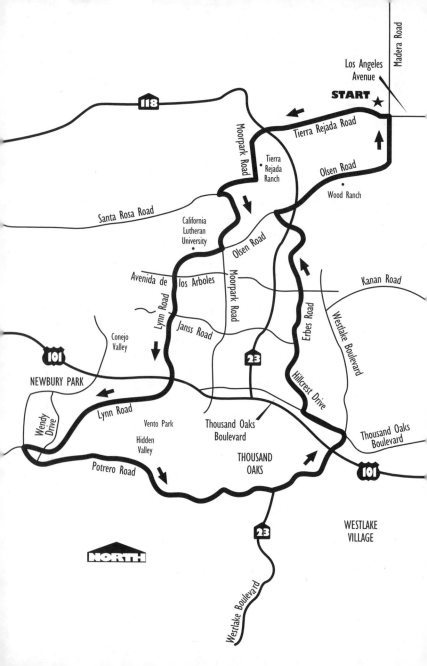

DIRECTIONS at a glance

0.0	Right (west) onto Tierra Rejada Road (toward the drive-in theater) from shopping center parking lot
3.5	Left onto Moorpark Road (first left after going under freeway)
4.5	Road bends right—continue on Moorpark Road
5.2	Road bends left—continue on Moorpark Road
5.6	Left at stop sign; continue on Moorpark Road (road looks like it should change names after the stop sign, but it doesn't)
7.1	Right onto Olsen Road
9.4	Olsen becomes Lynn Road
16.2	Left onto Wendy Drive
21.9	Right onto Lake Sherwood Drive
23.5	Right onto Potrero Road (at T)
24.2	Left onto Westlake Boulevard
25.8	Left onto Townsgate and immediate left into Carl's Jr. for rest stop
25.9	Left (north) onto Westlake Boulevard
29.2	Left onto Avenida de Los Arboles
30.2	Right onto Erbes Road
32.4	Right onto Olsen Road
34.0	Olsen becomes Madera Road
36.5	Left into parking lot on northwest corner

day-touring cyclists. The AM/PM is also a good place to drink your fill when the ride is over.

Simi Valley is at the same stage of development that the San Fernando Valley was in the sixties. It is primarily a bedroom community, where the people who work "over the hill" in the San Fernando Valley live. In the sixties the San Fernando Valley was a bedroom community for people who worked "over the hill" in downtown L.A., West L.A., and Santa Monica. The hills have changed but the urban ecology hasn't. Housing in Simi Valley is more affordable than in the

San Fernando Valley, and private housing development is rampant. Light industry is gradually moving into Simi Valley, and it appears that it is another San Fernando Valley in the making. Soon, Moorpark and the Conejo Valley will be the bedroom communities for people working in Simi Valley.

Start by riding west out of the parking lot on Tierra Rejada Road. Los Angeles Avenue changes its name at Madera Road. If you're at all confused, look for the drive-in theater and head toward it. You'll be faced with a hill almost immediately. Cyclists have dubbed it "Drive-in Hill" for obvious reasons. The theater used to have a good double bill, but more importantly, it has weekend swap meets whose traffic may be a minor inconvenience for cyclists. Just after you crest the hill, on the left side of the road is the site of a 1970's Western *Noon 'Till Three*. This movie, which I believe starred Charles Bronson, was what is known in the industry as a "SWAT" picture (Sank Without a Trace). The same was true of the sets, but the rolling hills remain most picturesque. Continue west on Tierra Rejada Road for 3.5 miles. (Incidentally, *tierra rejada* means "cracked earth" in Spanish.) Turn left on Moorpark Road, the second left after you pass under the SR–23 (Thousand Oaks) Freeway. Cars wanting to enter the northbound freeway as you pass under it are on a conflicting course with you, so be careful.

After turning left on Moorpark Road, you'll go through some heavily agricultural rolling terrain. On the left is **Tierra Rejada Ranch**, where you can pick your own veggies and berries in season, and which always has fresh orange juice—at a price—for thirsty cyclists. Across the road from the ranch is a large open field, now under cultivation.

The road takes a sharp right after 1.0 mile. There are some rolling hills along the way, but nothing too debilitating; about 0.7 mile after the right-hand bend in the road, there's an equally sharp bend to the left and a fairly steep downhill, followed by a stop sign. Do stop at it, because cross traffic, which is usually very light, does not. Turn left, and surprise of surprises, you're still on Moorpark Road. Follow it up the hill, known on even USGS maps as Norwegian Grade, 1.5 miles to Olsen Road. Norwegian Grade is one of the hills I said would get your attention, but it is quite survivable. Just stay with it. The late actor Joel McCrea's family, incidentally, owns all of the land around Norwegian Grade, and they have proposed that Moorpark Road be closed to all but local residents and bicyclists (son Steven McCrea is a cyclist), so that they can put in a large, gated real estate development. At the moment it appears to stand the chance of a snowball in Death Valley in August, although after climbing Norwegian Grade, you may not care if the road disappears from bicycling's repertoire. The scenery, incidentally, is typical of southern California coastal canyons—i.e., it is a deep, rocky canyon with a narrow two-lane road clinging to one side, elevated 50 to 100 feet above the bottom. Its sandstone slopes are covered with chaparral and prickly-pear cactus. In May and June there is a profusion of wildflowers, mostly California poppies and lupine, if there was sufficient rainfall during January and February.

Turn right at Olsen Road, which is about 0.4 mile beyond the crest of Norwegian Grade, and 1.0 mile later you'll pass **California Lutheran University**. About 2.3 miles after the turn, Olsen Road becomes Lynn Road. This is Conejo Valley. (*Conejo* means "rabbit" in Spanish, and indeed, there are lots of the critters here.) Stay on Lynn Road 6.5 miles to Wendy Drive. There are numerous new housing developments just completed and under construction in this area. The negative side to this is that the wild hills are disappearing; the positive side is that the roads are improving immensely to accommodate the influx of inhabitants. Turn left on Wendy Drive and stay on it for 0.6 mile to the T intersection with Potrero Road, where you turn left. (*Potrero* means "meadow" in Spanish. You can become a veritable linguist just riding on these roads!)

You are about to encounter another hill that will get your attention, and it doesn't even have a name. The scenery for the next 10 miles or so is absolutely spectacular, so dwell on that instead of the hill, which is only about a mile long. After cresting the hill you'll come down into **Hidden Valley**. There are some sharp curves, so be careful.

Hidden Valley is horse country. Two of the largest Arabian horse breeders in the nation have their "hindquarters" here. Off to the right, as you pass through the valley, is a multimillion-dollar stable that has been featured on a number of horse-oriented episodes of various TV dramas. Numerous car commercials have been filmed here as well. The odds are high that you will see this road on TV within twenty-four hours of your visit—assuming you turn on your television set, that is. Hidden Valley is long on scenery and great riding but short on history or interesting stories, so just enjoy it for what it is: probably the most beautiful little valley in southern California.

When you leave the valley, watch the right side of the road and the signs carefully. Turn right on Lake Sherwood Drive where you hug the shore of Lake Sherwood. Just before the turn is a new country club with a six-figure membership fee. Don't even bother to try getting in there on a bicycle. There is a brand-new road that goes straight where you should turn right. This road will take you up a steep hill and eventually rejoins our route, but ours is much more scenic and easier.

The ride along the lakeshore involves one steep, but mercifully short, climb, followed by an easy roll into the city of Westlake Village. If you watch carefully, you'll notice that Westlake Boulevard passes the northwest shore of **Westlake Lake** on the right. Westlake Village and its redundantly named lake were developed by ALCOA in the sixties, and the town was incorporated rather recently. In any event, on the right if you cross Hampshire Road (instead of turning left as this ride goes) is a large shopping center with a **Java City** and a couple of other places to eat. Java City takes special pains to accommodate cyclists, and there is limited, but delightful, outdoor seating amid giant California live oaks. Across the street at the corner of Westlake Boulevard and Townsgate Road is a **Carl's Jr.** that's a favorite stopping spot for bikies for miles around. Carl's, too, has a nice tree-shaded patio that's especially nice for cyclists. If you are a contrarian and stop for a rest at Java City instead of Carl's, you can take a left on Townsgate, ride for less than one block to Westlake Boulevard, and pick up the ride there by turning right onto Westlake.

Be careful crossing the freeway; it seems that there are several conflicting traffic lanes crossing the bike lane, which disconcertingly disappears at a very inopportune moment. About 100 yards or so after crossing over the freeway, there is an entrance to the Prominade Mall. Opened in 1997 this magnificent shopping center has numerous eating places, several of them arguably better than Carl's or Java City. These eateries are especially enticing because they have ample outdoor seating with a choice of sun or shade.

Immediately after crossing Thousand Oaks Boulevard, Westlake Boulevard climbs gradually through Thousand Oaks' high-rent district, known as North Ranch. Median house prices in the still somewhat depressed late nineties are in excess of $1,000,000.

With regard to the city of Thousand Oaks, wags are always remarking about the exact count of oak trees. A number of years ago, the city fathers, tiring of the pressure to confirm the oak population, took a census. The results were inconclusive, but everyone is certain that the actual figure is more like 10,000 than 1,000. It is, by the bye, illegal to cut down an oak tree more than 2 inches in diameter here. You may notice that some of the oaks have little white plaques on them; these particular trees are especially old (more than 200 years) and have been named and designated historic.

Westlake Boulevard climbs to a crest 0.5 mile after passing Kanan Road, and you'll be treated to one of the best downhills anywhere: a smooth, wide, traffic-free road to Avenida de los Arboles ("Tree Avenue") where you turn left. After a mile, turn right on Erbes (pronounced like "herbs") Road. Within a half mile you'll be at the summit and will be treated to another nice downhill, past a golf course to Olsen Road. You can let it all out, as the turns are wide and sweeping, and the pavement is in pretty good shape at this writing. Turn right at the stop sign at Olsen Road. This section of Olsen Road is somewhat east of the part where you were earlier. It will take you back into **Simi Valley**. At the crest of a mild hill, on the right, is **Wood Ranch**, a new development with a broad spectrum of housing, ranging from expensive to astronomical, and a golf course where major tournaments are played annually.

On the left after the sheriff's station and the crest of the hill is Presidential Drive, which goes to the **Ronald Reagan Presidential Library**. The library opened in late 1991, and it is accessible to bicyclists, but it sits atop a killer hill. The exterior features a garishly painted slab of the Berlin Wall. Like all presidential libraries, this one was built with private funds, but its upkeep is paid for, at least in major part, with public monies. President Reagan and Nancy Reagan have received permission from the appropriate Powers That Be to be buried on the library grounds. A visit to the library is worth the trip, as this is arguably the most spectacular presidential library yet built, but because of the hill leading up to it, the trip is best made by car.

At the sheriff's station at the top of the hill, the road changes name from Olsen to Madera Road. You'll like Madera Road. It has a perfectly wonderful downhill that doesn't end until you're almost back at your car, which is near the corner of Madera and Tierra Rejada. In short order you'll find yourself back at the parking lot and, local thieves permitting, your car. (The odds are in your favor, I should emphasize, because Simi Valley has the highest proportion of law-enforcement officers living within its boundaries of any city in the country.) In any event, I think you'll agree that this is one spectacular ride!

For Further Information

Ronald Reagan Presidential Library (805) 522–8444

Getting There

Take the SR–118 (Simi Valley/San Fernando Valley) Freeway west past the San Fernando Valley to the Madera exit, and go south 1.75 miles to the K-Mart, which is on the right side of the street, on the northwest corner.

Index